Archetype and Character

Also by the author

GATHERING THE LIGHT: A JUNGIAN VIEW OF MEDITATION
(*Foreword by Thomas Moore*)

JUNG AND POLITICS: THE POLITICAL AND SOCIAL IDEAS OF C. G. JUNG
(*Foreword by Marie-Louise von Franz*)

MARXISM AND EXISTENTIALISM

Archetype and Character

Power, Eros, Spirit, and Matter Personality Types

V. Walter Odajnyk
Pacifica Graduate Institute, USA

palgrave
macmillan

First published 2012 by
PALGRAVE MACMILLAN

Palgrave Macmillan in the UK is an imprint of Macmillan Publishers Limited, registered in England, company number 785998, of Houndmills, Basingstoke, Hampshire RG21 6XS.

Palgrave Macmillan in the US is a division of St Martin's Press LLC, 175 Fifth Avenue, New York, NY 10010.

Palgrave Macmillan is the global academic imprint of the above companies and has companies and representatives throughout the world.

Palgrave® and Macmillan® are registered trademarks in the United States, the United Kingdom, Europe and other countries.

ISBN 978–0–230–36401–1

This book is printed on paper suitable for recycling and made from fully managed and sustained forest sources. Logging, pulping and manufacturing processes are expected to conform to the environmental regulations of the country of origin.

A catalogue record for this book is available from the British Library.

Library of Congress Cataloging-in-Publication Data
Odajnyk, V. Walter, 1938–
Archetype and character : power, Eros, spirit, and matter personality types / V. Walter Odajnyk.
p. cm.
Includes bibliographical references and index.
ISBN 978–0–230–36401–1
1. Typology (Psychology) 2. Archetype (Psychology) 3. Motivation (Psychology) 4. Jung, C. G. (Carl Gustav), 1875–1961. 5. Freud, Sigmund, 1856–1939. 6. Adler, Alfred, 1870–1937. I. Title.
BF698.3.O33 2012
155.2'6—dc23 2012011171

10 9 8 7 6 5 4 3 2 1
21 20 19 18 17 16 15 14 13 12

Printed and bound in Great Britain by
CPI Antony Rowe, Chippenham and Eastbourne

Archetype: A psychological analogue of instinct. The organizing principle of psychological apprehensions, emotional reaction and external behavior.

Character: A combination of psychological qualities that distinguishes one person from another.

For my wife
and
in fond memory of Marie-Louise von Franz
and Edward F. Edinger

Contents

List of Figures

Foreword

Murray Stein

In an ambulatory conversation some years ago with my late dear friend, Raphael Lopez-Pedraza,[1] he told me that he thought Jung should have received the Nobel Peace Prize for his brilliant book, *Psychological Types*, which he considered to be the world's greatest treatise on tolerance. Jung's insight into the typological differences between Freud and Adler, which led them to formulate such different psychological theories, has been able to help many people to understand difference and appreciate it rather than to demonize it and try to eliminate the "other."

This conversation has remained with me, and I still find Raphael's insight brilliant. Books following up on Jung's work, like the ever popular *Please Understand Me* by Kiersey and Bates, have had a major impact on many people's lives. In addition, the much used psychological test, the Myers Briggs Type Indicator (MBTI), which is based on Jung's typology, has been used by millions in all walks of life and for a multitude of practical purposes to facilitate understanding among people of different persuasions who need to work and live together. The Gifts Compass Inventory (GCI),[2] which is a recent contribution to the still growing list of psychological tests based on Jung's typology, also promotes insight and understanding of character structure and preference and importantly with an accent on personal development. Maybe the world is indeed a better place today than it would have been without Jung's book, which was published originally in 1921.

Jung himself said of his work on types: "The book . . . yielded the insight that every judgment made by an individual is conditioned by his personality type and that every point of view is necessarily relative."[3] Further, he writes: "This work sprang originally from my need to define the ways in which my outlook differed from Freud's and Adler's. In attempting to answer this question, I came across the problem of types; for it is one's psychological type which from the outset determines and limits a person's judgment."[4]

The point is that no one speaks the absolute truth from his or her individual perspective, but few of us are able to put this insight into practice. The natural human tendency is to assume that I (the ego, the "little king") hold the truth ("They see the world as delineated by the ego," as the Jungian analyst, Joseph Henderson, in passing once said of narcissists[5]), while others may only approximate it, but in fact usually fall far short and stand in dire need of correction. *Psychological Types* relativizes this egoistic position, creates a mental space for doubt and further reflection and leads logically from certainty to the humility of a merely relatively sure posture. It is an intellectual position that all good scientists would subscribe to in their professional work, even if they often tend to ignore it egregiously in their personal lives. And Raphael has a very good point: if the human population as a whole were to adopt the perspective put forward by Jung in his *Types*, there would be a chance for world peace. War demands an enemy, and enemies are created out of what is not understood and declared intolerable. Of course, this is a two-way street: enemies create each other, and neither will pause to consider the degree to which the hated other reflects oneself in the mirror of shadow awareness.

That said, *Psychological Types*, despite its bulk (it consists of over 600 pages in the English translation and is Jung's longest work next to the late *Mysterium Coniunctionis*) and potential value for humanity, became something of a footnote in the field of Analytical Psychology due to Jung's much greater interest in discovering and exploring the processes active in the unconscious. *Psychological Types* "constitutes a psychology of consciousness,"[6] as Jung declares, whereas "the central concept of my psychology . . . [is] *the process of individuation*,"[7] and the study of this latter theme ran much deeper than type and the awareness of the limitations of consciousness and the relativity of conscious judgment. After the publication of *Psychological Types* in 1921, Jung put it to the side and worked intensively on the theory of the archetypes and their relation to personal and cultural individuation processes. There are occasional references to psychological type in his subsequent works, and he uses it, although infrequently, to interpret symbolic material, but he did not make it the centerpiece of a further study of any importance. Among Jungian analysts, type theory has been used clinically but only to a limited extent. In more recent times, however, there has been a renaissance of interest in psychological typology among Jungian thinkers, and the present work by V. Walter Odajnyk is a remarkable example of this trend.

Archetype and Character brings Jung's later work on the archetypal foundations of the psyche into relation with his earlier work on conscious judgment and typology. Perhaps this is what Jung himself would have done had he been so inclined later in life or had the opportunity to live another lifetime. As it was, he had his hands full enough with elaborating the thematics of the archetypal unconscious and showing how the processes of the unconscious play a role in psychological and spiritual development, that is, the individuation process. It has remained for others following him to bring the pieces of his life's work into relation with one another in new and generative ways. Walter Odajnyk has done this brilliantly in the present work by extending the notion of types from the rather limited consideration of conscious judment to the much larger terrain of character as a whole. He shows the archetypal foundations of the four functions—thinking rooted in the archetype of Power, feeling in Eros, sensation in Physis and intuition in Pneuma – and adds to this and to the introversion/extraversion vertex the important temperament archetypes, Soul (reflection) and Spirit (action). With this combination, which he accurately announces as Archetypal-Motivational Typology, he is able (far better than Jung himself did, incidentally) to account for the differences among the characters and theories of Freud, Adler and Jung, which was Jung's starting point for investigating psychological types in the first place. In addition, he is also able to offer prescient insight into various cultural creations, traditional and contemporary. Since he himself does such a complete job of laying out his position in the chapters of this book, I need say nothing further about it, only to compliment him on his thoroughness and intellectual rigor.

What I would want to add to the previous conversation with Rapheal Lopez-Pedraza, and this partially at least stemming from a reading of Walter Odajnyk's fine book, would be some reflections on how an understanding of one's own typology, and one's character, can foster and help advance the individuation process.

An understanding of type can be extremely useful clinically, as has been amply demonstrated by John Beebe's brilliant work in this area, for instance. Walter Odajnyk's book will contribute to this application of type. On a political and social level, Jung's *Psychological Types* may take us a good ways toward the ancient dream of turning swords into plowshares and creating a world where the lion will lie down with the lamb in peace. Tolerance of difference is the key. Whether this dream is realistic or not is certainly beside the point. But on a more intimate and personal level, I would like to add another dimension to the discussion. In order to have peace, whether locally in the family or team or more broadly in the community or nation, in a frutiful and creative sense, and not just a static and boring sense that mere tolerance of difference may tend to produce, with people merely accepting differences and letting it go at that – you live your truth and I will live mine; live and let live – there has to be another step. I would call this "embracing the other within." This implies a more active and spirited relationship to difference, not only tolerance of it. But this is more a matter of inner work and development than political and social work.

Jung clearly limits himself in *Psychological Types* to reflection. With his insight into type, we can reflect on differences in type and character, both individual and collective. We do not have to embrace them in the other, just keep a respectful distance. From a political and social perspective, this is about as far as one can go. Some cultural differences, which may well have a typological component, nevertheless cannot be tolerated without abrogation of human rights and ethical concerns, even if it is important to understand their typological, archetypal and historical reasons for being what they are. On the individual level, however, shadow awareness in a deeper sense of acceptance and embrace is possible even if very difficult. Indeed, it is necessary for individuation. This is a psychological move of great importance. Otherwise the difference and the "other" stays "out there." For individuation, one needs to bring it in and see it as a part of oneself. The other is me, too. It's a minority-me. Marie-Louise von Franz has addressed this issue with great insight and passion in her discussion of the inferior function.[8]

The basic insight is that each one of us contains all the types within, but much of their reality is unconscious to us. Our character as a whole is highly complex, and this fact is illuminated with great precision in the present work by Walter Odajnyk. The aspects of character and typology that are not available to us consciously are latent possibilities within us, even if they remain mostly asleep and show their faces only in projections onto unfamiliar others. Our realization of psychological wholeness depends on waking them up in ourselves and becoming aware of them. If we can hold up a mirror and see them as parts of ourselves, moreover, we won't demonize them quite so readily in the other, or overly idealize others either. We each need to find "the other" in ourselves and study it carefully. And if that could be done on a cultural level as well, maybe the world could resolve into an interesting state of peacefulness, not a boring one. The dour and hardworking Germans could see the slothful Greeks and the sensual Italians in their unconscious shadow tendencies; the proud French would see that the English with their bad food and lamentable loyalty to royals have a place in the their own less rigorous and democratic unconscious; the noisy Americans could find the place in their psyches where the quiet and polite Japanese reside. And vice versa, too, of course. We are all but small parts of a much larger whole.

However, and this is a big caveat: Such a state of individuation does not come without great suffering on a personal level. Books like this one by Walter Odajnyk may help to prepare the ground for such a development, but the work of bringing it about remains with the solitary individual and the single citizen of the global community.

Preface

This book has its origins in C. G. Jung's observation that although logically the opposite of love is hate, psychologically the opposite of love is a will to Power.[9] When I was an Assistant Professor of Political Science at Columbia University concerned with the theory and application of power, Jung's idea intrigued me. It certainly spoke directly to Machiavelli's maxim that it is better for a ruler to be feared than to be loved. The equation also explained the lack of attention to personal relations on the part of many individuals interested in power. Concurrently I observed that people devoted to furthering loving relationships were less involved with issues of power. I thought the contrast merited attention.

As I gradually changed my profession from Political Science to Analytical Psychology, the question of opposition continued to interest me. Like so many of my contemporaries, I was familiar with Freud's anal, oral, phallic and genital types, a model based on the vicissitudes of a person's psychological development. As a Jungian analyst, I also became conversant with Jung's typology and its classification of individuals into extraverts or introverts, and feeling, thinking, sensation and intuitive types. But neither schema addressed the psychological differences between what I began to think of as Power and Eros types.

In addition to Power and Eros, I took account of another evident difference—that between those individuals interested in the material universe, the world of objects, and others fascinated by the realm of spirit, the world of ideas. Again I found confirmation in Jung's statement, "that there are some people whose attitude is essentially spiritual and others whose attitude is essentially materialistic."[10] He continues, "It must not be imagined that such an attitude is acquired accidentally or springs from mere misunderstanding. Very often they are ingrained passions which no criticism and no persuasion can stamp out."[11] With the addition of the Matter and Spirit types, I felt I had a fairly comprehensive typology, particularly if I retained Jung's distinction between extraverts and introverts. I could then speak of extraverted and introverted Power and Eros types and extraverted and introverted Matter and Spirit types.

In contrast to Jung's typology, which describes a person's conscious orientation, my typology is concerned with unconscious motivations.

However, I am not using the term "unconscious motivations" in the Freudian sense, as repressed desires and impulses, but as referring to psychic energy that seeks expression in everyday attitudes and forms of behavior. In Jung's conception of the psyche, the personal unconscious is organized through feeling-toned clusters of energy or complexes, while the transpersonal or collective unconscious is structured by the psychic analogues of instincts or archetypes. My typology makes use of four of these archetypes: Power, Eros, Spirit and Matter. I define Power as an urge for domination and control; Eros as concern with relations and connections, and not only among people; Spirit as a fascination with the realm of art, fantasy and ideas; and Matter as interest in physical objects and the natural world. As archetypes they are not merely abstract, conceptual categories. Every archetype consists of a psychic image, an emotional charge and an energetic dynamism that seeks to realize the contents of the archetype in action.

By adding these four fundamental dynamics that provide the energy and a sense of direction for conscious functioning, archetypal-motivational typology deepens and completes Jung's typology. The combination of the two allows for a more dimensional grasp of personality than an assessment based on conscious preferences alone. For example, knowing someone is an introverted thinking sensation type does not disclose the motivational style or area of interest to which these functions are devoted. Archetypal-motivational typology, on the other hand, may reveal that the introversion, thinking and sensation are used in the pursuit of power. Many political scientists, incidentally, fit this typological profile. Because of their introversion, they rarely seek elected office, but, instead, find satisfaction in being the "power behind the throne." They use their thinking and capacity for organizing facts to teach and write books on politics or to advise those who wield power in the public arena.

As I continued to explore the relationship between the conscious functions and archetypal motivations, I realized that the above four archetypes are actually archetypal cores of the four functions. Power, which is closely related to Logos, is the archetypal core of the thinking function, Eros of the feeling function, Spirit of the intuitive function, and Matter of the sensation function. I elaborate upon this intriguing possibility in Chapter 1.

In addition to the motivations of Power, Eros, Spirit and Matter, I was always struck by the fact that many people have either a soulful or a spirited temperament. In other words, to use the Taoist concepts, some people tend to have more yin energy, others more yang energy.

Soulful or yin people like to feel their way into things; they tend to be reflective, slow and deliberate. Spirited or yang people, by contrast, are fiery, impatient and direct in their approach to life. I began to think of the soulful and spirited temperaments, therefore, as qualities that give a certain tone to the personality as a whole rather than as specific motivations or functions.

With the addition of the temperamental qualities of soulfulness and spiritedness my typology is complete. To free the terms *matter* and *spirit* from their religious and philosophical connotations, and to avoid confusion with the temperamental qualities of soulfulness and spiritedness, I use the Greek words *physis* for matter and *pneuma* for spirit. Furthermore, paralleling the dyads of thinking/feeling, sensation/intuition, judging/perceiving in Jungian typology, the archetypal motivations are also arranged in opposing pairs: Power/Eros, Physis/Pneuma, Soulfulness/Spiritedness. Each of the motivational dyads has a specific character: the first pair refers to a *style of functioning*, the second pair to an *area of interest* and the third pair to *temperamental predisposition*.

Again following the schema of dominant and auxiliary functions in Jungian typology, my typology also identifies dominant and secondary motivations and agrees that the secondary motivation can never be the opposing archetype of a pair. Thus, if the dominant motivation is a style of behavior, that is, either Power or Eros, the secondary motivation will be an area of interest, either Physis or Pneuma. On the other hand, if the dominant motivation is an area of interest, then the secondary motivation will be a style of behavior. This arrangement flows from the fact that the aims and motivations of Power are contrary to those of Eros, and the aims and the motivations of Physis are incompatible with those of Pneuma.

The basic eight permutations of archetypal-motivational typology, therefore, are as follows: Power Pneuma; Power Physis; Eros Pneuma; Eros Physis; Pneuma Power; Physis Power; Pneuma Eros; Physis Eros. With the addition of Jung's categories of introversion and extraversion and the temperamental qualities of soulfulness and spiritedness to the eight basic types, a fully elaborated archetypal-motivational typology reads, for example: extraverted soulful Pneuma Power type, or introverted spirited Physis Eros type. The first term describes the basic attitudinal orientation, the second the temperamental quality, the third the auxiliary motivation, and the last the dominant motivation. (Readers familiar with Jung's and Myers-Briggs' typology will note that I have reversed the order of the dominant and secondary categories, with the secondary motivation preceding the dominant one.) In keeping with the schema used in Jungian typology, each half of the two pairs that is not dominant or secondary becomes a tertiary or an inferior motivation. The dominant drive is opposed by the inferior motivation and the secondary drive by the tertiary motivation.[12] Figure 1 below illustrates the dynamics.

The inferior motivation is the most unconscious and least developed of the four archetypes. But that does not mean it has no influence on the personality. On the contrary, because the inferior motivation is rooted in the unconscious, it has an energetic charge that gives people a sense that they are expressing the deepest strivings of their personality. Power types, therefore, may swear they are profoundly interested in Eros and relationships, while Physis types will talk enthusiastically about their religious faith or fascination with occult phenomena. However, in quality, the inferior motivation is essentially a caricature, more of a black and white reaction when compared to the same motivation when it is either dominant or secondary and consciously expressed.

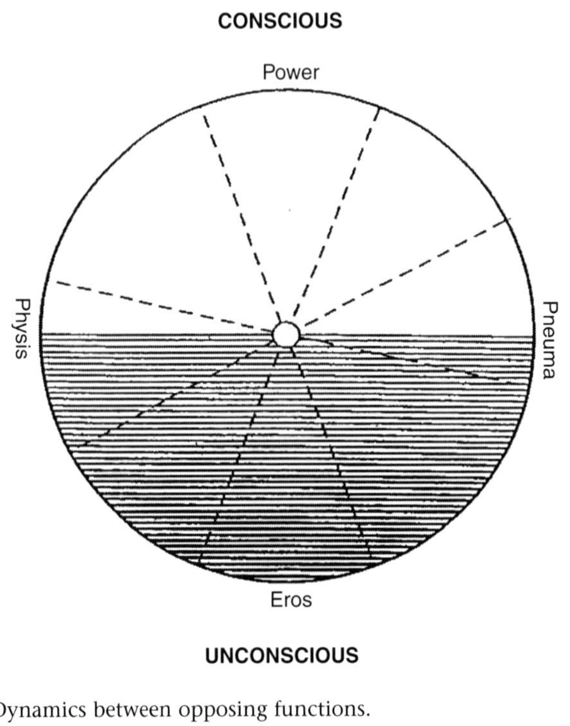

Figure 1 Dynamics between opposing functions.

Having developed a typology based on unconscious motivations, I thought it only fitting to demonstrate its validity with a typological assessment of the three founders of the psychology of the unconscious, Freud, Adler and Jung. In the course of that analysis, I discovered that I was completing the work begun by Jung when he became interested in the influence of temperament on psychological theory. Immediately after his break with Freud, he set out to create a typology which he hoped would enable him to understand the theoretical differences between Freud and Adler, who had also parted company with Freud, as well as his own standpoint.

Taking his cue from the pioneering American psychologist William James, who observed that temperament lies at the heart of many philosophical disputes,[13] Jung sought to discover the temperamental biases of Freud and Adler. Not satisfied with James' simple distinction between tough-minded empiricists and tender-minded rationalists, Jung fashioned a typology that encompassed a comprehensive range of psychological attitudes and functions. He also redefined the empiricist, who is oriented towards outer facts, as an *extravert*, and the rationalist, who is concerned with internal phenomena, as an *introvert*. Jung coined these terms and gave them psychological definitions: extraversion refers to the flow of psychic energy towards the outer world; introversion to the flow of psychic energy towards the inner contents of the psyche. The extravert, therefore, is objective in orientation, the introvert subjective.

Originally Jung linked extraversion with feeling and introversion with thinking, but upon further consideration he separated the pairs. Extraversion and introversion became the two paramount categories that combined with either feeling or thinking. He subsequently added sensing and intuiting to feeling and thinking and referred to these ways of either perceiving (sensation and intuition) or evaluating (feeling and thinking) reality as conscious *functions*. Jung regarded extraversion and introversion, as basic *attitudes* that determined whether the functions were focused on objective or subjective data. As already mentioned, he further arranged the two attitudes and the four functions in opposing pairs: extraversion/introversion; thinking/feeling; sensation/intuition.

With these categories Jung addressed the conflicting views of Freud and Adler. He decided that Freud's theory was extraverted since it was primarily concerned with outer objects, which either furthered or hindered the subject's desire for pleasure. Adler's theory, by contrast, was introverted because it emphasized the subject who sought to dominate external objects because they threatened the subject's internal well-being and sense of security. As a rule, Jung concluded, "the extraverted theory holds good for the extraverted type, the introverted theory for the introverted type."[14]

The problem with Jung's hypothesis is that Freud was not an extravert and Adler was not an introvert. When Jung became aware of these discrepancies he modified his stance and proposed that Freud's theory was the product of his inferior extraverted thinking. By way of explanation, Jung argued that originally Freud was an introverted feeling type who had suffered an emotional trauma and cultivated his thinking as a reaction formation: for "when feeling has been scared off," Jung stated, "one escapes into thinking!"[15] (See Chapter 5 for a discussion of the entire matter.) No similar argument was proposed for the extraverted Adler who, according to Jung, produced an introverted theory. We are therefore left to either speculate about the trauma responsible for the change from Adler's original extraversion to introversion or, more reasonably, simply to question Jung's explanatory hypothesis that extraversion and introversion account for the theoretical differences between Freud and Adler.

Thus, although Jung created a typology to understand the conflict between Freud and Adler, the effort did not serve his intent. The archetypal-motivational typology that I detail in this book seeks to remedy the situation by introducing categories that explain the theoretical differences, not only between Freud and Adler, but also between Jung and his two erstwhile colleagues

From my perspective, therefore, Freud is an introverted spirited Power Physis type, with Physis as his dominant archetypal motivation and Power as the secondary motivation. Adler is an extraverted soulful Physis Eros type, with Eros as his dominant motivation and Physis secondary. Jung is an introverted soulful Power Pneuma type, with Pneuma as his primary motivation and Power secondary.

As evident from the above classification, archetypal-motivational typology directly addresses the basic premises of the founders of depth psychology. Three of its main categories, Eros, Power and Pneuma, refer to the central theoretical orientations of Freud, Adler and Jung. The archetypal motivations of Eros and Power, not the attitudes of extraversion and introversion, are the principles that separate Freud and Adler and account for their conceptual differences. Furthermore, I disagree with Jung's initial idea that Freud was an extravert and with his later reformulation that Freud's theory was the product of inferior extraverted thinking. Similarly, I question Jung's conclusion that Adler was an introvert who consequently created an introverted theory. I argue instead, that both Freud and Adler were orientated towards material reality because they had the archetypal motivation of Physis in common. Jung, on the other hand, was a Pneuma type and opposite in motivation from the other two men.

When I assess the personalities of the three depth psychologists it appears that each created a theory based on his less developed archetypal motivations. As each man investigated his unconscious, he encountered the inferior sides of his conscious motivations and concluded that these motivations must be the dominant characteristic of the unconscious psyche. Thus, Freud's theory emphasized the archetype of Eros, the opposite of his secondary motivation, Power; however, as a dominant Physis type, he experienced Eros in spiritual terms and hence made it into a dogma. Adler's dominant motivation was Eros; consequently his inferior and most unconscious drive was Power. The issue of power, therefore, became the leitmotif of Adler's psychology. Jung's dominant motivation was Pneuma, which accounts for his fascination with alchemy, that is, with matter and its transformation. These conclusions will be elaborated upon in the subsequent chapters of the book.

A century has passed since 1912 when Jung delivered his lectures on "The Theory of Psychoanalysis" at Fordham University in New York City. In his Foreword to the volume of the lectures, he acknowledged that on various points he had arrived at similar conclusions to Adler, knowing quite well that in the previous year Adler had been unceremoniously drummed out of the Vienna Psychoanalytic Society. With the Fordham lectures and the appearance of his book, *Transformations and Symbols of the Libido* (the original title of *Symbols of Transformation*), Jung was publicly announcing his differences with Freud. He knew it was only a matter of time before he, too, would go his separate way. In *Psychological Types*, published in 1921, Jung made an effort to understand the role that temperament played in the divergent approaches to the psyche evident in his, Adler's and Freud's theoretical disagreements. He was, however, enmeshed in the situation and can therefore hardly be faulted for not being fully objective in his assessments. With the distance of many years, it is now possible to appraise in a dispassionate manner the personalities, the cultural atmosphere and the intellectual trends of the time when these disputes occurred. Thus, in addition to proposing a new typology based on archetypal unconscious motivations, this book also completes the work begun by Jung when he sought to understand the influence of temperament on the creative unfolding of depth psychology.

I discuss the above issue and apply the various categories of archetypal-motivational typology to the three pioneering explorers of the unconscious in the latter part of this book. To begin, however, Chapter 1 introduces the general topic of typology and outlines the basic model of archetypal-motivational typology. Because Power, Eros, Physis and Pneuma are archetypes and not merely abstract concepts, they are best elaborated through mythology, which depicts such dominants in personified images and stories. Chapter 2, therefore, outlines the mythological antecedents of these four archetypes. Chapter 3 describes eight basic personality types derived from the extraverted and introverted expression of the first four archetypes. Chapter 4 defines the archetypes of Soul and Spirit, again in mythological terms, and portrays the soulful or spirited temperament resulting from the predominance of one or the other. Chapter 5 addresses the influence of temperament and typology on the theories of Freud, Adler and Jung and begins to note the differences among them. Chapters 6 through 9 offer a detailed analysis of the life and work of Freud, Adler and Jung in light of the categories of archetypal-motivational typology. A concluding chapter summarizes the findings of the book, attempts to clear up possible areas of confusion, and addresses a number of important cultural and personal implications of the new typology.

After the conclusion, two appendices follow. The first, "Jungian Archetypal Typologies," outlines earlier typologies based on Jung's archetypal conception of the psyche in order to provide an historical and conceptual context for archetypal-motivational typology. The second appendix, "Primacy of Spirit in the *I Ching*," speaks to the imposition of a patriarchal bias by Confucius onto the original Taoist rendering of this ancient Chinese book of divination. Finally, an Addendum offers a self-administered archetypal-motivational typology test as a preliminary instrument for assessing the types described.

Acknowledgments

I am grateful to Pacifica Graduate Institute, its Chancellor, Dr. Stephen Aizenstat and its President, Dr. Carol S. Pearson, for providing the congenial academic environment that made this study possible. Dr. Murray Stein, Jungian analyst, author and President of the International School for Analytical Psychology, Zürich, was kind enough to write the Foreword, placing *Archetype and Character* in a historical and contemporary theoretical context. Dr. Patrick Mahaffey, chair of the Mythological Studies Program, and my colleagues Drs. Christine Downing, Ginette Paris, Glen Slater and Dennis Slattery all read and commented on Chapter 5. Christine Downing, in addition, engaged the contents of Chapters 2, 4 and 6 in a sustained dialogue with astute observations, reactions and corrections. Dr. Carl Levenson, Professor of Philosophy at the State University of Idaho, provided several references and read the entire manuscript in a thoughtful, responsive manner. Stephanie Westphal edited the first draft with skill, sensitivity and uncommon acumen. Mark Kelly, Reference Librarian; Richard Buchen, Special Collections Librarian; Alain Dussert, Director of Library Services; Paul Beck, PC/LAN Engineer; and other staff members of the Pacifica Graduate Institute were always available and helpful with their expertise and knowledge. My wife, Katherine Willner Odesmith, participated in the composition of this book from its very inception. She read, edited and reviewed all the essential components of the manuscript. Above all she generously allowed time and space for me to bring the book to a successful conclusion.

1
Introduction: Typology

Typology in the ancient world

Typology seeks to understand the differences among individuals based on the observation of their dominant personality traits. The earliest form of this endeavor is astrology which appears to have arisen spontaneously during the third millennium BC in different parts of the world: Mesopotamia, Egypt, India and China. Interestingly enough, 5000 years later astrology remains the most sophisticated and nuanced description of personality. Even without accepting the basic premise of astrology, that the position of the sun, moon, planets and constellations at the time of birth determines a personal character, one can appreciate its differentiated classification of personality types.[1]

The second ancient system of typology is associated with the classic theory of the four elements and appears in both the West and the East during the first millennium BC. In ancient Greece, fire, water, earth and air were considered the basic constituents of the material universe.[2] The Greek physician Hippocrates (*c.* 460–377 BC) correlated these elements with four bodily fluids or humors: fire with "yellow choler," or adrenaline in modern terms (*choler* is the archaic term for humor or fluid); water with "white choler," or lymph and mucous; earth with "black choler," or bile; and air with "red choler," or blood.[3] Hippocrates reasoned that illness was a consequence of an imbalance of the four humors, which in a healthy body are of equal proportion. The aim of medical treatment, then, was to restore the equilibrium. Claudius Galen, a second century AD Roman physician of Greek origin, introduced the link between the four humors and personality. Galen decided that a perfect balance among the four humors was a theoretical ideal. In practice he found that one of the humors tended to predominate and influence a person's temperament. The dominance of yellow choler, or adrenaline, gave rise to what he characterized as a choleric, volatile and angry temperament. An imbalance in favor of white choler, or phlegm, produced a phlegmatic, calm and easy going temperament. An excess of black choler, or bile, caused a melancholic or depressed temperament. The dominance of red choler, or blood, produced a sanguine or optimistic temperament. Throughout the centuries, the ancient science of astrology and Galen's typology remained the most widely accepted classifications of human character and behavior.[4] Physiognomy, phrenology and palmistry were other popular typologies; these were based on the body, on the external configuration of the face, head and hands.[5]

There were also purely psychological descriptions of character during the classic period. In the *Nicomachean Ethics*, Aristotle discussed various types of people in terms of their virtue, for example: the vainglorious, the contentious, the great-souled, the good-tempered and the self-detractor. Aristotle's pupil Theophrastus, in his book *The Characters* (*c*. 319 BC), ignored the criterion of virtue and simply provides a comprehensive outline of 30 different types of characters: for example, the flatterer, the show-off, the fabricator, the person without moral feeling, the slanderer, the penny pincher, the coward, the faultfinder. These character sketches of Theophrastus became the core of "character as a literary genre" and influenced the New Comedy of Menander and the later Roman comedy playwrights, although the "stock character" was already present in the Old Comedy of Aristophanes as well.

Aristotle's mentor, Plato, introduced a novel classification of types based on a tripartite division of the soul into the rational, the spirited and the instinctive. Each of these attributes of the soul had its own separate desire or goal: reason pursued wisdom; spirit, ambition and honor; and instinct, physical satisfaction or pleasure. In his dialogue *Phaedrus*, Plato uses the image of a charioteer driving a chariot pulled by a white and a black horse to describe the situation. The chariot represents the psyche itself, while the charioteer is the rational part, the white horse the spirited, and the black horse the instinctive. In most people one of the three tends to take the lead pulling the chariot in the direction it wants to go. In Plato's view, therefore, based on the dominance of one of the parts, there are three types of people: philosophic, spirited or instinctive. In *The Republic*, Plato associates these temperaments with three forms of government—philosophic, aristocratic and democratic. The first is the ideal form in which reason rules in the person of a philosopher-king. Honor is the ruling principle of aristocratic government. The satisfaction of human wants and desires is the goal of the democratic government. To these three, Plato adds two other forms of government: oligarchy, an intermediate state between aristocracy and democracy in which the spirited element pursues wealth rather than honor; and despotism or tyranny, a perversion of democracy, in which one man alone is allowed to exercise his instincts and desires in an unbridled manner.

Influenced by Plato, the Gnostics also proposed a tripartite typology but one that reflected their particular set of religious values. From their perspective, there were three types of human beings: the *pneumatikoi*, those ruled by the spirit; the *psychoi*, those responding to the promptings of the soul; and the *hylikoi*, those caught by the desires of the body. As with Plato, the classification had a hierarchical order, with the spiritual type superior to the soulful and instinctive types. Jung correlates the Gnostic schema to his thinking, feeling and sensation types, and would probably do the same with Plato's classification, although without the hierarchical correlation.[6]

The eighteenth-century empiricist Scottish philosopher David Hume outlined a typology similar to the Gnostic one: "The Epicurian, or the Man of Elegance and Pleasure"; "The Stoic, of the Man of Action and Virtue"; and "The Platonist, or the Man of Contemplation." But Hume also added a fourth type, "The Skeptic," a subset of the Man of Contemplation and one that apparently described his own philosophical attitude.[7]

In contrast, Hume's contemporary, the idealist German philosopher Immanuel Kant, adapted Galen's typology but arranged the temperaments according to the predominance of either feeling or volition. Thus, he considered the sanguine and melancholic types as feeling temperaments and the choleric and phlegmatic as volitional temperaments.

Another Enlightenment period German thinker, Friedrich Schiller, described two types of people, the realist and the idealist. He ascribed the difference between the two to the dominance of the *Sinnestrieb* ("the sensuous drive") in the realist and of the *Formtrieb* ("the formal drive") in the idealist. The two drives or instincts are in conflict with each other: the sensuous drive pursues a constant flow and alteration of sensuous feeling; the formal drive seeks to impose a conceptual and moral order on the world. Schiller thought the two can be reconciled through a third instinct, *Spieltrieb*, the instinct for play: "For, to declare it once and for all, Man plays only when he is in the full sense of the word a man, and *he is only wholly Man when he is playing*."[8]

A typology reminiscent of Schiller's formal and sensuous types was elaborated by the late nineteenth-century American philosopher and psychologist William James. James' typology, however, refers primarily to philosophers, whom he classifies as either empiricists or rationalists. The empiricists emphasize the primacy of sensation as the basis of knowledge. The rationalists, on the other hand, argue that the formal categories or structures of the mind determine the nature of human cognition. He called the first type of thinker "tough-minded" and the second type "tender-minded". In his first essay, "A Contribution to the Study of Psychological Types" (1913), Jung added that they could also be called "materially-minded" and "spiritually-minded."

In comparison to the essentially philosophical typologies noted above, the emotionally based typology described by the nineteenth-century French utopian theorist Charles Fourier is highly intricate and complex. In his view, there are 12 innate drives or passions that determined personality and character. Five are *luxurious* and associated with the desires of the five senses; four are *affective*, based on the need for other people; and three are *distributive*: that is, love of variety; love of intrigue; and a third, which was a composite of the 12 passions. The distributive drives govern the gratification of the other nine. Fourier amalgamates the 12 passions in various ways for a total of 810 different personality types. Consequently, his ideal community, called a *phalanx*, consists of 1620 people, with a male and female representative of each of the 810 types.

Jung's typology

The above outline presents the historical context in which Jung introduced his typology in 1921 with the publication of *Psychological Types*.[9] In this work he was primarily interested in describing how consciousness orients itself to reality. To begin with, he thought that most people can be divided into those who spontaneously embrace the world and those whose first impulse is to shy away from direct contact with outer reality. He coined the terms *extravert* and *introvert* to characterize these two modes of reaction.

Jung asserted that the difference between the two attitudes had to do with the flow of psychic libido. The extravert's libido streams outwards, toward people and external objects and is generally embracing and positive in its relation to the world. One should not, however, mistake extraversion for Eros. There are certainly extraverts whose dominant archetypal motivation, in terms of my typology, is Eros. But most extraverts' positive relationship to the world is simply the result of their extraversion. People are often surprised when the intense interest they receive from extraverts does not materialize into ongoing personal relationships. For extraverts with little or no Eros, the old adage holds true: out of sight is out of mind.

The introvert's libido, on the other hand, moves inwards toward the subjective realm of feelings, thought and fantasies. It recoils from the objects of the outer world and pursues, instead, the impressions these objects make within the psyche. One should keep in mind, however, that for an introvert, the inner images are as objective as the outer events are for an extravert. Nevertheless, introversion does not necessarily translate to depth of soul. There are introverted individuals who may plumb the depths of their souls; but for many people introversion is simply a way of being in the world and their inner concerns may be utterly banal.

Next, Jung reasoned that there are essentially four ways in which people apprehend reality: through thinking, feeling, intuition or sensation. Extraversion and introversion give people a sense of orientation or direction. But once the direction has been established, these four functions organize and evaluate reality. Sensation and intuition provide knowledge of the objects a person encounters. Thinking organizes this knowledge into a coherent structure and seeks to grasp the object's significance or meaning. Finally, the capacity for feeling provides a value judgment, which can be a highly differentiated evaluation, based on aesthetic or moral criteria, for example, or simply a subjective reaction of like and dislike.

Thinking, incidentally, is not to be equated with intelligence. Intelligence is the capacity for knowledge and understanding, while thinking is a psychological function which "brings the contents of ideation into conceptual connection with one another."[10] And I would add, thinking also compares and contrasts these contents. A thinking type can engage in such connective and discriminating activity but with little insight and understanding. It is intelligence that brings meaning to the thinking process. Similarly, a sensation type may collect and classify data, but only intelligence can make sense of the data.

As extraversion and introversion tend to be opposite in orientation, Jung proposed that thinking and feeling are opposite in function, as are sensation and intuition. Although one can move quickly back and forth between the opposing functions, each side of the pair is incompatible with the other: intuition seeks to grasp the whole, sensation is focused on the details; thinking is concerned with the coherence and structure of a phenomenon, feeling attempts to place a value on it. Strictly speaking, the two cannot occur at the same time. In reality, however, many people have not fully separated out the functions from each other and use them in a "contaminated" manner.

In any case, with the above categories, Jung defined eight basic psychological types: extraverted thinking, feeling, sensation and intuition types and introverted thinking, feeling, sensation and intuition types. He also found that most people habitually favor one of the four functions, but, in addition, rely upon another function in their interaction with reality. The second function, however, has to be compatible with the dominant one. A thinking type, for instance, cannot use feeling as the secondary function and a sensation type cannot use intuition as the auxiliary function. With the addition of the second function, Jung's typology now has 16 types, usually described in the following terms: extraverted intuitive feeling type or introverted thinking sensation type, with the dominant function placed first after extraversion or introversion. The orientation and functions not consciously deployed remain less developed and more unconscious. These are called the tertiary and the inferior functions. The inferior function is the one directly opposite the dominant function and the most undeveloped and unconscious of the four. A complete typological description, therefore, may read: extraverted thinking intuitive type with inferior feeling, or introverted feeling sensation type with inferior thinking.

Jung considered the above combinations of extraverted and introverted orientations and the thinking, feeling, intuitive and sensation functions to be psychological and mental categories that influence the manner in which human beings encounter and organize all phenomena presented to their ego consciousness. His typology appears to have a comprehensive scope because it is difficult to imagine any other conscious ways, aside from those he lists, in which human beings apprehend, organize and evaluate reality. Unlike earlier typologies, which were based on differences in temperament (for example, melancholic) or styles of functioning in the world (for example, Gemini), Jung's typology rests on operations of the psyche common to all human beings. Every person has and makes use of the four functions he describes and it is only a matter of temperament or habit that determines one's typology. Moreover, since everyone has the capacity to use all four of the functions, and can also alternate between introversion and extraversion, it means that it is possible to alter one's temperamental or habitual manner of apprehending reality and to change one's typology. He considered typology a dynamic and not a static phenomenon which changed with circumstances and during various stages of life. In fact, Jung's idea of psychological development includes the aim of consciously attempting to improve one's inferior orientations and functions to achieve a "well-rounded" personality.

Archetypal-motivational typology

In contrast to Jung's typology, with its focus on conscious orientation and functioning, archetypal-motivational typology explores the *unconscious archetypal motivations* that inform a person's conscious attitudes and behavior and outlines a typology based on these motivations. As previously mentioned, in Jung's conception of the psyche the personal unconscious is organized through feeling-toned clusters of energy or complexes, while the transpersonal or collective unconscious is structured by the archetypes, which he regards as psychic analogues of instincts. Actually, he thinks that every major archetype is connected to an instinct. Consequently, unconscious archetypal motivations are innate drives that seek expression in everyday attitudes and forms of behavior. They are not repressed or sublimated desires that undergo a process of displacement, but are basic drives that operate openly and directly. Archetypal-motivational typology makes use of four of these archetypes: Power, Eros, Pneuma (spirit), and Physis (matter). I define Power as the urge for domination and control; Eros as the desire for connections and union; Pneuma as fascination with art, fantasy and ideas; and Physis as interest in the natural universe.

As I indicated in the Preface, my interest in constructing a typology using the above four archetypes stems from Jung's observation that although logically it appears that "the opposite of love is hate . . . psychologically it is the will to power"; for where love reigns "there is no will to power; where the will to power is paramount, love is lacking."[11] In "The Franklin's Tale" of *The Canterbury Tales*, Chaucer, too, notes the opposition:

> Love will not be constrained by mastery;
> When mastery comes the god of love anon
> Stretches his wings and farewell! He is gone.[12]

Jung is correct in seeing the logical opposition between love and hate as erroneous, for both are part of the Eros archetype: love is a positive form of connection, hate, a negative one. (The reader needs to keep in mind that Eros is a drive for connection; love is a form of connection, but so is hatred. Since in the popular imagination Eros is usually linked with romantic or sexual love, I use the term *eros* with a small "e" to designate this partial aspect of the archetype of Eros, and a capital "E" for the more comprehensive notion of Eros as a drive for union or connection.) Edward Albee's play, *Who's Afraid of Virginia Woolf?* is a stark example of the negative aspects of Eros and its often desperate need for connection. The opposition between Power and Eros, on the other hand, is valid. Human experience, borne out by the poet, shows they tend to be exclusive of one another: if one is dominant, the other recedes in significance and value.

The opposition between Matter and Spirit may, at first glance, seem a logical rather than a psychological contrast, similar to that between high and low. But, actually, the opposition of these two archetypal principles is pre-logical and non-rational. It makes its appearance early in the human psyche with the rise of consciousness and a tendency to make a distinction between ordinary and spiritual reality, between the sacred and the profane. Hence, the duality of Matter and Spirit has a long religious and philosophical tradition. Jung observes that although the names for Matter and Spirit "are exceedingly relative, underlying them are very real opposites that are part of the energetic structure of the physical and of the psychic world, and without them no existence of any kind could be established."[13]

In "Psychological Factors Determining Human Behaviour," a 1936 lecture delivered at the Harvard Tercentenary Conference of Arts and Sciences, Jung argued for the presence of three psychological modalities that influence human behavior: the conscious and the unconscious; extraversion and introversion; spirit and matter. The reality of matter is attested to by sense-perceptions; while the existence of spirit is confirmed by psychic experience. In the end, he felt, "it would not be too much to say that the most crucial problems of the individual and of society turn upon the way the psyche functions in regard to spirit and matter."[14] In the construction of my typology, it therefore seems appropriate to take into account this significant duality.

As we shall see, I also make use of the modality of extraversion and introversion. But at this point, I wish to emphasize that archetypal-motivational typology acknowledges the essential modality of conscious and unconscious by describing the *unconscious motivations that inform the aims toward which the conscious attitudes and functions that characterize Jung's typology are directed*. An analogy may be drawn with the structure of a home: the first floor and the upper stories, with doors and windows open to the world, represent the four functions. The four archetypes are in the basement, sealed off from the rest of the house and not visible to the outside world. But like the electricity, the plumbing and the heating, they sustain the environment which allows the inhabitants of the house to pursue their daily life. More than that—and here is where the analogy breaks down—these archetypes not only supply the energy for the upper stories, they also provide the direction for the conscious orientations and functions.

Like the four functions, the four archetypes are arranged in opposing pairs: Power–Eros; Physis–Pneuma. I also make a distinction between the two pairs. Power and Eros are *styles* or ways of functioning; Physis and Pneuma are the two *areas* in which the functioning takes place. Individuals who use Power as a style of functioning, have a desire to exercise dominance or control in all areas of life—inner or outer reality, personal and social relations. Those with Eros as the main style are primarily concerned with union, again, in all areas of life—in mental or imaginal constructs, in the physical universe and in human relationships. People with Physis (Matter) as their preferred realm of interest, are interested in everything that has material existence, everything that can be perceived and apprehended by the senses. And those with Pneuma (Spirit) as their area of interest are concerned with the life of the mind or the psyche—imagination, spirituality, feeling, thinking. At first sight, it may appear that Physis is a form of extraversion and Pneuma a form of introversion. But, as I will demonstrate, an introvert can be motivated by the archetype of Physis and an extravert by the archetype of Pneuma.

I am aware that traditionally, the distinction is between Eros as desire and Logos as reason and not between Eros and Power. Moreover, the classical Greek opposition was between Eros as harmony and Eris as discord or strife. Freud introduced his own pairing, with Eros as the life instinct and Thanathos as the death drive. (See Chapter 5 for a discussion of Freud's thesis and Jung's response.) I agree that Eros and Logos are the basic opposites, but I also think that the expression of Logos is closely associated with the exercise and manifestation of Power. (See the mythological illustrations of the archetype of Power in Chapter 2.) Archetypal-motivational typology, therefore, highlights the Power aspects of Logos, and contrasts Power with Eros because that is the opposing pair encountered in human attitudes and behavior. The contrast between Logos and Eros is a conceptual one and not primarily behavioral.

In contrast to the variability of the Eros pairings noted above, the opposition between Physis and Pneuma is historically stable and well established. It is present in many creation myths with the separation of heaven and earth. The animism of early cultures assumes the existence of a spirit realm as distinct from the physical world. In Taoism, the opposition is a complementary interaction between the universal principle of yin and yang. Philosophically, the distinction is present in Plato's concepts of being and becoming and Kant's noumena and phenomena. In religious hermeneutics, the difference between Physis and Pneuma makes itself felt in the centuries-old conflict between those who insist on an historical and literal reading of the scriptures and those who favor a symbolic or allegorical exegesis. The emphasis on "the letter of the law" versus "the spirit of the law" is another illustration of how these two archetypal orientations influence fundamental attitudes toward reality. More than that, they determine what is regarded as true or false, both in a religious and philosophic sense.

The Physis and Pneuma orientations also provide the basis for valuation, defining what is to be considered important and what is to be disparaged or ignored. For example, the philosopher's love of truth for its own sake or the artist's love of art for its own sake are meaningless to a Physis type whose temperamental tendency is always to ask: "What good is truth if it can't be applied or used in some practical manner? And what exactly is the point of art for art's sake?" On the other hand, these questions are without merit to the Pneuma type who loves theory and art for their own sake, and sees their practical application as a debasement of their essential nature.

The above distinction between Physis and Pneuma does not preclude the Physis type from becoming a philosopher. The distinction between Platonic and Aristotelian and between the idealist and empiricist types of thinkers is a traditional one in philosophy. If interested in philosophy, Power types will gravitate toward political theory and Eros types will espouse the idea of the great chain of being either in its metaphysical or secular evolutionary form.[15]

As Physis types can be philosophers, Pneuma types can be scientists. But, while the Physis types will be drawn to applied science, the Pneuma types will pursue its theoretical formulations. This does not mean, however, that Pneuma types want nothing to do with concrete reality. On the contrary, many seek to shape the world according to their internal image of it, through art or politics, for example. If religiously inclined, they tend to sanctify or ritualize their relationship to matter.

To the above four archetypal motivations I append the temperamental qualities of soulfulness and spiritedness, which confer a particular inflection to the entire personality. In a purely formal way, these qualities are analogous to the judging and perceiving orientations in the Myers-Briggs typology or to the attitudes of introversion and extraversion in Jung's. They add a certain tone to each of the four archetypes and influence the manner of their expression. Even though there is a connection between soulfulness and Eros and between spiritedness and Pneuma, they are different archetypes. (Please see Chapters 2 and 4.) Eros is a specific motivational style of behavior while Pneuma refers to an area of interest. Soulfulness and spiritedness, on the other hand, describe a characteristic quality of the entire personality. Each of the four motivational archetypes, therefore, is modified by the two attitudes of extraversion and introversion and by the two temperamental qualities of soulfulness or spiritedness.

All six of these archetypes employed in archetypal-motivational typology are present in the psyche of every person. My hypothesis is that an inborn tendency determines which archetypes become dominant in the formation of personality. In other words, I think an individual has a natural predisposition for either Power or Eros as a *motivational style*, or way of being in the world, Pneuma or Physis as an *area of interest*, and soulfulness or spiritedness as a *temperamental quality*. It is also true that culture and circumstances may favor or force the development of a certain style, interest and temperament and, in that case, people work against their natural bent and become proficient in expressing the motivations required by the external demands. We know, for instance, that in an extraverted culture, such as the United States, introverts adopt an extroverted style. Similarly, in many cultures young men are expected to be spirited rather than soulful, and in those cultures a soulful young man may repress his natural inclination and cultivate a spirited demeanor. Some people are more flexible in this regard than others; the difference stems from the relative strength of the libido inherent in the motivational drives and temperamental biases.

Furthermore, there is a tendency on the part of people in the second half of life to embrace the neglected sides of their personality. A Power type will begin to develop Eros, a Pneuma type will start to appreciate the perspectives of the Physis type, and soulful types will seek to express their spirited side. The reversal in temperament is particularly noticeable among mature men and women: women who were soulful in their youth become spirited at mid-life; and previously spirited men become soulful as they mature and age. A drive toward the integration of personality and wholeness makes itself felt at this time, uniting the opposites. Consequently, an older person's typology is more complex than that of a younger person and more difficult to measure accurately.

A resistant or defended attitude on the part of an older person toward typological assessment may reflect the transitional phase at mid-life, in which libido flows toward the previously neglected functions. Ideally, therefore, assessment measures should allow for differences among developmental stages.

Archetypal cores of the four functions

In the course of exploring the relationship between the conscious functions of thinking, feeling, intuition, sensation, and the archetypal motivations of Power, Eros, Pneuma/Spirit and Physis/Matter, it dawned on me that these four archetypes were, in fact, the archetypal cores of the four functions. The thinking, feeling, intuiting and sensing functions are in the same category as complexes. In more specific terms, they are connected to the ego and deployed as part of the persona. A thinking type, for example, may identify with the thinking function and consider that manner of encountering the world and interacting with others as key to her or his integral personality.

In Jung's conception of the psyche, a complex is defined as a cluster of associated feelings around a specific psychological content and every complex is considered to have an archetypal core. Each of the four functions is certainly a cluster of associated feelings related to a specific content, namely, to thinking, feeling, sensing and intuiting. Feeling types, for instance, love to exercise their feeling function and will avoid thinking at all costs; intuitive types have no difficulty in gaining an inclusive general impression of a situation, but hate to be pinned down about the specific details.

The theoretical connection between the four archetypes and the four functions, however, does not mean that every Eros motivated person is a feeling type, every Power type relies upon thinking as the dominant function, every Spirit type is an intuitive and all Matter types prefer sensation. These universally shared basic motivations and functions are malleable and influenced by historical, sociological and cultural conditions. There is nothing to prevent an Eros motivated individual, for example, from developing thinking as the dominant function or a Spirit oriented person favoring sensation.

A prior attempt to connect archetypes with the four functions can be found in the work of the Jungian analyst and author, John Beebe. However, Beebe links the archetypes to the dominant, secondary, tertiary and inferior functions, regardless of what these may be, and not to the specific functions of thinking, feeling, intuition and sensation.

Thus, he argues that the dominant function is tied to the hero archetype, the secondary function to the parental archetypes of father and mother, the tertiary function to the eternal child archetype (*puer* and *puella*), and the inferior function to the animus and anima archetypes. He also adds archetypal shadows to the positive archetypes of the four functions. The shadow of the hero is the opposing personality: avoidant, passive-aggressive and paranoid. The rigid, rule-bound *senex* and the controlling, immobilizing witch are the shadows of the helpful parental archetypes. The trickster is the shadow of the puer and puella archetypes. And the anima and animus are shadowed by the demonic personality, which undermines one's sense of self and relationships with others.[16]

In my opinion, Beebe's attribution of the above positive and shadow archetypes to the dominant, secondary, tertiary and inferior functions seems somewhat arbitrary. Perhaps these are the archetypal forces related to his personal typology, but I do not think they have a more general application. The connections, on the other hand, between thinking and Logos, feeling and Eros, intuition and Spirit, and sensation and Matter are not derived from personal psychology, but have an established conceptual and philosophical foundation.

Archetypal-motivational typology: Cultural implications

With some care, archetypal-motivational typology can be applied to historical, cultural and social activities and events. For example, a political convention is an extraverted spirited Power event, while an evangelical revival meeting is an extraverted spirited Pneuma event. Introverted soulful Eros fascinations may range from watching soap operas or reading the novels of D. H. Lawrence and Marcel Proust. There are hard-driving, deal-making Power lunches and seductive, flirtatious Eros lunches. There are Physis lunches where gourmets focus on the taste and quality of the food. In contrast, during Pneuma lunches, the food receives scant attention, or lies uneaten, while the diners commune in a meeting of minds, oblivious to their surroundings, carried off on the wings of thought.

As everyone knows, opposites tend to attract, not only physiologically, but also psychologically. Eros types, therefore, will be attracted to Power types, Physis types to Pneuma types. True, there are Power couples, like FDR and Eleanor Roosevelt or Hillary and Bill Clinton; but even then, one member of the couple will carry the Eros side. People sometimes mistake the Eros charm of either member of the Power couple for affection and friendship. These may certainly be present, but they are, at the same time, consciously cultivated virtues in the service of the Power drive. Hence, the importance of the corporate or political wife, who is expected to embody Eros, but who may, in fact, be as much interested in power as the husband. When she is not, difficulties arise as evidenced by the incidence of depression, alcoholism and divorce among spouses of political and corporate Power types. Incidentally, in a Power type, Eros is less developed and more unconscious than the dominant motivation and therefore sometimes expressed in compulsive sexual or romantic encounters.

Each of the four archetypes can confer a specific character to a historical period or culture. For example, Physis was the dominant archetype of the ancient Egyptians exemplified by the massive pyramids, monumental sculptures and the art of mummification. The Roman Empire and the Age of Imperialism were manifestations of the archetype of Power. These periods were marked by Power considerations as a style of behavior: the seizure of territory was motivated by the Power drive and not by cultural or economic interest in the conquered areas. The Romantic Era, with its emphasis on a relationship to nature and its attempt to speak directly to and connect with the feelings and emotions of the reader, listener or viewer of art, was under the sway of Eros. The Romantic writers, artists and thinkers approached all things, whether material or spiritual, in a feeling and soulful manner. Periclean Athens, the Middle Ages, the Renaissance, the Reformation and the Enlightenment were various expressions of the archetype of Pneuma or Spirit. Interest in matters of spirit dominated these periods and movements. Our modern era, possibly as a counterbalance to the previous dominance of Spirit, is under the influence of the archetype of Matter. The physical world is our main area of preoccupation, with science, technology and massive production and consumption of material goods leading the way. In fact, in the not too distant future, we may achieve the foremost aspiration of the Egyptian civilization—the survival of the life of the body.

In this regard, the intellectual and cultural ethos of the United States, as opposed to that of Europe, for example, tends to be pragmatic and practical in its orientation. Behavioral and experimental psychology are the dominant schools of psychology in the United States, the influence of Freudian depth psychology notwithstanding. Freud actually complained about the American tendency to de-emphasize theory and proceed as quickly as possible to its practical application.[17] The difference between theory and practice, or speaking archetypally, between Spirit and Matter, was more pronounced during the Middle Ages than it is today. So much of the libido of the medieval culture focused on the issue of the conflict between spirit and matter. That opposition was expressed in various ways, as a conflict between Church and State, between reason and faith, between a worldly or a saintly life. Toward the end of the Middle Ages, Cervantes caricatured that polarity in the contrasting figures of Don Quixote and Sancho Panza. In our contemporary Western culture, Matter has conquered Spirit and the conflict between them holds little energy and interest. Instead, a good deal of cultural energy today is centered on the other archetypal pair, Power and Eros. The Power fascination is evident in the dominance of politics in everyday life, and, as befits a Physis oriented culture, the emphasis on sexuality as the expression of Eros. Not matter and spirit, but politics and sex are the driving archetypal forces of our day.

Limitations of typology

Earlier, I mentioned the limitations of Jungian typology: it does not specify the areas of interest to which the four functions are applied or describe the style of behavior through which these interests are pursued; and it gives no indication of the unconscious motivations that determine a person's goals and activities. These limitations, I believe, hold true for other typologies as well: one can be an Aries (astrology), phlegmatic (Galen), Vata (Ayurvedic), sensuous (Schiller), Apollonian (Nietzsche), tough-minded (James), anal (Freud), motor (Adler), moving against people (K. Horney), mesomorph (W. Sheldon), perfectionist (Enneagram), narcissistic (A. Lowen), left-brained (R. Ornstein); in business-centered typologies one may be a company man (M. Maccoby), collaborative (J. Corbett), or a country-club manager (R. R. Blake and J. S. Mouton); and in various Jungian typologies one may be a puer or a senex, or live out the archetypes of Aphrodite or Hera, or of the hero, the warrior or the trickster—but none of these temperamental attitudes, styles or roles will convey anything about the areas of interest to which these possible ways of being and functioning will be applied.[18] Someone with a "country-club management" style, for instance, may have absolutely no interest in business and will use that approach in academics or sports. A warrior type can apply that style to a religious quest, for example, the Knights Templar, the Salvation Army, Shambhala or Rinzai Zen. An Aries is a pioneer, but one can pioneer in politics, business, science, industry, religion, art or culture.

The same limitations are encountered in another popular typology, the Enneagram of Personality developed by the Bolivian-born founder of the Arica school, Oscar Ichazo. Ichazo identified nine ego fixations and accompanying vices that provide the underlying motivations for each of the Enneagram personalities. The vices are anger, pride, envy, avarice, gluttony, lust, sloth, fear and deceit. The list is almost identical with the Seven Deadly Sins in Catholicism and reminiscent of the Three Poisons in Buddhism—anger, desire and delusion. Their negative attributes notwithstanding, these chief features or passions of the Enneagram function as unconscious motivations that inform and define the resulting personalities. For example, the romantic is driven by envy, the mediator by sloth, the perfectionist by anger. Nevertheless, even in these cases, the chief passion will not disclose the area of life to which it will be directed. A romantic can be motivated by envy in personal relationships, in politics, in scientific endeavors, or in acquiring works of art. The same holds true for the chief features and personality traits of all the other Enneagram types. A person's chief passion and resulting personality will not disclose the area of life in which she or he will function or be interested.

Typology and stereotypes

From its inception in astrology to the various personality assessments of today, the purpose of typology is to make sense of the differences encountered among individuals and groups in attitudes and behavior. The impulse to classify different types of human beings stems from scientific curiosity and the desire for knowledge. By its very nature, typology consists of abstract categories. Consequently, it easily lends itself to stereotyping, which is a distortion of its intent, for stereotypes are rigidly held opinions or beliefs. Typology, on the other hand, is a flexible enterprise and those who make use of it are capable of modifying the categories in accordance with newly discovered facts. The advent of psychology in the 19th and early 20th centuries, for instance, led to a re-evaluation of earlier typologies which were based on physiology or on external bodily, cranial and facial features. Nevertheless, every typology illuminates only a circumscribed area of the psyche and should not be seen as exclusive of other typologies. Typologies are heuristic devices or tools and valid only to the extent that they are useful in describing certain attributes of human psychology and behavior. The nature of the psyche or behavior that one seeks to describe should determine the typology one applies. In this regard, typologies function as a form of differential diagnosis. It is important to keep in mind, though, that every typology represents an abstract schema that hardly ever perfectly applies to individuals in the conceptually clear manner that it appears in graphs. Individual variations often contradict the neatly arranged and delineated concepts.

Like all scientific observation and classification, in its best form typology is simply an objective description of differences. Unfortunately, not just typological categories, but every distinction among human beings can be used in a stereotypical manner to buttress prejudice, particularly if that distinction carries connotations of inferiority and superiority. The introduction of cultural, ethical and political evaluations of differences among human beings, therefore, is responsible for such irrational use of typological categories. The fact that sometimes people and institutions wrongfully use typology in this manner does not impugn its validity. These are two separate matters and should not be confused.

2
The Archetypes of Power, Eros, Pneuma and Physis

This chapter is devoted to a detailed description of the four archetypes, Power, Eros, Pneuma and Physis, that serve as the core of archetypal-motivational typology. Because archetypes are fundamental to the human psyche, their earliest expression is found in mythology, which offers the richest illustration of archetypal contents and dynamics. Following the mythological description of each archetype, I provide historical and psychological examples of that archetype's influence on cultural and personal attitudes and behavior.

Power

I begin with Power because Western civilization appears to be motivated primarily by this archetype, even though, as noted above, certain cultural periods were influenced by one or another of the remaining three principles. But the governing archetype of our contemporary civilization seems to be Power. As an expression of dominance and control, there is hardly a more impressive manifestation of power than God's command, "Let there be light, and there was light" (Genesis 1:3). I know of no other creation myth that begins with such a striking display of power and it is noteworthy that the founding myth of our culture is based upon such exercise of will. In most other mythologies, creation is depicted as a spontaneous, organic development, more of an emergence than the consequence of a command. Jehovah's encounter with Job, in which he responds to Job's plea for justice with a litany of his impressive works of creation, provides another occasion for the display of supreme power and essentially a declaration of "might makes right."

Power is closely linked with Logos, whose etymological root *lego* means "to count, tell, say or speak". Thus Psalm 33 states: "By the word of the Lord were the heavens made . . . For he spake, and it was done; he commanded, and it stood fast" (verses 6 and 9). Similarly, the Gospel of St John commences with these words: "In the beginning was the Word and the Word was with God, and the Word was God . . . . All things were made by him; and without him was not any thing made that was made" (verses 1 and 3). Amplifying the concept of Logos in relation to alchemy, Jungian analyst Edward F. Edinger writes: "Logos is the great agent of *separatio* that brings consciousness and power over nature—both within and without—by its capacity to divide, name, and categorize."[1]

In his use of the term "Word" as synonymous with God, St John may have been aware of the classic Greek idea that Logos was the animating spirit and underlying organizing principle of the universe. Aristotle linked Logos to rational persuasion, which proves or disproves a point, and argued that the distinguishing characteristic of human beings is that they are reasoning or rational animals. (The Latin translation of Logos is *ratio*, the root of our word "reason," which together with the word "logic" directly connects the archetypal principle of Logos to the thinking function even as that principle remains associated with the archetype of Power.)

The power theme in our culture continues with the emphasis on the chief attributes of God as the "King of Kings" and "Lord of Lords," and with the first commandment insisting on the primacy of that God. As a symbol, the king manifests the archetype of Power, as does the law with which the king is invariably associated. His word is law. He is both sovereign authority and supreme judge.

The theme of kingship and power persists in the Old Testament anticipation of the Messiah and his millenarian rule. In the New Testament there is a similar expectation of a kingdom of God with Christ enthroned at the right hand of the Father, judging the living and the dead, meting out eternal punishment or reward. Even the Lord's Prayer emphasizes the themes of kingship and power: "Thy kingdom come. Thy will be done in earth, as it is in heaven . . . For thine is the kingdom, and the power, and the glory, for ever" (Matt. 6:13). One can argue that the reason for placing all power in the hand of God is to prevent human beings from becoming megalomaniacal through identification with the archetype of Power. Still, the displacement demonstrates the dominance of the Power drive in a culture where such a move in necessary.

The mythology of the Greeks and the Romans, the other Western religious traditions, also emphasizes power, with Zeus-Jupiter as "King of the Gods". Homer calls him the supreme sovereign and patriarch, father of both gods and men. Zeus presides over the physical, social and moral laws that govern the universe and wields the thunderbolt to enforce his will. The eagle, king of the birds and associated with the sun, is a chief attribute of Zeus and a symbol of Imperial Rome. In other mythologies, the Nordic Thor with his hammer and thunderbolts, the Indian lord of the sky, Indra, with his lightning, and the Egyptian sun-god Ra, king over both gods and men, are other manifestations of the archetype of Power. In every culture the king's power and authority stems from his serving as a representative of the ruling deity on the earth. In Western Europe this archetypal form of legitimacy was codified in the principle of "the divine right of kings."

An interesting attribute of the archetype of Power is that over time, power loses its force or becomes inflexible and rigid and periodically needs to be renewed and rejuvenated. In the modern era periodic elections acknowledge this aspect of power. In ancient Egypt the renewal was institutionalized in the 30 year Sed festival devoted to the restoration and renewal of the pharaoh's vitality. The motif is also found in Sir James Frazer's *The Golden Bough*, with accounts of tribal customs of killing kings when their strength begins to fail and replacing them with younger ones. The rebellion of Zeus against Kronos is the Greco-Roman version of the same phenomenon.

It appears that the archetype of Power, characterized as it is by domination and control, does not allow for change or creativity, hence the need for periodic renewal. Eros, Physis and Pneuma, on the other hand, are characterized by growth, change and motion. These archetypes have other problems and limitations, but generally, rigidity and stagnation are not among them.

Cultural and personal manifestations of the power archetype

Totalitarianism, with its attempt to control every aspect of life including belief, is a graphic illustration of the Power archetype operating with little or no restraints.[2] The two totalitarian movements of the twentieth century, communism and fascism, were based on political theories informed by the power principle. Communism has its philosophical roots in Hegel who envisioned history as a progressive development governed by the ultimate design of the "Absolute Spirit". Marx translated this theological formula into an economic one, with the "laws of production" replacing the Absolute Spirit, and on that basis concluded that capitalism will inevitably give way to socialism and the rule of the proletariat.

Fascism, with its emphasis on "will" as opposed to reason, and its ideas of social Darwinism and Aryan supremacy, has its philosophical roots in Nietzsche. And for Nietzsche the "will to power" is the dominant drive of humanity, superior even to the survival instinct. His idea of the *Übermensch* conceives of future human beings who have overcome the traditional dichotomy of good and evil, and glory in the full expression of their instinctive life.

The archetype of Power is also present in the religious sphere, where the priest or minister, as agent of the divine power, expounder of divine law and administrator of divine grace, is an archetypal power figure. In a theocracy the high priest is the wielder of ultimate power, both spiritual and secular. The earlier religious personalities, the shaman and the magician, are also power figures capable of commanding the spirits and the "animal powers" to do their bidding.

Cultures and individuals ruled by the archetype of Power will find pleasure and meaning in the exercise of control and domination in the area of life in which they happen to have an interest. Power motivated individuals interested, for instance, in religion or spirituality will find pleasure in positions of responsibility and authority in their particular congregation or church, seek to live a disciplined life in accord with the tenets of their religion, or pursue a spiritual practice based on self-control and mindfulness. Scientifically oriented Power individuals will find meaning in the precision required in their experiments or observations and in the careful and methodical reporting of their findings. Of course people interested in political power will be fighting for the dominant political structure or against it. They may associate themselves with it or work in opposition to it, as revolutionaries or anarchists, but in any case they remain engaged with the issue of power.

Power oriented individuals invariably make enemies. In fact, they look for enemies as a way of defining themselves and their standpoint. A certain amount of paranoia, therefore, is a predictable aspect of power, serving both an identifying and defensive function. Paranoid purges, consequently, are inevitable in totalitarian regimes. Offers of accommodation or attempts at appeasement by identified enemies engender disdain, not appreciation or respect. In aristocratic and chivalric times the enemy had to be a noble or a worthy opponent. But most of the time, once identified, the enemy is the target of every conceivable negative projection. Power oriented individuals, with their undeveloped Eros, are, in fact, prone to prejudice and negative stereotyping. Also, for Power types, friendly feelings toward others and close or intimate relationships are periodically subject to tests of loyalty.

In conclusion, cultures and individuals dominated by the archetypal motivation of Power will emphasize, in both their personal and professional lives, the values of self-control, domination, will, authority, discipline, loyalty, law and order. They will seek and identify enemies; personal, political or doctrinal. Their good will and friendly feelings will be limited to those who support and share their cultural and personal values, for their aim is the attainment of specific goals and accomplishments. Alfred Adler, one of the pioneers of depth psychology, offers a comprehensive exposition of the psychology of Power and his work will receive due attention in subsequent chapters.

Eros

Although in the popular imagination Eros is seen in personal and human terms as love, it is primarily an abstract and cosmic principle. As I will be using the term, Eros is the force in the universe that seeks union, not through domination, will or control, but through connection or relation. One should keep in mind, however, that connections and relationships can be either positive or negative, for conflict is also a connection. The first sentence of Jung's *Mysterium Coniunctionis: An Inquiry into the Separation and Synthesis of Psychic Opposites* states: "The factors which come together in the coniunctio are conceived as opposites, either confronting one another in enmity or attracting one another in love."[3] Both love and hate, harmony and strife, therefore, are under the purview of Eros and where possible, it seeks to unite them, even if the union is a paradoxical one, as the epigraph to Jung's other alchemical treatise, *The Psychology of the Transference*, makes clear: "A warring peace, a sweet wound, a mild evil."[4] Eros holds the universe together, whether in enmity or love, keeping it from splitting into meaningless, disconnected, chaotic fragments.

In an Orphic myth, for instance, Eros was the first deity hatched out of the "cosmic egg" and the first opposites, heaven and earth, were formed from the two halves of the broken shell. As the first being to emerge out of the primordial unity of the cosmic egg, Eros retains the chief characteristic of its origins, namely oneness and wholeness, and forever strives to bring about that original state of unity and unite all the opposites once again. Consequently, one could see Eros as a regressive force, supremely conservative. It functions in a compensatory manner to the innovative, expansive creative principle and seeks a reintegration, a return to the source. In human beings that compensatory function is experienced as nostalgia. In its negative expression, Eros is also behind the destructive impulse that seeks to return all forms and beings to their original undifferentiated condition. (Freud's description of the death instinct as the drive that seeks a return to the inorganic primeval state of being discloses this aspect of Eros. From my perspective, however, Freud's distinction between the death drive and Eros is essentially a distinction within the archetype of Eros itself.) Watching children at play, one can see both creative and destructive sides of Eros.[5] At the beach, for instance, both boys and girls love building sand castles and derive equal pleasure from destroying them.

The representations of Eros as a winged youth with bow and arrow (the Hindu Kama, the Greek Eros), refer to the human and personal aspects of this cosmic principle. His arrows, representing the projection of the romantic urge, with its amalgam of biological and psychological drives, inflict wounds and passion (literally, "suffering") that can only be healed by a union with the beloved. Originally the ancient Greeks regarded Eros as one of the winged Spites, such as old age, disease, labor and vice, that were let loose upon the world when Pandora opened the box in which Prometheus had imprisoned them. Only in later antiquity did Eros become "sentimentalized as a beautiful youth."[6] The Renaissance images of "erotes", cherubic children and infants, represent the "love child," the fruit of love, whether as an actual child or as the loving feelings born of the mutual attraction.

Romantic love, coitus and marriage, with their positive and negative potentialities, therefore, are expressions of the underlying meaning of the archetype of Eros, as the force desirous of the cohesion and continuity of the cosmos. In its striving for reintegration and oneness, Eros must reconcile differences and overcome the conflict and separation of opposites.

The cross, with its horizontal and vertical lines meeting in the center, is one of the symbols of the union of opposites; it seems fitting, therefore, that in Christian mythology the God of Love sacrificed himself and redeemed humankind on the cross. The Taoist yin/yang emblem and the intertwined downward and upward pointing triangles of the Star of David are other symbols depicting the paradoxical and all-encompassing aim of this archetype.

Alchemy never tired of creating new images of the union of opposites, among them, the philosophers' stone, the golden flower, the hermaphrodite. Actually, given the goal of the alchemical opus, one could see the work guided not only by Hermes/Mercurius, who—as the *prima materia* at the beginning of the work and the *lapis* at the end of the work—embodies all universal opposites, but equally by the archetype of Eros. In this way, the alchemical Mercurius needs to be seen as an aspect of Eros.

The alchemists' dedication to the investigation of spirit or soul embodied in matter and its redemption through the work of humankind, remind us that the arrows of Eros may fall not just onto human beings, but also onto nature or onto God. In fact, participation in any human endeavor, science, religion, politics, business, art, literature or music for example, may be a passion, again for good or ill, inspired by the arrows of Eros. Many Eros types find more personal satisfaction in these cultural areas than in personal love or human relationships.

Symbolically, the "arrow" and the "net" are the chief objects with which Eros seeks to accomplish its purpose. As we have seen, the arrows represent the psychological process of projection. (I use the term "projection" in the Jungian sense, referring to the spontaneous tendency of the psyche to project its unconscious contents unto the external world and not in the Freudian sense as a defense mechanism.) Projection creates a bridge between our psyche and the world and fosters relationships. Without projection there would be no connection, no fascination, no passion and no desire to know the universe and others.

The veil of Maya is the Indian image of this projection-making tendency of the psyche. The veil of Maya is the "net" that envelops the entire universe and holds it together. Never mind that Maya is an illusory, deceptive, ephemeral unity that must be "seen through" to attain knowledge of ultimate reality and unity with Brahma. The projections of romantic Eros are also illusory and, in time, fall away to reveal the possibilities of a real, or more objective, relationship and love. Paradoxically, these illusions lead to reality and ultimately aim at connection and unity.

In our culture the spider and its "net" are regarded as symbols of the destructive entanglement in the web of illusions. But in many non-Western mythologies the spider is a creator god, a culture hero or a psychopomp; that is, a guide of the soul. The spider's thread is considered the umbilical cord, the golden chain or the link between the created and the creator, and can be used to climb back up and return to one's origins.

In Mid-Eastern myths, gods have nets to catch human beings and bind them to their will. In Persia, the mystics arm themselves with nets to capture God and become one with their Beloved. In Greek myth it seems fitting that Hephaistos captures his wife, Aphrodite, and her lover, Ares, *in flagrante delicto* with an invisible net: here, for all the gods to see, the God of War and the Goddess of Love are caught in a union with the entangling strands of Eros. For unlike the gods of Power, who rely upon overt commands and force to achieve their ends, Eros is more subtle, though no less effective, in attaining its ends, relying upon illusion, deception, seduction and fascination, as well as empathy, compassion, relatedness and love.

Cultural and personal manifestations of the Eros archetype

Individuals and cultures that embody the positive archetype of Eros will tend to have a "holistic" perspective. They will emphasize the interrelatedness of all things, value harmony, charity and altruism, and, ideally, appreciate differences and practice a good deal of tolerance. On the other hand, such cultures and individuals may easily succumb to romantic delusions and cling to naïve, idealistic expectations of people, of gods and reality.

In personal relations, in contrast to the Power types who need to have enemies, positive Eros types place a premium on friendship. Eros extraverts generally manage to make more friends than they can realistically handle. The introverts, on the other hand, prefer a few close friends and view the extraverts' profligacy as superficial and shallow. Power types achieve their goal of dominance and control through force of will, through reward and punishment, intimidation and fear. Eros types are no less adept at domination and control—through uncompromising demands for relatedness and shared feelings. The vices of Power are arrogance, rivalry and ambition, those of Eros are jealousy and possessiveness. As every parent, spouse and family member knows "the ties that bind" are difficult to break. There is such a thing as the tyranny of love just as there is the tyranny of power. Two days after he became engaged to his wife, Freud confessed, "I am so exclusive where I love" . . . and "certainly have a disposition to tyranny."[7] How many family members, out of undying enmity, do not speak to each other? And need I cite the statistics for domestic violence or for the sexual abuse of women and children? Physical violence and emotional torture, the negative sides of Eros, are integral to all intimate relationships. Communities based on the principle of Eros are no less controlling and intolerant than those based on Power: if you do not share the community values or act in a selfish way, you will be reprimanded, in the name of love of course, and ultimately ostracized. In the context of speaking about an overdeveloped maternal complex, Jung even argues that "unconscious Eros always expresses itself as will to power."[8] In other words, at its extreme, an enantiodromia takes place and Eros reverts to its opposite.

But, as noted earlier, one should not think of Eros as only or primarily concerned with the human realm. Eros is a cosmic principle and its positive forms expressed in such notions as the Pythagorian idea of "the harmony of the spheres," Jan Christiaan Smuts' "holism" and Arthur Lovejoy's "the great chain of being." Eros types find meaning and pleasure in seeing how things are intertwined and connected. They seek to live in harmony with nature, marveling at its inherent balance and coherence; the Power types, on the other hand, find pleasure in civilizing and dominating nature. In this respect, the Western religious and scientific traditions are clearly more Power than Eros oriented.

In philosophy, positive Eros types are synthesizers rather than analytical philosophers or deconstructionists.[9] St Augustine, the Renaissance philosopher Marsilio Ficino, the Jewish religious thinker Martin Buber, and the early twentieth-century German phenomenologist Max Scheler are examples of Eros philosophers. In psychology, Eros tends to appear in such movements as Roberto Assagioli's Psychosynthesis, in Carl Rogers' client-centered therapy and empathic listening, and in current attempts at holistic medicine and psychotherapy. I think it is significant that Adler, who as we shall see was an Eros type, referred to his school of thought as individual psychology and avoided the terms "analysis" and "analytical." He admired Jan Christiaan Smuts' philosophy of holism (see his *Holism and Evolution*), felt it confirmed his ideas, and provided a philosophical basis for individual psychology.[10]

Pneuma

The term *Pneuma* in Greek means "breath, wind, spirit". All three synonyms are frequently associated with creation myths and the beginning of life. Thus, "In the beginning," according to Genesis, the Spirit of God "hovered over the face of the waters" and, in some readings of the event, God's breath brought order to the primordial chaos, called "tohu-bohu." God also formed Adam out of "the dust of the ground" and "breathed into his nostrils the breath of life" (Genesis 2:7). In Egyptian mythology, the god Shu holds heaven and earth apart making space for the creation of the world; he is also the air, the wind and the breath of life. The Vedic wind god Vayu, the Blower, is Lord of the Wind and the breath of life; as the air he unites heaven and earth. In China air is the home of *chi*, the breath or vital spirit of universal life. According to a Taoist conception of the Han Dynasty, nine breaths intertwine with each other to fill the space between heaven and earth. And mastery over breath, in Yogic and Taoist meditation practice, is an essential component of spiritual development.

With space and air as primary manifestations of Pneuma, it is easy to see why birds often represent spirit and play a central role in many creation myths. In Egyptian mythology, for instance, the Benu bird brought the cosmic egg from which the world was created to Heliopolis and the sun first broke out of this primeval egg in the form of a goose. The Egyptian god Thoth, inventor of the hieroglyphs and bringer of culture, is represented as an ibis. According to the *Rig Veda* "intelligence . . . is the swiftest of winged creatures."[11] In the New Testament, the dove is one of the personifications of the Holy Spirit. Biblical and Islamic angels, the messengers of God, are often imaged with wings. Similarly, Mercury, the Roman messenger of the gods, has winged feet. The wings symbolize not just locomotion but indicate the spiritual nature of these denizens of the heavenly realms.

Closely associated with the breath is the spoken word. Thus the word is the first manifestation of creator gods in many cultures. In Vedic tradition, "AUM" is the primeval sound, the word that created the universe.[12] In Egypt, Ptah created the world through the thoughts of his heart and the words of his mouth. And as we have seen, the Genesis creation myth begins with, "And God said, Let there be light." The Gospel of St John opens with, "In the beginning was the Word, and the Word was with God, and the Word was God" (1:1). As the active manifestation of spirit, the word carries the seeds of creation and is a fecundating, impregnating and inspiring force. The Virgin Mary, for example, was impregnated by a *logos spermatikos*, the spermatic word: "be it unto me according to thy word" (St Luke 1:38).

The destructive and harmful use of the power of the word is the curse. But even breath can be damaging. The Celts spoke of "druids' breath" that could kill enemies and cause evil and harm. Slavic priests held their breath as they swept out Svantovit's temples, for fear of polluting the atmosphere with evil spirits.[13]

The air is also the realm of light and in many creation myths light is among the first manifestations of the Spirit god. Thus the Egyptian sun god, Ra, is born of the cosmic egg brought by the Benu bird. In alchemy, which can be traced to ancient Egypt, the word as light descends from the sun to take material form in the earth's womb as reddish copper. And in contrast to his earthly, serpent form, Satan has his spiritual or heavenly manifestation as the winged Lucifer: the name means "carrier of light."

Cultural and personal manifestations of the Pneuma archetype

Cultures and individuals marked by the dominance of Pneuma (or Spirit) are devoted to religion, music, art, literature and ideas. They value insight, inspiration and vision. The material world, the body and economic concerns are deemed secondary in importance to these manifestations of spirit. These cultures and individuals are not necessarily interested in making the world sacred but in sublimating the instincts and spiritualizing matter.

In philosophy, the primacy of abstract ideas will be championed over empirical data and personal experience. Philosophic issues are taken seriously and debated in the public arena and given wide currency. Examples of this idealistic bias are found in Plato's notion of the world of "forms" as the source of all material manifestations, Hegel and his idea of the "world spirit" as the determining factor in history, and the Enlightenment philosophers with their emphasis on reason as the universal principle.

In religion, if the culture is introverted, mysticism and monasticism characterize its attitude and practice. Marriage and family, and the pursuit of fame and fortune have less hold on individuals living in these cultures than the exploration of the inner world and spiritual realization. The study of scriptures, prayer, meditation and ritual observance take precedence over secular concerns and economic interests.

If the culture is more secular than religious in orientation, then the arts and sciences will be accorded a place of honor. In science, however, the pursuit of knowledge for its own sake takes precedence over its practical application. In the humanities, artists, musicians, writers, sculptors and architects are the culture heroes. Poets and novelists are expected to give voice not only to the aesthetic but also to the moral sensibilities of their time. The aesthetic sensibility is cultivated and imbues every facet of life. Education reflects these idealistic, theoretical, spiritual and aesthetic considerations.

The vices of cultures ruled by the Pneuma archetype are those of perfectionism, dogmatism and neglect of material reality. A one-sided emphasis on spirituality may make the culture joyless, lifeless and sterile. With their love of religious and philosophical abstractions, such cultures tend to ignore unpleasant material and social conditions. An extreme example is the refusal of medical treatment by strict Jehovah's Witnesses and Christian Science devotees. For after all, this world and its reality are illusory or unimportant in comparison to the essential purity and eternal being of the metaphysical realms.

Physis

While Pneuma refers to heaven and air and the life of the spirit, Physis is associated with the natural, material and soulful manifestations of life. *Physis* is the Greek term for the Latin *materia*; etymologically, both words refer to growth associated with nature. Physis derives from *phusis*, meaning "nature"; its verb is *phuein*, "to bring forth," or "to make grow." The root of the English word "matter" is the Latin *mater*, that is, "mother" and among its variations is *materia*, meaning "tree trunk."

The name of the Greek goddess of grain, Demeter, is a compound of *de*, possibly meaning "earth," and a variation of *mater*. As an archetype, therefore, Physis (or Matter) refers to natural, physical life. From both an etymological and archetypal perspective, it is a modern prejudice to speak of "dead matter." Matter is not dead; on the contrary, it is the *mater*, the mother of all life.

For early Greek philosophers, *physis* was composed of four elements that were arranged in polarities: earth–air; water–fire. This "fourfold Physis," as Jung refers to it, was symbolized by the cross, which appropriately enough appears in the astrological signs for Earth.[14] But the most widespread mythological image of Physis is the serpent or dragon. The "uroboros", the serpent biting its own tail, is an ancient Egyptian and Democritean emblem of Physis—an image of the self-fructifying, never-ending cycle of nature.

The connection between the serpent and life was acknowledged by the ancient Chaldeans who used the same word for both serpent and life. In Arabic the words for serpent, *el-hayyah*, and for life, *el-hayat*, are linked. Given these associations between serpent and life, it is not surprising, therefore, that the serpent is an attribute of all mother goddesses. In fact, in many mythologies, the "cosmic serpent" is the wellspring, the source of all manifestation. It stands for the primal matter or the limitless ocean out of which life emerged. In ancient Egypt, Nun, the primordial water, is most often depicted as a serpent. In Greece, Typhon is the dragon son of Gaia, Mother Earth. Often the dismemberment of the cosmic serpent precipitates the creation of the universe and its multiple manifestations. There are also anthropomorphic parallels to this motif with the dismemberment of the Nordic Ymir, the Persian Gayomart and the Chinese P'an Ku. Nor should we forget Adam, whose name is derived from *adamah*, meaning "earth," and who was formed from the "dust of the ground," which is the realm of the serpent, and whose "rib" provided the *materia* out of which Eve was created.

In Judaism and Christianity the serpent is regarded as the enemy of spirit. Given its ancient association with the earth and the great mother, it is not surprising that with the emergence of the patriarchal archetype in Western religion and culture, the serpent became a symbol of the enemy that had to be overcome: hence Jehovah's curse, "and *dust* shalt thou eat all the days of they life . . . " (Genesis 3:14, emphasis added); and in Christian iconography, this antagonism can be seen in images of St George and the Archangel Michael slaying the dragon.

The Gnostics held a similarly negative view of Physis with myths of the divine Nous (Spirit) caught in the embrace of Physis and of *anima mundi*—the "world soul" and counterpart of the heavenly spirit—imprisoned in the realm of matter. The task of salvation consisted of helping to reassemble the divine sparks of Nous, or to liberate the soul, and return both to their heavenly abode from which they accidentally or inadvertently fell. Jung alludes to this theme of the "fall" when writing about the materialistic tendency of the modern era:

> the human mind has sunk deeply into the sublunary world of matter, thus repeating the Gnostic myth of the Nous, who, beholding his reflection in the depths below, plunged down and was swallowed in the embrace of Physis. The climax of this development was marked in the eighteenth century by the French Revolution, in the nineteenth century by scientific materialism, and in the twentieth century by political and social "realism."[15]

Contrary to appearances, Jung is not being critical in his assessment; he is simply noting that the archetypal psyche is beginning to correct the one-sided emphasis of the patriarchal spirit that had dissociated or split-off the Western psyche from the realms of Physis and soul. Only from the patriarchal perspective is the presence of the soul in matter conceived as a fall into or an imprisonment in matter. From the matriarchal point of view, the world soul is *sui generis*: it arises within matter and does not fall from heaven; nor does it ever separate from matter.

Basing himself on the alchemical tradition, Jung makes a distinction between soul and spirit. (See Chapter 4.) "Spirit" refers to an invisible presence, like the air, and is therefore associated with heaven. "Soul", on the other hand, is the living manifestation of matter and in human beings closely connected with the body and its instinctive and emotional life. In the Taoist formulation of this differentiation, *p'o*, the personal anima or soul resides in the abdomen and at death returns to the earth, while *hun*, the personal animus or spirit, lives in the eyes and at death ascends to heaven. The ancient Egyptians also make a distinction between the spirit as *ka* and the soul as *ba*. However in Egypt the earth, personified as the god Geb, is masculine and associated with spirit, while the sky, imaged as the goddess Nut, is feminine and associated with soul. Thus after death, the *ka* has to remain attached to the mummified corpse while the *ba* is free to roam the cosmos.

Cultural and personal manifestations of the Physis archetype

Cultures and individuals ruled by this archetype focus on the material and instinctive aspects of life. They are preoccupied with the natural and physical manifestations of reality and have almost a religious sense of awe about the miracles wrought by science and technology. The other important aspect of these societies is the emphasis on the production and acquisition of material goods. In the modern era, capitalism, socialism and communism are the accepted ideologies and economic systems. The disintegration of the Soviet Union was the result of its inability to compete in the production of material goods and military armaments with the capitalist West. It did not fall apart because of its authoritarian form of government. Not the absence of personal freedom, but the lack of capitalism was responsible for its demise. The lesson has not been lost on the leaders of communist China who now embrace capitalism, a more efficient system for the production and distribution of material goods than communism.

Individuals and cultures of the Physis type know that time is money and excel at calculating the cost of all things. These societies also favor laws that are predictable and stable so that the pursuit of material well-being is given a free reign. Nevertheless, litigation is the norm because of the constant attention to property rights and monetary compensation for any actual or perceived injury to the material well-being of a group or individual. Emphasis is placed on physical health, on exercise and eating right. The physical satisfactions of sex take precedence over romance. And everything is done to prolong life. Concern with ecology, nature preserves, species survival and sustainability are the enlightened manifestations of this archetypal constellation.

Materialism and pragmatism are the ruling philosophies. "What works" is the accepted definition of truth, or as the popular adage has it, "the proof of the pudding is in the eating." Ludwig Feuerbach, the nineteenth-century German philosopher, in an essay entitled, "Concerning Spiritualism and Materialism," even went so far as to say, *"Der Mensch ist, was er isst,"* a man is what he eats. Marx, who admired Feuerbach, gave this facile aphorism a theoretical underpinning with his thesis that the division of labor and the means of production determine all social and historical events. Religion, aesthetics, politics, laws, ideas of justice and freedom are all conditioned by economic developments and class interests. He considered these cultural manifestations the "superstructure" used to justify the economic interests and social privileges of the economically dominant and politically ruling classes. For Marx there is no such thing as a unique individual. Every person is simply "an ensemble of social relations" defined by the economic conditions of a particular time and place.

The Physis dominated culture and individual, seeks paradise in this world, and not in the world to come. Emphasis is placed on life in the here and now. And if there is a world to come, then it must be based on the satisfaction of the same physical and material desires as those of this world. For the Physis oriented ancient Egyptians, for example, life after death was exactly like this life; absent illness, suffering, labor and death.

3
Power, Eros, Pneuma and Physis Personality Types

This chapter provides a description of the Power, Eros, Pneuma and Physis personalities. The addition of Jung's categories of introversion and extraversion to each of these dominant motivations makes a total of eight different types. The description takes into account the inferior motivation of each type, for example, extraverted Eros type with inferior introverted Power. (Please note that the inferior motivation is usually opposite in the attitude of extraversion or introversion to the dominant motivation.) The dominant motivation is consciously deployed and usually well differentiated and socially adapted. The inferior motivation, on the other hand, is essentially unconscious. But because of that, it has a more intense psychic charge and tends to be expressed in a naïve, exaggerated, all-or-nothing manner.[1]

The reader should keep in mind that a typology is an abstract schema and few individuals fit a specific type perfectly. Moreover, the motivational typology I describe is hardly static, but a dynamic interaction of each individual with a given environment. Both Jung's and my typology are formulated in dyads comprised of opposites that by definition exclude one another. In real life, of course, individuals are not bound by these abstract rules. Because of circumstances, some people readily alternate between Power and Eros, or between their extraverted and introverted expression. Other people find themselves somewhere in a middle position in one or more of the dyads, which, not unusual. When this happens, the opposition between the two categories is essentially negated and the person makes use of both in a relatively balanced manner. A combination of innate tendencies, habitual predisposition, cultural attitudes and one's life situation determines which motivation becomes dominant or which tends to be balanced by its opposite. There is at least anecdotal evidence that in the second half of life, many people turn to their undeveloped motivations and seek to balance out the opposites.

Jung distinguishes between extraversion and introversion in terms of the flow of psychic energy toward either external or internal objects. Introverts tend to withdraw their libido from the external object and instead, direct it towards internal objects—images, feelings, ideas. Extraverts, on the other hand, have a positive attitude toward the external object and are not particularly interested in pursuing their inner ruminations or feelings. In my opinion, however, it is important to note that both introversion and extraversion are ultimately motivated by the archetype of Eros; the flow of energy, whether extraverted or introverted, seeks a connection with the objects of either the internal or external universe. When Jung wrote *Psychological Types*, he had not yet formulated his hypothesis of archetypes. He theorized that "the type antithesis" between extraversion and introversion "must have some kind of biological foundation" probably based on two different modes of adaptation to preserve the living organism:

> There are in nature two fundamentally different modes of adaptation which ensure the continued existence of the living organism. The one consists in a high rate of fertility, with low powers of defense and short duration of life for the single individual; the other consists in equipping the individual with numerous means of self-preservation plus a low fertility rate. The biological difference, it seems to me, is not merely analogous to, but the actual foundation of, our two psychological modes of adaptation. I must content myself with this broad hint. It is sufficient to note that the peculiar nature of the extravert constantly urges him to expend and propagate himself in every way, while the tendency of the introvert is to defend himself against all demands from outside, to conserve his energy by withdrawing it from objects, thereby consolidating his own position. Blake's intuition did not err when he described the two classes of men as "prolific" and "devouring." Just as, biologically, the two modes of adaptation work equally well and are successful in their own way, so too with the typical attitudes. The one achieves its end by a multiplicity of relationships, the other by monopoly.[2]

When reading the depictions of the four types and their introverted and extraverted modes, one should keep in mind the mythological or archetypal images associated with each, for there will be a tendency on the part of the individuals ruled by these archetypes to act out the underlying motifs. Thus, the Power type will tend to behave like a god or a king. The Eros type will try to hold on to people that ought to be dropped or to remain in situations that call for change. The Pneuma type may assume a lofty, superior attitude toward material concerns, while the Physis type will tend to ignore or downplay the value of abstract ideas that appear to have no basis in material reality. In addition, if people become too identified with their ruling archetype, they tend to lose their individuality and act as spokespersons or pawns of that archetype. The ego then becomes absorbed by the archetype and an inflated or charismatic personality results. In reality, however, such inflation beyond the boundaries of one's ego is a form of possession. The possession feels satisfying because it provides the person with energy, self-confidence, influence and the admiration of others. The problem is that such a charismatic person is rooted in a collective role while his or her individual personality fails to develop. Inside the collective persona there may be a deformed, immature creature or an empty shell of a person.

Extraverted Physis type

With inferior introverted spirit

Generally speaking, the extraverted Physis type regards speculation based on anything other than materially verifiable facts as pure fantasy.[3] For this type, the marvelous operations of nature is philosophy enough, and a well-oiled engine—poetry. The extraverted Physis, or material type, will be attracted to professions, occupations and preoccupations where the primary focus is on manipulating, utilizing and understanding material reality. Scientists, doctors, computer programmers, engineers, businessmen, industrialists, architects, farmers, craftsmen, technicians, athletes, artisans and laborers are some of the occupations compatible with this archetype. These are the people who develop and maintain our physical, technological and economic well-being. If this type of person has an aesthetic sense, it will be expressed in design, fashion, sculpture or architecture. They will also be the collectors, consumers, gourmets and sensualists. If they are artistic, the art will tend toward illustration, portraiture, realism and naturalism. Moreover, if they are philosophically inclined, they will be the realists, empiricists and materialists, Aristotelians rather than Platonists. If they are religious in orientation, they will stress works over faith, dogma and organization, ritual and the concrete expression of devotion. They will be suspicious of miracle workers, visionaries and mystics. For them, religion is a practical matter, and they tend to take things somewhat literally and concretely. For example, they can imagine paradise only as a sensuous place, essentially a continuation of life in this world, but without its evils and travails. For this type of person, the pleasures of the flesh take precedence over the pleasures of spirit, or more precisely, their way to the experience of the sublime is through the senses. The sexual practice of *tantra* is another example of this concretizing tendency.

The inferior motivation of the extraverted Physis type makes itself felt in an attraction to religious and mystical cults. Because Southern California seems to have a good number of these types, it is home to every conceivable cult imaginable. Wealthy extraverted Physis types donate significant amounts of money and time to these organizations. They feel that even though they may not be able personally to participate at least they can make it possible for others to do so. They admire and even envy the people who devote their life to these causes. At the same time they are a bit baffled by it all, but would never admit it. If they are secular and rationalistic in their orientation, the inferior motivation then shows up in conspiracy theories or in an interest in parapsychology, for example, ESP, UFO sightings and alien abductions.

Introverted Physis type

With inferior extraverted spirit

While the extraverted Physis type would like to take in the whole world, and all at once, if possible, the introvert will be very selective about the number of impressions and amount of sense data that he or she takes in. Introverts in general, and not only the material type, are easily overwhelmed by too much information and too many impressions. They need to process things slowly, preferably one at a time. As a result the introverted Physis type has an exquisite sense for and love of detail.

The introverted type will be attracted to the same occupations as the extravert but will pursue them in an introverted manner. Research scientists or computer programmers, for instance, can spend days and weeks talking to hardly anyone, so completely are they absorbed in their work. Introverted technicians, engineers or architects like nothing better than to be left alone to draw up their plans or tinker with their models. There are, of course, many introverted farmers, craftsmen and artisans who enjoy their professions, in part because these occupations afford them the opportunity to work alone. Introverted businessmen or fashion designers are harder to find, but they do exist, working behind the scenes and hiring extraverts to do their promotions, public relations and selling.

Of course, the introverted Physis artists or philosophers will have no difficulty in pursuing their chosen professions. Jan Vermeer and Thomas Mann are examples of introverted materialist artists and writers. All the qualities that characterize the extraverted Physis type of religious person apply to the introverted type as well, save that the introvert prefers not to make too much of a display of his or her spiritual activities, devotional practices, adherence to dogma and suspicion of their more free-spirited co-religionists. I suspect that the classical alchemists were introverted Physis types seeking to ground their religious beliefs in the world of matter. Having spent some years in Switzerland, I would hazard a guess that a good percentage of the Swiss population consist of introverted Physis types.

In its positive manifestation, the extraverted Pneuma compensating the introverted Physis motivation will make itself manifest in a fascination with theater, ballet, concerts and sports events. People with an inferior Physis motivation love the rituals associated with these events and are mesmerized by the bands marching in formation and the elaborate half-time shows. They enjoy being swept away by audience particiaption and crowd enthusiasm. If, for some reason, they happen to attend a religious revival meeting, in spite of their skepticism and resistance, they may suddenly find themselves walking to the front and publicly dedicating their life to Jesus. Moreover, they have a tendency to be carried away by the latest scientific, political or religious movement that advocates a solution to the varied ills of humanity. Only their introverted temperament stops them from completely losing their bearings.

Extraverted Pneuma type

With inferior introverted Physis

An extravert motivated by the archetype of Pneuma or Spirit is interested in the various cultural expressions of the psyche or spirit: drama, dance, film, literature, music, art and religion. For such a person life's meaning is held within these forms. They may appreciate the material side of life but primarily as a means to pursue these interests. Their pleasures are those of the spirit rather than of the senses and the body.

As a psychoanalyst I have frequently encountered individuals who are more-or-less equally motivated by these two, essentially opposite, archetypes, and constantly torn between their desire for material status and well-being and their spiritual and idealistic impulses. If the tension is not too extreme, a compromise between the two poles can be achieved;

such people then seem to have the best of both worlds. If the tension between the two sides is too extreme, a different resolution needs to be discovered often requiring a unique, creative solution.

The extraverted Pneuma types are the musicians, dancers, actors, directors, producers, teachers, counselors, priests. They are also the patrons and consumers of culture, the public that fills the theaters, concert halls, movie houses, museums and churches, that attends lectures and buys the books, the CDs, works of art and antiques. In the religious area the extraverted Pneuma type will be found among pastors, preachers, evangelists and missionaries. Their main motivation will not be Power or Eros, but Spirit; they are inspired by the Holy Spirit and feel a compelling need to spread the news, whether fire and brimstone or the Kingdom of God. For better or worse, extraverted Pneuma types comprise the host of individuals who are vocal and active in their appreciation, support, cultivation and furtherance of the intellectual, artistic, cultural and religious life of a nation.

The inferior introverted Physis motivation of the extraverted Pneuma type tends to balance the conscious emphasis on the outer world. It forces one to pay attention to the body, often because of real or imagined symptoms, and periodically makes one concerned about one's financial well-being. At such times, extraverted Pneuma types fall into a black depression and actually become ill. They then entertain suicidal thoughts and become fixated on some idea or feelings of inadequacy that overwhelm them. This side of their personality will also lead them to seek the pleasures of the flesh and turn them into sexual, alcohol or drug addicts.

On the positive side, the unconscious Spirit archetype can turn a concrete experience into mystical insight. The sight of a beautiful child, a gnarled old tree, a majestic mountain or a colorful sunset can inspire these types with religious feelings they never knew they had. If scientifically inclined, such individuals are moved by the wonders of the universe seen, for instance, in the intricate patterns of microbes under the electron microscope or in the spiraling galaxies visible through the Hubble telescope. And if they have such an experience, their extraverted Pneuma steps in and makes them feel they need to let others see and experience the same thing. They want to share it with the whole world.

Introverted Pneuma type

With inferior extraverted Physis

Introverted spiritual or idealistic (Pneuma) types of people are primarily moved by inner rather than outer images, ideas and values. Together with their extraverted colleagues, they provide and sustain the communal and cultural life of a nation. Introverted Pneuma types are the philosophers, theologians, scholars, ideologues and theoreticians—whether in the sciences or the humanities. They make up the ranks from which come the composers, artists, writers, poets, academics and the creative types who love to play with images, fantasies and ideas. And needless to say, they are also the people who respond to the religious or spiritual call, devoting their lives to interior, rather than outer spiritual endeavors. Hermits, monastics and mystics are spiritually inclined introverted Pneuma types.

The so-called disheveled artists and the absent-minded professors who live in an "ivory tower" are caricatures of some introverted Pneuma types with a tendency to renounce, disdain and neglect the material side of life. In a defensive posture they may look down upon those who pursue material goals as "philistines." Many, however, secretly envy the material well-being of the Physis types, and are jealous of their more extraverted colleagues, who seem to thrive socially and economically. Victims of their own feelings of inadequacy in this regard, they sometimes compensate with a sense of elitism and superiority and accuse their more extraverted colleagues of having compromised their principles and "sold out."

The inferior extraverted Physis side of the introverted Pneuma types shows up in their love of gadgets and, if they have an aesthetic sense, in their appreciation of the union between beauty and function. Depending on their interests, they may even become collectors of books, art, pottery or kitschy objects. When they have the time to work on material things, whether cleaning the kitchen or carving a stone, they fall into a meditative state and feel at one with the world. They enjoy reading popular books on science, especially if these tie the scientific data to an overarching vision of the universe: for example, Fritjof Capra's *The Tao of Physics* or Lewis Thomas' *The Lives of a Cell: Notes of a Biology Watcher.*

In their eating habits, their natural tendency is to attack food with gusto and sometimes stuff themselves to excess. Their sexual fantasies are frequently coarse and vulgar and they prefer fantasizing about sex to getting involved with an actual person, unless it is to play out the fantasy. However, sometimes they experience sex as a religious sacrament or a mystical union and feel completely cleansed by it. A similar experience can happen with outer reality: the sight of a statue or a stained glass window can suddenly transport them to paradise. Like the poet William Blake, they know what it means:

> To see a World in a grain of Sand
> And Heaven in a Wild Flower,

> Hold Infinity in the palm of your hand
> And Eternity in an hour.

Because they are *introverted* Pneuma types, however, they want to keep these experiences to themselves as a treasured secret. At most, they may join a group that shares the same perspective on reality and considers such experiences normal.

Extraverted Power type

With inferior Eros

The extraverted Power types are natural leaders. Without much thought and reflection, they are simply impelled to take charge and assume the mantle of authority. It does not matter whether the situation is family life, romantic relationships or community affairs. Jung pointed out that there is an unspoken relationship between power oriented individuals and the community at large: each uses the other to accomplish their ends. The power driven individuals gain a leadership position and status, while the community makes use of their desire for power to achieve its social, economic and political aims. They rely on control, domination and, if need be, on threats, intimidation, rewards and punishments to attain their ends.

A common misconception abounds that people interested in power gravitate toward the field of politics. In reality the military, business and even religious establishments are more suitable areas for the exercise of domination and control in a direct and unrestricted manner. In politics only authoritarian and tyrannical forms of government allow for such express use of power.

Also, whether in politics, religion or business, there are many different ways of employing power. One can be a charismatic or an inspirational leader, or lead by example, through persuasion and oratory, by wheeling and dealing, by intimidation, or through compromise. One can be authoritarian, dictatorial, democratic, bureaucratic, or one can be a rebel, a revolutionary, an innovator, a liberal, a reactionary or a conservative. Ideology notwithstanding, these are simply styles of exercising leadership and power.

In fact, extraverted Power types, because of their need for a socially recognized power position, will adopt the ideological currency of the day. With the collapse of the Soviet Union, for instance, the former communist leaders quickly transformed themselves into nationalists, thereby maintaining their power. If popularity is the route to winning elections, the extraverted Power type will pursue popularity as a means of attaining power. On the other hand, if power is to be obtained by currying favor with powerful interest groups, or even with a dictator, the power driven individual will do that.

Because so many extraverted Power types interested in politics pursue power at almost any cost, many people consider politicians as unprincipled and view politics as a dirty business. But all power oriented individuals, whether extraverted or introverted, will look for opportunities to make use of any of their talents or capabilities to obtain power: skill, wealth, ability, celebrity, knowledge, social status, even their energy level and capacity for work. The neurotic or pathological aspects of the Power types, whether introverted or extraverted, include tendencies toward paranoia, dogmatism and perfectionism—getting things right, which often means "doing it my way."

Inferior introverted Eros has a number of possible ways of making its presence felt in the life of the extraverted Power type. The desire for connections and union which characterizes Eros may reveal itself in their personal life as an intense attachment to a close friend or associate: Ronald Reagan's bond with Nancy, for example, or JFK's love for his brother Robert. But the same motivation can be expressed in a humanitarian impulse: for example, Jimmy Carter's and Bill Clinton's philanthropic work. Incidentally the two former presidents' turn from their dominant to their inferior archetypal motivation demonstrates the typical mid-life change that aims at psychological balance and wholeness in the lives of individuals.

The Eros side of an artistically inclined Power type may find an outlet in painting or music. But this will be a side of that individual only his or her intimates know. This is also true of any religious feelings. However, in the present political climate in the United States, professional politicians will be prompted to reveal to the voting public their religious inclination.

In its less sophisticated manifestations, inferior Eros will be responsible for flirtations, affairs and sexual addictions. It can also account for periodic personal expressions of affection or more general humanitarian gestures, but ones which are not followed through. The inferior Eros of the extraverted Power type accounts for other mischief: for feelings of betrayal by people who one thought of as good friends when actually there was no basis for those friendships except in one's mind. Contrariwise, these types may imagine all sorts of envious feelings on the part of close friends and associates for which, again, there is no basis in fact.

Introverted Power type

With inferior extraverted Eros

By nature more retiring and shy than their extraverted colleagues, introverted Power types are keenly sensitive to issues of hierarchy, domination and control. They see every situation in terms of power. From their perspective, power is not limited to politics but permeates every field of human endeavor: the arts, literature, aesthetics, ethics, philosophy, religion, economics and human relations. Roger Bacon's dictum "knowledge is power" exemplifies this sensibility.

Generally, people assume that power has to do with control of external matters. Bacon's statement, for instance, implies that knowledge is useful because it can provide a means for controlling and changing the world. A distinguished political scientist, Harold D. Lasswell, once defined power as "who gets what, when, and how."[4] But this is an extraverted view of power. The introverted version defines power as "who *thinks* what, when, and how." Unlike the extraverted Power type, such as Genghis Khan, Alexander the Great or Napoleon—to use the classic historical examples—who aim to conquer the world or create an empire, similarly globally-ambitious introverted Power types seek to attain the same ends through a world-conquering ideology. Hence, the appeal of Marxism to many introverted intellectuals and academics. Karl Marx himself was certainly an introverted Power type. His economic and socio-political critique of the ruling ideas, laws and values of various societies, past and present, and his expectation of a proletarian revolution that would establish a radically new world order is an example of how the archetype of Power can dominate an entire *Weltanschauung*. The introverted Power type, therefore, can also be found among philosophers, ideologues and academics, for example, Plato, Machiavelli, Hobbes, Jefferson, Marx and Lenin.

Of course not every introverted Power type has such wide-ranging ambitions as Marx or Plato, who also wanted to establish a utopian society on the basis of his theories. Many introverted Power types have a much more limited drive and are satisfied with power and influence within their immediate family, community, occupation or profession. On the whole they keep a low profile, working quietly behind the scenes. Often they are "the power behind the throne," either as trusted advisors or as power brokers who nominate and appoint leaders they favor or can easily manipulate and control.

Government and corporate bureaucracy, therefore, is an area in which this type of power person can obtain enormous influence, and sometimes, like Stalin, even translate that bureaucratic power into an overt leadership position. On the surface, therefore, the bureaucratic and ideological infighting that takes place within the government (or academia) is concerned with ideas or policy, but, in reality, these are merely the coin or medium with which introverts pursue their power struggles. Similarly the struggle among political parties is not only over control of a nation's resources but often even more about the dominance of a specific ideology, with its array of values and beliefs.

Politics, however, is not the only area that accords opportunities to the lovers of power. In *Birth of Tragedy* Nietzsche, for example, pointed out that the religious ascetic is driven by a will to power. Many religious people, in fact, pursue their spiritual aims by controlling and dominating their physical, emotional and mental life. Their approach is in stark contrast to the Eros types whose spiritual life is expressed through relatedness, love, devotion and faithfulness. Of course the former envision God as a powerful Father, the latter see God as Love. Every religion has these two ways of approaching spirituality. One need only contrast the religious attitudes of such figures as Savonarola, Calvin or Khomeini with those of Buber, Rumi or Gandhi.

The inferior extraverted Eros of the introverted Power type reveals itself in sudden bursts of extraverted activity and in the love of crowds: of people singing, chanting and moving as one. Participation in such collective assemblies, where there is an emotional feeling of unison, fills introverted Power types with ecstasy. Add a little alcohol or drugs and they readily fall into a Dionysian frenzy and lovefest.

The inferior extraverted Eros of these types, however, makes them genuinely warm and disarming. There is little or no guile in their love, and people, who sense this genuine warmth, are perturbed when the ostensibly sincere Eros connection is ignored or utilized in a calculating pursuit of power.

But that is only one side of the inferior extraverted Eros of the introverted Power types. The other side is their blind loyalty to a leader they happen to admire. They will cleave to such a leader through thick and thin and find excuses for his or her faults and transgressions. They are often the sycophants surrounding a leader and will readily sacrifice themselves when the leader they chose to follow is disgraced or deposed.

Loyalty is their supreme value. They are loyal and demand loyalty in return. Oddly enough, at the same time, they are easily swayed by the negative reactions of others who can undermine their feelings of loyalty and friendship. Their susceptibility in this regard has to do with their inferior Eros; they just don't trust their feeling judgment, which then leads to overcompensation and fanaticism. Often they neglect or drop close friends because the new person or group they associate with disapprove of their previous allegiances. Moreover, their feelings about people are black and white; they feel either positive or negative about someone, there is no in between. They can't imagine that the person they like can have serious faults and the person they dislike may have positive attributes.

Extraverted Eros type

With inferior introverted power

Similar to the misconception that the Power oriented individual is primarily interested in politics, is the notion that the Eros type is mostly interested in human relationships. *Eros is an archetype whose principal aim is union*—connections and relationships are only the means through which it pursues its goal. Because Eros also makes use of love—and fascination—to attain its goal, it tends to be equated with love, and love of course is seen as primarily having to do with personal relationships. But the fact is that the world is full of things to love and to be fascinated by, besides human beings. One can love animals, flowers, nature, beauty, music, ideas, art, literature, theater, Fashion, gadgets, food, wine, not to speak of philosophy, law, medicine and all the other professions. Many extraverted Eros types will fall in love with any one of these areas of interest and devote their entire life to it. Sometimes their fascination with or devotion to their chosen field is so great that they sacrifice their personal relations and families to it, in the same manner that Power types do.

Then there are people who sincerely love humankind but shy away from personal relationships. And there are, of course, those who love God above all else. But on the whole it is also true that extraverted Eros types weave a network of social bonds that provide connections and a sense of unity in the family, the community and society at large. They are the "glue" that binds people and the world together.

The extraverted Eros types will be open about the things they love. They wear their hearts on their sleeves, so to speak. Since love, as we have seen, is not limited to human beings, this type can be found in all walks of life. Many people devote themselves to politics, for instance, out of love and not because of a need to dominate or control. They like the public service aspect of politics, or are fascinated by the intellectual and emotional challenges of political life, or simply love the give and take and camaraderie. Social reformers, educators, philanthropists and missionaries also tend to be extraverted Eros types.

Extraverted love is infectious and easily able to carry one away on the wings of love. This is why extraverted Eros types who love people and relationships are so magnetic and seductive. In their desire to connect with people, they will overlook many faults and sometimes are not very discriminating about their friends. People who fall under their spell feel special, understood, related to, connected with—and keep coming back for more. But chances are they will be disappointed. For extraverted Eros types are butterflies, flitting from one flower to the next and before you know it, they are involved with new friends and acquaintances who have succumbed to their charms. Many extraverted Eros types, aware of what they are doing, feel guilty about the people with whom they made a passing but close connection, and sincerely regret that they just don't have enough time and energy to stay in touch with everybody. The other side of this equation is that they themselves often merge with others to such an extent they lose their sense of identity and become a sort of "collective" person, or as Marx aptly put it, "an ensemble of social relations."

More often than not, extraverted Eros types are not aware of their Power drive. Like horses with blinders, they move through life in a blithe manner pursuing their Eros goals and in the process ignoring the expressed desires of others. One sees this dynamic with couples, where the extraverted Eros type, whose partner is often introverted, arranges an active social life and simply expects the partner to go along. When the partner protests, the extraverted Eros person is convinced of being right and the partner wrong: besides, so the rationalization goes, the socializing, after all, is for the partner's own good. There may be some truth to that, but the point is that the introverted partner's desires are simply ignored and the inferior unconscious Power drive of the extraverted Eros type takes over the situation.

But there is a good reason why extraverted Eros types try to ignore their inferior Power drive: it caries a self-deprecating and judgmental tone and makes the extraverted Eros type feel inadequate, weak and inferior. Alfred Adler was an extraverted Eros type and when he analyzed his unconscious, discovered his inferior Power drive with strong feelings of inadequacy. That discovery led him to formulate a theory that all human beings suffer from feelings of inferiority and strive to overcome them with a compensating sense of superiority.

When extended to the realm of politics or society, the critical attitude associated with the inferior introverted Power drive finds expression in conspiracy theories and in suspicions about the motives of people in authority. When coupled with racial, ethnic, gender or religious prejudice, this attitude seeks to blame some group for trying to dominate the culture or the economy, or even to take over the whole world through secret machinations. In fact, it is the inferior introverted Power motivation that is responsible for harboring these fantastic power schemes which, under normal circumstances, the extraverted Eros side does not permit to come to the surface—except through unconscious projections. The exception is when, because of external or internal pressures, such a person becomes neurotic and the dominant motivation loses its hold. Then the controlling side comes out and the individual becomes compulsive in behavior and fanatical in attitude.

Introverted Eros type

With inferior extraverted power

The introverted Eros type is also motivated by a desire for relationship and connection, for a union with people, ideas and things. But they are less open about the things they are fascinated by or that they love. Put another way, their relationship to the people or the things they love is based primarily on their fascination with the internal image activated by the outer person or thing. It was the poet Rainer Maria Rilke, evidently an introverted Eros type, who said: "I love you, but it's none of your business." This attitude is something inconceivable for the extraverted Eros types; if they love you, you will hear about it and they will make certain that it is your business.

But the fact is that the introverted Eros types have all sorts of inner relationships, connections and friendly feelings that are never openly expressed or revealed. The result is that they are often disappointed and even feel betrayed by people with whom they thought they had a close connection, when in reality, these people know nothing about it and then don't understand what it is they may have done or said to hurt them.

Like their extraverted counterpart, the introverted Eros type may love and be fascinated by art, music, ideas, nature or their work, as well as other areas of interest, but they will pursue these loves in a quiet, unobtrusive, sometimes almost secretive manner. Only their partners or an intimate circle of like-minded friends will know about their consuming interests and the depth of their love. This is where the introverted Eros types may lose their sense of identity, merging and identifying with their consuming interests. If they are artistic, they may give expression to these feelings in poetry, music, literature and other works of art. These are people who believe in "art for art's sake." Actually, what they really mean to say is "art for the love of art." This is, in fact, how we know that Plato's auxiliary archetypal motivation was Power and not Eros, for he wished to control art and use it for purposes other than art itself. His dominant archetypal motivation, of course, was Pneuma.

Among the introverted Eros types are the mathematicians, scientists and academics who are fascinated by the ideas they investigate, as well as the engineers, architects, artisans and mechanics who love the designs and the materials they work with. Many musicians and poets are introverted Eros types devoted to the audible harmonic aspects of Eros. The love of wisdom is pursued by the introverted classic philosophers; the love of God, by hermits and monastics to the exclusion of everything else. There are also the introverted humanitarians and philanthropists whose love of the arts, or of people, or animals is expressed by their generosity and behind the scenes devotion and work. Then there are the quiet lovers of beauty who surround themselves with exquisite furnishings, objects and works of art. These are some of the ways that the introverted Eros types contribute to the cultural, intellectual, social and spiritual life of a community.

Introverted Eros types with inferior extraverted Power often are highly sensitive to the power relations among people. If in a position of power, they take into account issues of disloyalty and betrayal and will readily cut off or ostracize anyone who challenges their authority. In religious circles, this tendency is expressed in a search for heresy and heretics. While the inferior introverted Power drive of extraverted Eros types makes them prone to spin conspiracy theories, the extraverted Power drive of the introverted Eros types makes them focus on actual events and people as conspiring against them, or against the group with which they identify.

In personal life this extraverted unconscious Power drive makes itself evident in an orderly life and predictable habits. Introverted Eros types are not tolerant or forgiving of people who upset their plans and expectations. They like to dominate and control their environment and can become quite adamant about it. Freud, as we shall see, is an example of this type.

Auxiliary archetypes and qualities

In addition to Jung's distinction between introverts and extraverts, I also make use of his idea of a dominant and secondary or auxiliary function.

Thus most people are motivated by a dominant archetypal style or a dominant area of interest. Those whose primary archetype is a style of functioning will have an auxiliary area of interest in which they will exercise that style, while those whose dominant archetype is an area of interest will have an auxiliary style through which they pursue that area. People who are principally motivated by the archetypes of Power or Eros will have either Physis or Pneuma as their secondary archetypes, and individuals whose ruling archetypes are Physis or Pneuma, will have Power or Eros as their auxiliaries. For example, a predominantly Eros motivated person can use that style of functioning either in the Pneuma or Physis areas. On the other hand, a predominantly Pneuma motivated person can pursue that area of interest using either Power or Eros as the auxiliary archetype. The possibilities add up to eight types: Power Physis; Power Pneuma; Eros Physis; Eros Pneuma; Physis Eros; Physis Power; Pneuma Eros; Pneuma Power. (Please see Figure 3.1.)

If one adds the extraverted and introverted attitudes to each of these eight types, there are a total of 16 types, which parallel the 16 types of classical Jungian typology. I will soon complicate matters by adding a soulful and spirited temperament to each of the above types. At this point, however, a fully differentiated Jungian typology, based on both conscious functions and unconscious motivations, will read, for example, as follows: introverted sensation feeling, Power Physis type. (The reader should keep in mind that in Jungian typology the dominant function is placed first and the secondary function last. In archetypal-motivational typology the secondary motivation is placed first and the primary motivation last.) The combined typology entails a total of 32 which admittedly, makes for a somewhat unwieldy schema, but no more so than a fully articulated astrological chart, with its rising signs and the placement and juxtapositions of planets in the 12 houses. Moreover, it is not necessary to use the two typologies together. Testing can be done either for the conscious functions or for the unconscious motivations alone, depending on the characteristics one seeks to identify.

In Jung's typology there are gradations in the development of the four functions and in the expression of the two basic orientations of introversion and extraversion. For instance, a person can be balanced equally between extraversion and introversion, or swing to either extreme. Similarly, it is possible that a person can be equally strong in thinking and feeling, or in sensation and intuition—even though *theoretically* these pairs are opposites and exclusive of each other. Various gradations are also possible: for example, one can be an intuitive type with no sensation to speak of, or an intuitive type with very good sensation.

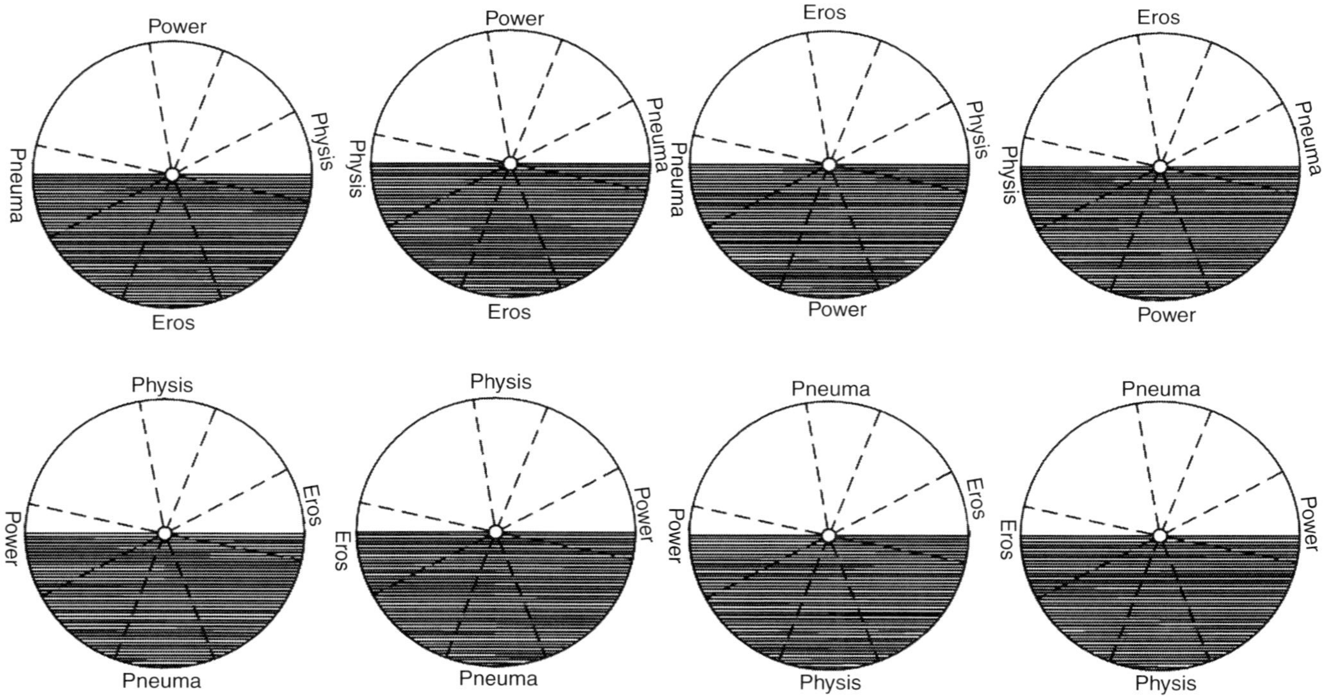

Figure 3.1 The basic eight personality types with the dominant conscious motivations above and their unconscious inferior opposite motivations below. The secondary motivations are on the right side and are more conscious than the tertiary opposed motivations.

Also, some people are able to develop their inferior function, while others, no matter how hard they try, simply cannot make any significant improvement in that function.

In terms of the differentiation of the four functions, it should also be kept in mind that the auxiliary function alters or adds certain characteristics to the primary function. For example, thinking intuitive types will be more theoretical and flexible in their formulations, than thinking sensation types. Similarly, feeling intuitives are more generalized in their feelings than feeling sensation types, whose feelings are invariably tied to identifiable contents or objects. The latter qualifications apply to archetypal-motivational typology as well: for example, a Pneuma Power type will express power in more conceptual or ideological terms than a Physis Power type; a Pneuma Eros type functions in a more inclusive manner than a Power Eros type.

In both Jung's typology and in archetypal-motivational typology the overall conscious functioning of the personality is also modified by the auxiliary function or archetype because, being less developed, it contains an element of unconsciousness. Thus, in terms of my typology, the auxiliary or secondary archetype is more in the shadow than the primary archetype and, when caught off guard, brings with it a primitive, emotionally disturbing quality of expression and behavior that contrasts with the otherwise smooth functioning of the individual. These shadow characteristics of the auxiliary archetypes will become clearer when I illustrate the typology with the examples of Freud, Adler and Jung.

4
Soulful and Spirited Temperaments

My observation of various types of behavior and attitudes has led me to conclude that the pursuit and expression of every archetypal style and interest is characterized by either a *soulful* or *spirited* quality of temperament. I therefore make a distinction between the archetype of Pneuma/Spirit as a motivational drive and 'spirit' as a temperamental characteristic. The use of the same archetype in two different ways is possible because every archetype has multiple manifestations, each one with its own specific attributes. For instance, the great mother archetype includes the Virgin Mary, the sky goddess, the earth mother and Kali. It can also be represented by such impersonal objects as the moon, the ocean, a tree or a cave. Although the great mother archetype is the source of all these representations, each possesses its unique characteristics, a separate frame of reference and a different meaning. This multifaceted nature of every archetype is also true of the archetype of Spirit. Thus, Spirit can appear as a wise old man, as Mercurius in alchemy, or wind, breath, light or fire. Archetypal-motivational typology relies upon two psychological attributes of this archetype, as a motivational drive and as a temperamental quality.

The soulful and spirited temperaments cut across the four motivational archetypes and influence their manifestation. For example, a person can be an Eros type and pursue that style of behavior either in a soulful or spirited way. Or someone can be a Pneuma type and follow that area of interest in a soulful or spirited manner. Theoretically, it might seem possible for an individual to pursue the dominant archetype in a spirited way and the auxiliary archetype in a soulful way, or vice versa. But in practical terms, the archetypes of Soul and Spirit will affect the entire personality in the same way that the extraverted/introverted orientation cuts across the permutations of the four functions.[1] Introversion and extraversion also affect the temperamental predispositions of soul and spirit so that one may speak of extraverted or introverted soulful and spirited types. In this connection, it is important to keep in mind that people with a spirited temperament are sometimes mistaken for extraverts and soulful types for introverts.

As was true with the four basic motivations, temperament is flexible and some individuals move easily between the temperamental archetypes of Soul and Spirit in keeping with their personal developmental needs and circumstances. For instance, it seems that many men cultivate a spirited temperament during the first half of life and become somewhat more soulful as they mature. Initially soulful women, on the other hand, may become spirited at mid-life.

In the sections that follow, I define the archetypes of Soul and Spirit, provide mythological illustrations of each and offer a vignette of the soulful and spirited temperaments.

Archetype of soul

Etymologically the term "soul" evolved from the Old English *sawol*, the Gothic *saiwola* and the Proto-Germanic *saiwalo*, meaning "coming from the sea," or "belonging to the sea." The etymology gives expression to the belief that the sea was a stopping place of the soul before its birth and after its death. Botticelli's painting of Aphrodite's birth from the foam of the sea is a representational depiction of this myth. The water from which souls emerge and to which they return is a metaphor for the source, or origin of life. Numerous creation myths refer to water as the original "matter." Freud literalized the notion as the amniotic fluid; his literal idea can be extended by evolutionary theory which hypothesizes that life first emerged from the seas. Jung, however, felt that mythology expresses and elaborates upon internal psychic events; he, therefore, interpreted the references to water from which the soul emerged as analogous to the unconscious.

The Chinese version of the soul's watery origins is the belief that at death the soul sinks to the earth and lives in the ground water near the Yellow Springs. These springs are the Land of the Dead, yet, paradoxically, the reservoir of life as well, and from there, having become rejuvenated, the soul comes back to life. In Homer, the afterworld is not underground but at the far end of the ocean, beyond where the sun sets. In both Nordic and Egyptian mythology, ships transport the soul to the land of the beyond. In Greek mythology, the Sirens, sea creatures with heads and breasts of women and bodies of birds, lure passing sailors into the sea where they devour them. The Greek Sirens are reminiscent of the Egyptian soul bird, Ba, which separates from the body at death and takes the form of a bird with a human head. The Greek Sirens were regarded as the souls of the dead who had turned into vampires, although they also had a positive side, charming the dead with their songs on the Isles of the Blessed. The Northern European versions of the Sirens are the mermaids, or the Lorelei, water nymphs whose singing lures men to their death. The parallel Slavic figure is the *rusalka*, the ghost of a drowned girl who bewitches and drowns passing men. In part, these myths are probably based on actual events of love-sick youths committing suicide by drowning. But psychologically, the myths represent, on the one hand, a regressive tendency of the psyche, namely the temptation to return to one's unconscious origins, and on the other hand, a desire on the part of the soul, as a personification of the unconscious, for a relationship with ego consciousness. The death and the drowning are not to be taken literally, although in a pre-psychological era or in an un-psychological person, the impulse may be acted out rather than responded to in a conscious way.

In various myths and folktales swans, geese and doves are other soul birds. The allusion to wings, and the fact that these soul birds are imagined at home both in water or in the air, alludes to the otherworldly nature of the soul, namely, that it is capable of living and moving in the watery realm and in the invisible element of air. In contrast to the soul birds, there are spirit birds, the falcon or the eagle, for example. These represent spirit, that is, the spiritual component of the psyche and its connection to transcendent reality. But soul birds are different from spirit birds: they are "feminine" in nature and associated with Eros and Physis; spirit birds are "masculine" and connected to Power and Logos.

As a personification of the feminine, or yin aspects of the unconscious, soul is characterized by fantasy, vague feelings, memories, moods, anxieties, fears, instinctual urges, prophetic hunches, dreams, inspiration, imagination, reflection, receptiveness to the irrational, capacity for personal love, feeling for beauty, for nature, and relationship with the unconscious.[2] The *I Ching* regards receptivity as the chief attribute of yin. Receptivity presupposes openness and emptiness, and *emptiness*, Jung remarks, is the great secret of femininity.[3] In this respect it is important to keep in mind that the concept of femininity is not circumscribed by gender. I am reminded of Lao-tze's description of Tao:

> There is something formless yet complete
> That existed before heaven and earth,
> How still! How empty!

> Dependent on nothing, unchanging,
> All pervading, unfailing.
> One may think of it as the mother of all things under heaven.
> I do not know its name,
> But I call it "Meaning."
> If I had to give it a name, I should call it "The Great."[4]

As for the value of emptiness, here are some examples from the *Tao Te Ching*:

> We put thirty spokes together and call it a wheel;
> But it is on the space where there is nothing that the utility of the wheel depends.
> We turn clay to make a vessel;
> But it is on the space where there is nothing that the utility of the vessel depends.
> We pierce doors and windows to make a house;
> And it is on these spaces were there is nothing that the utility of the house depends.
> Therefore just as we take advantage of what is, we should recognize the utility of what is not.[5]

With the principle of opposites always in play, it is not surprising that next to emptiness, the other important attribute of the soul and of the feminine is that of giving form, substance and specificity to things. In alchemy, Luna, the moon, governs the process of *coagulatio*. Traditional folklore of many cultures calls the moon the place where souls gather after death before they journey to higher spiritual realms; and it is also the place where spirits and souls take on material substance before their return to earth.

The moon is the alchemical source of moisture: "Luna secretes the dew or sap of life," which ties in with the idea of the soul's origins in the waters.[6] Both the waters and the moon, therefore, are places of cyclical transformation, where shapes are dissolved and from which they emanate. Jung continues, "the relation of the moon to the soul, much stressed in antiquity, also occurs in alchemy though with a different nuance. Usually it is said that from the moon comes the dew, but the moon is also the *aqua mirifica* that extracts the souls from the bodies or gives the bodies life and soul."[7]

In fantasy, myth and literature, the soul is usually personified as a woman. A phenomenological purview of her characteristics reveals that she likes diversity, the unique, the personal and the atypical. She is polyvalent, polygamous, polytheistic. In contrast, spirit prefers uniformity, similarity and abstraction; it is monotheistic, monogamous, and one. In addition, Soul is elemental, animistic, warlike, adventurous, romantic. She loves life, the adventure of it, and seeks experience and immersion in the hustle and bustle of daily existence. Consequently, Jung defines Soul as "the archetype of life itself."[8] For Soul ties one to instinctive, material reality, to the earth, to country, church, community, family and personal relationships. She is responsible for our likes and dislikes, our loves and hatreds, our vocation and avocations. Soul is the source of artistic and intellectual pursuits, making one loyal to these endeavors. In the Slavic countries, hobbies, such as playing a musical instrument or painting, are said to be done "for the soul." The Soul is also the font of religious devotion and of the mystic's passionate desire for a relationship with God. And finally, Soul is the wise old woman of folklore and the Biblical Sophia, a personification of wisdom.

In her negative guise, Soul turns into a death demon, as depicted by the Sirens and the Lorelei. She can seduce human beings away from life, into the world of unreality, sterile fantasy, pedantic thought, insanity, depression and psychological or physical suicide. Here she reveals her ghostly side, the dark side of the moon, and becomes "the archetype of death."[9]

The soulful temperament

People with a soulful psychological temperament are receptive, reflective, often deliberate and slow. When speed is of the essence, do not ask a soulful type. They like to take their time and feel their way into things.[10] The 19th-century composer Johannes Brahms, for example, took 21 years to complete his *Symphony No. 1* and discarded 24 drafts of a chamber music piece for strings. Contrast that working style and pace of the soulful Brahms with the lightning speed of composition by the spirited Mozart!

When soulful types are upset, or matters are not going well, they turn moody, morose and sulky. If introverted, a sense of melancholy and retreat are natural to them; if extraverted, they impose their moods and deliberations onto the surrounding environment. They give credence to hunches and have no difficulty with irrational, fantastic, emotional and even contradictory perspectives. They can play with various schemes and scenarios. But, unless soulful types are impassioned or highly extraverted, they prefer to think, or rather, to reflect before they act.

Soulful individuals are emotionally and personally connected to the physical world and to other people. They tend to be loyal, take things personally and are loathe to do something out of mere principle, or for abstract logical reasons. They love beauty and harbor an almost mystical connection to nature. As the romantics on the typological spectrum, they are easily swept away by their fantasies, passions and irrational notions, sometimes even indulging in fits of unreality. If blessed or cursed with a modicum of creativity, they will tend to pursue their creative fantasies and not understand why the world does not follow suit; their vision seems so real and compelling. For the soulful, John Keats' words in his *Ode on a Grecian Urn* have the ring of eternity: "'Beauty is truth, truth beauty,' that is all ye know on earth and all ye need to know."

Archetype of spirit

Complementary to the soulful temperament is the spirited one, for which the supreme value lies in meaning, rather than beauty. The word "spirit" comes from the Latin *spiritus*, derived from *spirare*, meaning "to breathe". The term *spiritus* was used in Latin translations for the Greek *pneuma* and the Hebrew *ruach*. These terms, as we saw in the description of the archetype of Pneuma, refer to breath, wind, air, heaven or sky, the light that fills the air and that comes from above. Birds, angels and other winged creatures represent the realm of spirit and serve as intermediaries and messengers between the heavenly and earthly realms. By extension, breath becomes "the word," and then, idea, thought and meaning. While soul is expressed through fantasies, images and the irrational, spirit is at home in the realms of thought, reason and meaning. Both mythically and psychologically, soul prefers low, shaded, hidden, dark places. Spirit, on the other hand, is enamored of the heights; it favors bright, open, sunny spaces. Soul is slow, watery, heavy, earth-bound, body-bound. Spirit is quick, fiery, light, airy and immaterial.

In the classic Taoist distinction between these two principles, yin as soul and yang as spirit, the basic meaning of yin is "cloudy" or "overcast," while that of yang is "banners waving in the sun," something "shone upon" or bright.[11] In the *I Ching* soul is *K'un* and described as the receptive. Its main attribute is devotion, its image the earth, and it is symbolized by a mare wandering over the earth. Spirit is *Ch'ien* and defined as the creative. Its main attribute is power or energy, its image heaven. *Ch'ien* is symbolized by a dragon flying in the heavens and is "light giving, active, strong and of the spirit."[12] Like soul and sprit, or yin and yang, the creative and the receptive are not opposites; they complement each other. Still they are distinct: the receptive "represents nature in contrast to spirit, earth in contrast to heaven, space as against time, the female-maternal as against the male-paternal."[13]

The energy of *Ch'ien* is "unrestricted by any fixed conditions in space and is therefore conceived of as motion."[14] This mobility of spirit and its power to move over great distances in the flick of an eyelid is also true of the other attribute of spirit, namely, light. In human beings, thought is characterized by similar speed and mobility. The unrestricted quality of spirit is expressed by the Biblical image that the "wind bloweth where it listeth" (John 3:8) and its transmutability is encountered in the ancient Taoist, Egyptian and Roman descriptions of the metamorphoses of spirit and its ability to take any and every form.

One form the spirit takes is fire. There is even a relationship between movement of birds in flight and the flickering tongues of fire. The upward movement of both has come to represent impulses or strivings toward spirituality: "my soul takes flight," or "my heart burns with love for Thee, O Lord." Like birds and other winged creatures, fire also connects heaven and earth and is regarded as a vehicle of offerings to the gods. Since time immemorial fire has been used ritually as a form of purification. In alchemy, fire purifies gross matter and is the means of forging the philosophers' gold. Entering fire without being burned is a sign of purity and spirituality. The Sanskrit word for "fire" and "pure" is the same. Fire is the major attribute and symbol of the heavenly gods. Thus, a Zoroastrian temple was known as "the house of fire" and fire festivals marked the ancient Persian sacred calendar. Originally, the Biblical god Elohim, like the Greek Zeus and the Nordic Thor, was a god of the thunderbolt. In Daniel's vision, Jehovah's face flashes like lightning (Daniel 10:6) and in Job, His hands are covered with lightnings (Job 36:32). The Thrones and Cherubim that surround the throne of God glow with fire. In the New Testament, the Holy Spirit descends on Christ's disciples in "tongues of fire." The *Bhagavad Gita* equates fire with Brahman and with intuitive spiritual knowledge and wisdom. In the *I Ching,* breath and wind are chief attributes of the trigram Li, defined as sun and fire: "Fire has the same nature as heaven, to which it flames up. It is strengthened in this trend by the . . . trigram Sun [Li], wind . . . The wind which blows everywhere."[15] Lightning, the fire descending from heaven, is considered fertilizing, inseminating, purifying. Spiritually, lightning alludes to sudden inspiration or enlightenment as in, for instance, the Zen experience of *kensho* or *satori.*

Like every archetype, Spirit too has its negative and destructive side. A flash of lightning can kill, or turn one speechless, blind, dumb and insane. Then there is the fire of hell and the human experience of the "fires" of hate, anger and war, that devour, burn and destroy. The sun, as well, can scorch the earth, dry up all the water and bring life to an end; and to the extent that the forces of nature were once regarded as manifestations of the gods, this destructive aspect of the sun was seen as a power of the heavenly Spirit. Sekhmet, the lion goddess of ancient Egypt, personified this raging side of the sun god Ra.

The spirited temperament

In human beings the upward striving of spirit, its tendency toward purity and perfection, can make a person abstract, distant and cold. Like the fairy tale princess in her tower, spirit can isolate one from human contact, its critical eye discerning every fault and blemish. Discriminating, judging, phallic, assertive words and actions can castrate and utterly destroy all feeling, connection and relationship. As the Jungian psychologist James Hillman notes, spirit tends to mistake "above" for "superior" and looks down upon soul and its desires, fantasies and involvements with the human and material realms.[16] In this context, Jung speaks of "the crime of sainthood," for saints often "murder" ordinary human impulses, the love of family, for example.

Thus spirit, when allowed to run its course unchecked by humanity, by soul and Eros, easily turns into dogmatism, fanaticism and authoritarianism. It demands discipline, order, rules and regulations—doing things the "right way," whether in one's personal, social or spiritual life. When turned inward, the perfectionistic and judgmental demands of spirit can deprive a person of all self-esteem or self-confidence, and bring an individual to the brink of suicide. In this way, as we saw with soul in its negative form, spirit turns into a death demon that can destroy a person's life, figuratively and actually. These are the dangers that can afflict people whose personality becomes too narrowly identified with spirit.

Even in well-balanced individuals, spirited types will be fiery, impatient, mobile and aggressive in their approach to matters at hand. They may be inconsiderate, not seeing the point of getting into all the details of a problem or issue. They will be decisive, judgmental, cutting and somewhat rough at the edges. On the other hand, they do bring a great deal of "fire" and "spirit" to things and are not afraid to try new approaches. In the process they may not always take into account people's feelings or even what appear to be insurmountable obstacles and difficulties. Spirited people favor Napoleon's maxim, *"On s'engage, puis on voit,"* first you engage and then you see. When necessary, they may rely on charm and seduction, but generally will prefer bold strokes. They emphasize the force of character and will. It may seem as though spirited types are under the sway of the archetype of Power, but that is not necessarily the case. They can apply their spirited temperament and attributes in the area of Eros and seek union and connections in a spirited, forceful, aggressive and willful manner. Furthermore, they bring these qualities of personality to bear on any area of interest—spiritual or material, intellectual or worldly. Extraverted spirited types will use these temperamental qualities when engaging the outer world; introverted types will apply them to their inner life.

5
Temperament and Theory: Freud, Adler and Jung

In a manner of speaking, it is not an exaggeration to consider Freud, Adler and Jung as mythologists of the soul—in its broad connotation as *psyche*—because they perform the same function for the psyche that mythology carries for the world: explain its origins, purpose and final goals. Furthermore, they work with dreams, visions and stories—the stuff of mythology. Freud and Jung were aware of the connection between their psychological theories and mythological motifs, while Adler was less so.[1] It is precisely because Freud and Jung made a conscious effort to link their ideas with mythology that their theories continue to engage the imagination of countless individuals, while those of Adler do not. Pure mental constructs or clinical terminology, for example, "compensation" or "inferiority complex", leave little for the imagination to work upon. On the other hand, Freud's "Oedipus complex", "narcissism", "castration anxiety", the "primal horde" and "eros", and Jung's concepts of "self", "shadow", "*anima*", "*animus*", "wise old man" and "wise old woman" all have mythological antecedents and, as such, enduring imaginative resonance.

In addition to their contribution to a modern mythology of the soul, Freud, Adler and Jung were highly creative individuals and therefore, also artists of the soul. Each was inspired to fashion a new image of the human psyche. A dynamic creative impulse was evident in their work and accounted for the poetic license with which they, at times, molded objective data. Despite attempts to present their theories in terms of the scientific bias of their day, all three ignored facts or even distorted them in the service of their vision. For example, Freud knew that Lamarck's hypothesis of acquired characteristics was scientifically untenable. Nevertheless, he insisted on using it because he felt he could not otherwise fully account for the transmission of culture from one generation to the next. Similarly, he insisted on the universality of the Oedipal complex, on the validity of his notion of the inferiority of women and their penis envy, on the origin of society and culture through the murder of the patriarch of the "primal horde", and on Moses as an Egyptian prince in the court of the monotheistic pharaoh Akhenaton. At least with his speculations about Moses, he was aware of the tenuous nature of his claims, but that did not prevent him from elaborating the notion and asserting its accuracy, if only as a psychological truth. The fact is that Freud was as much a creative individual as a scientist, and creative endeavors have their own internal dynamics and validity.

Adler's theory of organ inferiority and inferiority feelings compensated by striving for superiority is another original reading of human nature and one which he, too, maintained was universally applicable.[2] Adler's creative spirit, however, was most visible in his ardent desire to improve society through education informed by psychological knowledge and the deliberate cultivation of *Gemeinschaftsgefühl*, or "community feeling".

With Jung, there is almost no need to emphasize the originality of his theoretical constructs and perspectives. The mainstream scientific world had always dismissed him as a mystic and Jung himself was keenly aware of the unusual nature of his creative research and output. "I have had much trouble getting along with my ideas,"[3] he mused in the final pages of his autobiography, and concluded that, for better or for worse, "the daimon of creativity has ruthlessly had its way with me."[4] In the Preface to his book *Ego and Archetype*, Edward F. Edinger writes:

> It is only beginning to dawn on the educated world, what a magnificent synthesis of human knowledge has been achieved by C.G. Jung. Starting as a psychiatrist and psychotherapist he discovered in his patients and in himself the *reality of the psyche* and the phenomenology of its manifestations at a depth never before observed systematically. As a result of this experience, he could then recognize the same phenomenology expressed in the culture-products of mankind—myth, religion, philosophy, art and literature. He has penetrated to the root source of all religion and culture and thus has discovered the basis for a new organic syncretism of human knowledge and experience. The new view point thus achieved, is so comprehensive and all-embracing that, once grasped, it cannot fail to have revolutionary consequences for man's view of himself and the world.[5]

Edinger's comments clearly indicate the mythological compass of Jung's accomplishment—a radically new vision of the human soul and its place in the world.

Since my typology has its roots in depth psychology, it seems appropriate, therefore, to illustrate its practical application to the personalities of the founders of that discipline. Today, when Adler's name is often merely a footnote in the field of psychology, it is difficult to imagine that in the decades preceding World War II, the newly emerging discipline of psychoanalysis was invariably associated, as Laurens van der Post writes, with "the awesome psychological trinity of Freud, Adler, and Jung."[6] Of the three, in the 1930's, it was Adler who achieved the greatest popularity, particularly in the United States. There is even an anecdote about this patriarchal trinity. It appears that during one of his visits to London, Jung stopped at the British Museum, which, at the time, also housed the British Library, to undertake some research. When he signed in, the librarian looked up in amazement, "You mean Adler, Jung and Freud?" "No, no," Jung answered, "just Jung."

After his break with Freud in 1913, Jung devoted a great deal of thought to typology, in part as a way to account for his and Adler's disagreements with Freud. (The precise nature of those disagreements will be delineated in the ensuing chapters.) The result of that effort was *Psychological Types*, published in 1921. Apparently, Jung was struck by the fact that he and his psychoanalytic colleagues could examine similar clinical data and come to different, even diametrically opposed, conclusions. His attempt to understand the disagreements among his colleagues in terms of differences in temperament was influenced by William James, whose work he knew and whom he met briefly in 1909, during his visit to the United States.

Jung was aware of Nietzsche's distinction between the Apollonian and Dionysian temperaments, but still credits James with "being the first to draw attention to the extraordinary importance of temperament in colouring philosophical thought."[7] In *Pragmatism*, James observed that "the history of philosophy is to a great extent that of a certain clash of human temperaments,"[8] disguised as disputes over abstract ideas. James noted that in these arguments temperament, this "potentest of all . . . [philosophical] premises is never mentioned," for it could lay no claim to "superior discernment or authority."[9]

As noted previously, James described two philosophical types: the "rationalist", guided by principles, and the "empiricist", oriented toward facts. James characterized the first as tender-minded, the second as tough-minded. He listed a number of other qualities that distinguish the two. The rationalist is intellectualistic, idealistic, optimistic, religious, a believer in free-will, monistic and dogmatic. (James uses the term "dogmatic" as the antonym of "skeptical" and not in its usual sense as authoritarian or inflexible.) The empiricist is sensationalistic, materialistic, pessimistic, irreligious, fatalistic, pluralistic and skeptical. In James' schema, therefore, Adler and Jung are rationalists, Freud, an empiricist.

Jung subjected the above pairings and their characteristics to a critique and found that in many instances they simply did not hold. The empiricist Darwin, for example, was not pessimistic in his assessment of reality, while Schopenhauer, though a rationalist, held a decidedly negative view of the world. He, therefore, proposed an alternative set of categories to account for the difference between the tender-minded rationalist and the tough-minded empiricist: the rationalist, who is concerned with internal principles, is an introvert; while the empiricist, who is oriented toward outer facts, is an extravert.

Freud's extraversion and Adler's introversion

As Jung proceeded to outline his typology, he began to see the difference between Adler and Freud in terms of the above categories. In *Two Essays on Analytical Psychology*, Jung illustrated the clash of opinion with a brilliant presentation of a Freudian and an Adlerian interpretation of the same case material. In his view each theory adequately explained the material. Consequently, he concluded, there must be both a Freudian and an Adlerian side to a neurosis, even though each school insists that its reading of the case is the valid one. Since the neurosis being treated by the two approaches is the same, the divergence in interpretation must stem from the different psychological perspectives the two analysts brought to bear on the case. Adler's focus is on the *subject*, who struggles against objects that threaten its security and works to gain control or mastery over them. Freud, in contrast, places the emphasis on the outer *object*, that either furthers or hinders the subject's desire for pleasure.[10] These differences in perspective, Jung argues, must be rooted in temperament: one in which "the determining agency" is the subject and the other in which it is the object.[11] The dispute between Freud and Adler, therefore, stems from these temperamental biases: "Freud's view is essentially extraverted, Adler's introverted. The extraverted theory holds good for the extraverted type, the introverted theory for the introverted type."[12]

Problems emerge, however, if one examines Jung's analysis in a dispassionate manner. To begin with, if temperament determines the clinical and theoretical disposition, and particularly one's basic premises, then Freud's "pleasure principle" and Adler's "striving for superiority," for example, should correspond to their extraverted and introverted perspectives. In other words, Jung should argue that striving for superiority is an introverted bias and the desire for pleasure an extraverted one. He fails to do so because the argument has no basis in fact. Introverts derive as much pleasure from internal objects as extroverts derive from external objects and both may seek to control, dominate and strive for superiority over objects, whether internal and external.

The more serious problem with Jung's argument is simply that Freud was not an extravert and Adler was not an introvert. By all accounts, Freud was an introvert and Adler an extravert. It is difficult to imagine that Jung was unaware of these facts—although in a 1919 letter to Sabina Spielrein, he wrote that he was not certain of Freud's typology because he knew him "too little on a personal level."[13] The statement is disingenuous and at variance with what we know of their relationship. Jung met Freud in the spring of 1907 and until their break in 1913 they had many personal dealings with each other. Freud liked Jung and they were quite informal in each other's company. They corresponded regularly, organized and attended psychoanalytic conferences, traveled together to the United States and analyzed each other's dreams. Jung had seen Freud function in both a personal and a social context and was certainly able to make an assessment of his personality, particularly in terms of such readily discernible categories as introversion and extraversion.

In his letter to Spielrein, the only specific observation Jung made concerning Freud's typology was that Freud's "neurotic predisposition" made him an extravert.[14] In a 1953 conversation with the Freudian analyst Kurt Eissler, Jung elaborated on the statement. He said that by natural temperament Freud was a feeling type and as a child or adolescent must have suffered a severe trauma that impelled him to develop his thinking function: for "when feeling has been scared off, one escapes into thinking!"[15] As far as Jung was concerned, originally Freud "wasn't a thinker at all, but began to think secondarily, and with difficulty."[16] The implication of Jung's argument is that innately, Freud was a feeling introvert, but because of an emotional shock to his interior feeling life, "the accent of value" was deflected to his thinking and extraversion and he became an extraverted thinking type.[17]

Similarly, in a letter dated 18 February 1957 to a Zurich physician and colleague, Ernst Hanhart, Jung wrote that originally Freud was "an introverted feeling type with inferior thinking. When I got to know him in 1907 this original type was already neurotically blurred. . . . Freud, then as later, presented the picture of an extraverted thinker and empiricist."[18] In addition, according to Jung, Freud's original auxiliary function was intuition, but that, too, was "replaced by a somewhat deficient" sensation function. Jung writes that when one got to know Freud personally, he displayed a well-differentiated feeling function and good intuition. "Yet the superficial picture he presented to the world was that of an extraverted thinker and empiricist."[19] As evidence of Freud's poor sensation, Jung cites his *Studies in Hysteria*, which proposes an etiology of hysteria based on childhood sexual abuse by the father. Within two years after the publication of the book, however, Freud concluded that most of the seductions never took place and were products of pure fantasy on the part of his patients. Freud himself noticed his inadequacy when it came to careful observation of facts: "the case histories I write read like novellas, and... lack the serious stamp of scientific method."[20] Yet, he persisted in his efforts to elaborate his intuitive ideas in empirical terms.

In a subsequent letter to Hanhart, Jung sought to clarify his designation of Freud as an extravert and Adler as an introvert, stating that he was not referring

> to them personally but only to their outward demeanour. The question of the real personal type still remains open . . . Freud's thinking had a definitely extraverted character, i.e., pleasure and unpleasure in the object. Adler's character, on the contrary, was introverted in so far as he gave paramount importance to the power of the ego.[21]

But even if we take the above statement about Adler's introverted character as unintentional and accept Jung's prior statement that he is speaking of two men's outward demeanor and not of their "real personal type," Jung still has to account for the extraverted Adler developing an introverted theory. Unfortunately, Jung never does address the issue and we are left to speculate and arrive at our own conclusion. I make an attempt to come to terms with this conundrum in the chapter devoted to Adler.

Freud's extraverted thinking

Marie-Louise von Franz, Jung's brilliant and loyal colleague, elaborates on Jung's hypothesis for the secondary development of Freud's thinking in her essay, "The Inferior Function." She agrees with Jung that by natural inclination, Freud "was an introverted feeling type."[22] Basing her observations on biographical material, von Franz finds evidence of Freud's feeling nature in the highly differentiated way he dealt with people, meaning that his feeling function was consciously deployed. He adapted and modulated his behavior and emotional response in keeping with the circumstances and the personalities involved. His feeling temperament, von Franz adds, also accounted for a "kind of 'gentlemanliness' which had a positive influence upon his patients and upon his surroundings."[23]

Von Franz then proceeds to characterize the inferior thinking of an introverted feeling type as "simple, clear and intelligible."[24] At first glance her depiction seems like a contradiction in terms, but in fact, superior thinking is complex, highly qualified and not easy to follow: for example, the writings of Hegel, Kant and Heidegger. Another characteristic of inferior thinking, according to von Franz, is a tendency to subsume a great deal of data under the rubric of one or two basic ideas. Introverted feeling types with inferior thinking, von Franz argues, "actually have only one or two thoughts with which they race through a tremendous amount of material."[25] She describes this propensity as an "intellectual monomania" and believes that Freudian theory suffers from that symptom. Freud himself, she notes, complained that his dream interpretations felt monotonous and boring.

I agree with von Franz's characterization of Freud's thinking. However, I believe Freud's tendency to subsume a myriad of facts under one or two explanatory principles was influenced by the intellectual bias of his day. Enlightenment thinkers and their nineteenth-century adherents, in keeping with the laws of causality, reason and logic, sought to identify a basic explanatory principle in every field of study. In addition, I think the materialistically oriented Enlightenment thinkers, having rejected causality from top down, that is, with God as the primal cause, based their theories on "bottom-up" causal premises. In other words, the causal archetype structured their thinking; they merely applied it in a concrete manner. For Darwin, that causal premise was natural selection, for Marx, the division of labor, and for Freud, sexual libido.

Von Franz further observes that another aspect of inferior extraverted thinking is its tendency to become "tyrannical, stiff and unyielding."[26] Such thinking is not primarily oriented by outer reality but forces a theoretical structure onto it. In his conversation with Kurt Eissler, Jung provided an illustration of this dogmatic quality of Freud's thinking. He recalled a disagreement with Freud concerning some theoretical issue and ventured to say that in his "opinion it wasn't so at all." Freud countered with, "Yes, it is, it must be so!" "But why?" Jung asked. "Because after all I thought it!" Freud replied.[27] In later years, reflecting upon Freud's response, Jung concluded that since Freud's thinking was not fully conscious, when an idea came to him, he himself was surprised by it; and because the idea had its roots in the unconscious, it carried a connotation of rightness.[28] (An analogous occurrence is a lover's conviction concerning the rightness of his or her feelings for the beloved: for love, too, is not a conscious process, but a surprise and the result of "falling" into an archetypal state of mind.)

Further corroboration of Freud's belief in the validity of his ideas is found in a letter to Jung in which he wrote about his work on *Totem and Taboo*. Freud complains that he has little time to consult books and reports, "besides, my interest is diminished by the conviction that I am already in possession of the truths I am trying to prove."[29] He adds: "I can see from the difficulties I encounter in this work that I was not cut out for inductive investigation, that my whole make-up is intuitive, and that in setting out to establish the purely empirical science of [psychoanalysis] I subjected myself to an extraordinary discipline."[30] Here, Freud confirms Jung's assessment of him as a feeling intuitive type. In terms of my typology, Freud's attempt to ground psychoanalysis in empirical science illustrates how the primary archetypal motivation, Physis in the case of Freud, overrides an individual's conscious orientation.

Aside from the inferior quality of Freud's extraverted thinking, with all of its attendant problems, the chief characteristic of extraverted thinking (whether inferior or superior), according to Jung, is that it is conditioned by "objective data transmitted by sense-perception" and directed toward external facts in its theoretical conclusions.[31] In Jung's and von Franz's view, this attribute of extraverted thinking accounts for Freud's dominant orientation toward objective reality and the empirical character of his theories.

There is one other important aspect of extraverted thinking: a tendency to derive its ideas from tradition or from "the intellectual atmosphere of the time."[32] Again, Freud's materialistic and scientific orientation is a case in point. One can hardly consider Freud's ideas traditional, but they are, in fact, derived from ideas current in his day; and that holds true even for his sexual theories. In *The Discovery of the Unconscious*, Henri Ellenberger argues that although mid-twentieth-century accounts of Freud's life "state that the publication of his sexual theories aroused anger because of their unheard-of novelty in a 'Victorian' society," documentary evidence does not support their conclusion.[33] In reality Freud's *Three Essays on Sexual Theory* "appeared in the midst of a flood of contemporary literature on sexology and were favorably received."[34] His main contribution, Ellenberger states, consisted of synthesizing the extant ideas and applying them to psychotherapy. In the process Freud sought to base his theories on objective data, but the tendency to proceed along those lines was also part of the intellectual atmosphere of his time.

Adler's introverted thinking

Although it is my contention, which I hope to demonstrate in the following chapter, that Freud was an introvert, it is possible to provide a rationale for Jung's view of Freud's extraversion by arguing, as von Franz does, that Freud's *style of thinking* was extraverted. The same argument will then have to be made with respect to Adler's style of thinking, namely, that it was introverted. But in terms of Jung's description of the introverted thinking type, with Kant as the chief example, it is difficult to subsume Adler under that rubric. Briefly stated, introverted thinking, whether concerned with concrete or abstract objects, always begins and ends with the subject. Objective data are of secondary importance for the introverted thinker and used only to buttress the development of a subjective idea or symbolic image. Introverted thinking, Jung writes, "creates theories for their own sake."[35] The latter could never be said of Adler, who always insisted on the practical application of his ideas. Adler's thinking invariably referred to outer reality. For example, as far as Adler was concerned, the inferiority complex, its compensation and striving for superiority, was always played out in the context of a relationship between the individual and the surrounding physical and cultural environment. Adler's extraverted tendency was also apparent in his early interest in social medicine and in his emphasis on social interest and community feeling as the measure of psychological health and maturity.

If Adler is an extravert, how will Jung account for what he conceives to be Adler's primary focus on the subject—on subjective feelings rather than on objective data? Are we to suppose that Adler's introverted thinking was also inferior and the consequence of a trauma that forced his originally extraverted feelings into introverted thinking? Or, are we again going to conclude that Adler's inferior introverted thinking was simply the shadow side of his superior extraverted feelings? For, in all likelihood, Adler was an extraverted feeling type, which makes it possible to argue that his inferior orientation was introversion and his inferior function, thinking. In these terms, then, his theories could be seen as displaying the usual characteristics of inferior introverted thinking: negative judgments about oneself and others, avoidance of abstractions and philosophical issues, and a tendency to propound general platitudes and nostrums, for example, *Gemeinschaftsgefühl.*

Heinz and Rowena Ansbachers' classification of Freud and Adler

I think it noteworthy that Heinz and Rowena Ansbacher, who compiled a comprehensive summary of Adler's writings, also seek to demarcate the difference between Freud and Adler in typological terms. In their Introduction to *The Individual Psychology of Alfred Adler,* the editors rely upon philosopher Karl Jaspers' distinction between objective and subjective approaches to the study of psychology, and William James' delineation of the tough-minded and tender-minded temperaments to characterize the difference between the two Viennese founders of depth psychology.

For Jaspers, the term "*objective* corresponds to the psyche as seen from without, by the observer, and *subjective* corresponds to the psyche seen from within, by the subject himself."[36] Jaspers' distinction between objective and subjective is not based on typology; the distinction simply implies that there are two ways of observing the psyche. His use of the terms has no relation to Jung's characterization of the extraverted and introverted points of view. For by *objective,* Jung means the tendency to focus upon external reality and not just to look at the psyche from without; and by *subjective,* he means the tendency to refer both inner and outer reality to the perceiving subject.

The Ansbachers, however, make use of Jaspers' definitions and argue that Adler examined the psyche from within, Freud from without. But, if one looks at the differences they list between the theories of the two men, the distinction is somewhat forced and arbitrary. For example, as the objectively oriented psychologist, Freud is seen as minimizing consciousness, that is, in contrast to his emphasis on the powerful drives of the unconscious. Moreover, he favors molecular units of analysis and static structuralism, while his approach to the psyche is reductive, mechanistic and deterministic. In my opinion, it is difficult to say why the objective or external approach to psychology necessarily implies the above categories. Adler, by contrast, as the subjective psychologist, is appreciative of the role of consciousness. He prefers molar units of analysis and functional relativism, while his approach to the psyche is holistic, organismic and teleological. Again, there is no basis for arguing that the subjective point of view necessarily emphasizes the role of consciousness or, for that matter, pursues a holistic and teleological approach to the psyche.

With respect to James' differentiation between the tough-minded and tender-minded thinkers, the Ansbachers place Freud in the tough-minded category: empiricist, materialistic, pessimistic, irreligious, fatalistic and skeptical. Adler, on the other hand, is a tender-minded thinker, and, therefore, rationalist, intellectualistic, optimistic, religious, free-willist and dogmatical. The last two stylistically awkward terms are meant as contrasts to fatalistic and skeptical. The point is that tender-minded thinkers tend to stress free will. They are also less skeptical of abstract principles and more receptive toward religious beliefs than their tough-minded counterparts. Needless to say, the two types invariably tend to have a low opinion of each other.

The manner in which the Ansbachers apply the categories introduced by Jaspers and James discloses their anti-Freudian and pro-Adlerian bias. Also, they have no other categories to characterize the difference between Freud and Adler, which forces them into the inadequate, yet available classifications.

Freud and Adler as Physis types

Similarly, Jung and von Franz seek to understand the apparently opposing theories and orientations of Freud and Adler as best as they can within the parameters of Jung's typology. Extraversion and introversion, thinking and feeling, whether superior or inferior, are the only categories they can rely upon to explain these differences. On the other hand, my typology is able to explain Freud's emphasis on the object by the fact that his dominant archetypal motivation was Physis. He was a Physis type, an Aristotelian who, through historical circumstance, also happened to share the materialistic world-view of many scientifically-minded people of his day: material cause and effect rule the entire universe, psychology included; there is no eternal soul or spirit that animates the body; all creations of the mind, no matter how sublime, have their origins in evolutionary biology; human psychological development and resulting character, health or neurosis are determined by the vicissitudes of inner and outer stimuli brought to bear upon the organism.

Adler too, as we shall see, was a Physis type. That was the archetypal motivation he and Freud had in common. Freud's Physis orientation, however, was expressed in an introverted manner—evidenced by his intense scrutiny of intra-psychic processes, by his insistence on grounding all his theories in physiological processes, and by the nature of his therapeutic method. Adler's Physis orientation, on the other hand, was displayed in an extraverted manner. He emphasized the family and social context of all psychological processes, sought to apply his ideas through education and favored the "team" approach in dealing with disturbed adolescents.

Given Freud's Physis bias for objective data, it is not surprising that his main criticism of *Psychological Types* was that Jung claimed "there could be no 'objective truth' in psychology because of 'personal differences in the observer's constitution.'"[37] In other words, Freud questioned Jung's assumption that temperamental bias colors the perception of objective reality. He regarded the conclusion as much too subjective, with no basis in fact.

At one point, however, Freud did acknowledge the importance of "personal differences in the observer's constitution." The cultural historian, Peter Gay, reports that during debates about Otto Rank's book, *Trauma of Birth*, Freud warned his close followers that "'complete unanimity in all questions of scientific detail and on all newly broached themes' is not possible or even desirable, 'among half a dozen people of differing nature.'"[38] Note Freud's restriction about "scientific detail" and "newly broached themes." Disagreements stemming from temperamental differences were permitted on minor matters and during initial discussions of new theories. Once agreement was reached, which in practical terms meant that Freud had made up his mind about the matter, the objective validity of the theory was established. Freud would never agree that his temperamental bias determined the dominant features of his theories and the criteria by which he defined "objective truth."

Eros and Power

An example of the above process is Freud's introduction of the death drive in *Beyond the Pleasure Principle*. No doubt, confronted with the extensive violence of World War I, he finally overcame his earlier resistance to a separate aggressive drive, an idea proposed by Adler over a decade earlier. Freud always held a dualistic conception of the psyche and of the libido, but now he placed that dualism on an instinctive, biological foundation. In his new formulation, libido had two separate sources: the drive for life, ruled by the pleasure principle and expressed in the desire for sex and procreation; and the drive for death, which ignores the pleasure principle and pursues a covertly masochistic and externally aggressive agenda for a return of the primeval inorganic state of being from which all life originated. Put in other terms, the instinct for life, present in every living cell, is concerned with building up larger organisms; it is countered by an equally present cellular tendency toward the dissolution of the complex living organisms and their return to a state of inorganic matter. In Freud's formulation, the death drive is more fundamental than the life drive and he therefore concludes with the statement: "*the aim of all life is death.*"[39]

Commenting on Freud's presentation of the above thesis in *Beyond the Pleasure Principle*, Max Schur, Freud's sympathetic follower and personal physician, saw it as "an example of *ad hoc* reasoning to prove a preformed hypothesis."[40] Freud himself was somewhat disconcerted by the results of his theoretical speculations. "At the beginning," he writes, "I advocated the views here put forward only tentatively, but in the course of time they have acquired such a power over me that I can no longer think differently."[41] The very formulation of his statement tends to corroborate Jung's contention that for Freud, ideas had an autonomous character combined with a belief in their unassailable truthfulness. As for the pairing of the death drive (soon dubbed "Thanatos" by his followers) with Eros, Freud must have known that it ran contrary to the classic pairing of Eros with strife, and life with death. His creative vision, however, led him to propose a completely new and different set of opposites.

Freud's revised theory with a new set of opposite drives posed no difficulty for Jung, since already in *Symbols of Transformation*, he argued that libido aims equally at life and death. In fact, Jung felt he anticipated and probably influenced Freud's revision. But Jung was critical of the specific nature of the new dualism:

> It was a concession to intellectual logic on the one hand and to psychological prejudice on the other that impelled Freud to name the opposite of Eros the destructive or death instinct. For in the first place, Eros is not equivalent to life; but for anyone who thinks it is, the opposite of Eros will naturally appear to be death. And in the second place, we all feel that the opposite of our own highest principle must be purely destructive, deadly, and evil. We refuse to endow it with any positive life-force; hence we avoid and fear it.[42]

Consistent with his notion that typology determines one's basic orientation, Jung reasons that even the issue of how psychic opposites are envisioned is largely influenced by temperament. He also thinks that with

Freud's emphasis on Eros and Adler's on power, a temperamental clash of opposites is present in the history of psychoanalytic theories of neuroses.

In view of that historical fact, Jung offers his own unique set of opposites, namely, Eros and power. He argues that even though logically the opposite of love is hate, and of power, weakness, *psychologically* the opposite of Eros is the will to power.[43] He continues:

> Where love reigns, there is no will to power; and where the will to power is paramount, love is lacking. The one is but the shadow of the other: the man who adopts the standpoint of Eros finds his compensatory opposite in the will to power, and that of the man who puts the accent on power is Eros.[44]

Since for Jung, every conscious standpoint has its unconscious shadow side, it follows that the person "who adopts the standpoint of Eros finds his compensatory opposite in the will to power, and . . . the man who puts the accent on power" will balance that emphasis with Eros.[45] In Jung's opinion therefore, Freud harbored an unconscious will to power and Adler an unconscious desire for pleasure.

Jung is correct in identifying a will to power in Freud and a desire for pleasure and love in Adler. But contrary to Jung's reading, and as I demonstrate in the subsequent chapters, Freud's power drive was part of his everyday personal style of functioning, as was Adler's commitment to Eros. If I am accurate in my assessment, then the compensatory unconscious archetype for Freud was Eros and for Adler, Power. This is why each turned that compensatory archetype into the explanatory premise and dominant motivation of the unconscious. In other words, when Freud analyzed his unconscious he discovered that it was characterized by erotic fantasies and desires. Adler, on the other hand, found that his unconscious harbored feelings of inferiority and a drive for power. Freud's fascination with Eros and Adler's with power, therefore, stemmed from these unconscious feelings and desires which provided the impetus not only for the formulation of their theories, but also for a firm conviction in their validity. Their theories were not conscious constructs; if that were the case, they could be readily altered or adapted to varying circumstances. Instead, their ideas had a personal hold on them, and because these ideas were archetypal in nature, each felt them to be universally applicable and valid. In this respect their theories, as many critics have suspected, were actually mythologies.

Perhaps Adler would not have seen his contribution to depth psychology in these terms, although his idea of "guiding fictions" playing the central role in individual psychology and his advocacy of *Gemeinschaftsgefühl* in the social realm has the import of a mythological standpoint. By contrast, Jung knew he was creating a myth to replace the Christian one which no longer held meaning for him. Similarly, in the *New Introductory Lectures on Psychoanalysis*, Freud writes, "The theory of the drives is so to say our mythology. The drives are mythical beings, superb in their indefiniteness."[46] And in a 1932 letter responding to Einstein's query about the human propensity for aggression and war, after explaining his idea of the death drive, Freud adds: "It may perhaps seem to you as though our theories are a kind of mythology and, in the present case, not even an agreeable one. But does not every science come in the end to a kind of mythology like this? Cannot the same be said today of your own Physics?"[47]

Myth and numinosity

The fact that the theories of Freud, Adler and Jung have a mythological underpinning does not mean they had no empirical value. Every perspective on the nature of reality or on the nature of the psyche is mythological, in the sense that it is largely determined first by the dominant archetypes that inform one's temperament and then by the ruling myths of the day. The scientific outlook, for example, the accepted mythology of our day, is actually only one way of apprehending reality—romanticism, aestheticism and mysticism are other possible *Weltanschauungen*. But given the scientific temper of the twentieth century, Freud, Adler and Jung often sought to present their ideas in those terms.[48]

Aside from taking into consideration their divergent temperaments, another way of describing the differences among the three founders of depth psychology is to see where each located the "value of numinosity." Clearly for Freud, sexuality was a numinous area and that numinosity accounted for his unswerving life-long insistence on making it the keystone of his theories and the *shibboleth* with which to separate his allies from his enemies. Jung recounts Freud's attempt to obtain his commitment: "My dear Jung, promise me never to abandon the sexual theory. This is the most essential thing of all. You see, we must make a dogma of it, an unshakable bulwark."[49] Already at their first meeting, Jung was struck by the intensity of Freud's emotional attachment to his sexual theory:

> when he spoke of it, his tone became urgent, almost anxious, and all signs of his normally critical and skeptical manner vanished.

> A strange, deeply moved expression came over his face, the cause of which I was at a loss to understand. I had a strong intuition that for him sexuality was a sort of *numinosum*.[50]

For Adler the accent of numinosity fell on his notion of *Gemeinschaftsgefühl*, "community feeling". The term is related directly to Ferdinand Tönnies' influential book *Gemeinschaft und Gesellschaft* ("Community and Civil Society"), originally published in 1887. In Germany and Austria its 1912 edition touched off a core of deep nostalgia for the pre-industrial society with its personal community ties. In addition, Adler's personal need for community and Eros was clearly a response to his traumatic experiences as a military physician on the Russian front during World War I. One of his duties was to determine which soldiers were fit to return to the trenches. He had also lost a good number of his friends and colleagues. The war had sobered and focused his previously cheerful and extravagant personality.

When Adler was once again holding court in his favorite Viennese café, his colleagues eagerly awaited his comments and insights concerning the disturbing events all had witnessed. "*Nun, Adler—was gibt's Neues?*" one of them asked. "It seems to me," said Adler, looking seriously at everyone around the table, "that what the world chiefly wants today is *Gemeinschaftsgefühl*."[51] They were stunned. The British novelist Phyllis Bottome, one of Adler's friends and earliest biographers, describes the scene: "Here they were, these picked brains of Vienna, hard-bitten intellectuals, scientists, writers, teachers, journalists—waiting for the wisdom of a great philosopher; and what did he offer them—a mere generalization of 'good-will.'"[52] One of them objected, "*Gemeinschaftsgefühl* . . . what a word to use—it does not even exist in philosophy!" Nevertheless, Adler repeated quietly, "It is what the world wants."[53] They sensed that this was not a mere theoretical notion but a deeply felt conviction. That conviction, indeed, informed his theories from then on and alienated many of his colleagues and adherents. As one of them recounted:

> We were all prepared to accept what further he had to teach us; but this stuff for everybody—this sudden missionary idea of *Gemeinschaftsgefühl*—how could we deal with it? The medical profession must keep its science above the crowd! Adler should, as a scientist, have known this, and he should have known that if he insisted on spreading this sort of religious science through the laity we, as a profession, could not support him.[54]

It speaks well of Adler's ethical character that in the face of the horrors of World War I he did not succumb to pessimism but instead responded with Eros and hope. The fact that *Gemeinschaftsgefühl* was a restatement of the Christian ideal of "Love thy neighbor as thyself" only confirmed for Adler that his ideal was a perennial goal of humanity. But Adler, Bottome writes, "was prepared to do what no man of science had as yet adventured—to harness his science to a religious goal."[55] Actually, Adler's proposal was not that radical given his previous psychological theories: he had never considered striving for power a salutary drive, but always an illusory, distorted attempt at self-cure that isolates the neurotic individual from the community. From now on, however, he insisted that the striving for superiority was not only the primary source of neuroses but also of war; and that neurotic and troubling impulse needed to be replaced with the ideals of community feeling and community service. He thought this humanistic aim could be accomplished through a sustained program of psychologically informed education of children and adults.

In contrast to the numinosity of sexuality for Freud and of community feeling for Adler, for Jung, *spirit* was numinous. A perusal of his autobiography, *Memories, Dreams, Reflections*, as well as a cursory glance at the titles of his other writings, disclose his overarching interest in the spiritual aspects of psychology. Almost all of Jung's mature writings deal with the topics of religion and spirituality: *Psychology and Religion*; *Aion: Researches into the Phenomenology of the Self*; *Psychology and Alchemy*; and his magnum opus, *Mysterium Coniunctionis: An Inquiry into the Separation and Synthesis of Psychic Opposites in Alchemy*. I think an impartial examination of Jung's research and writing indicates that just as Freud established a scientific method for the exploration of the unconscious, Jung placed the study of religious and spiritual phenomena on an empirical basis. Given his focus on these aspects of the psyche, it is not surprising therefore, that Jung came to regard Freud's fascination with sexuality as a displaced form of spirituality. In his memoirs, Jung writes of Sigmund Freud:

> In retrospect I can say that I alone logically pursued the two problems which most interested Freud: the problem of "archaic vestiges," and that of sexuality. It is a widespread error to imagine that I do not see the value of sexuality. On the contrary, it plays a large part in my psychology as an essential—though not the sole—expression of psychic wholeness. But my main concern has been to investigate, over and above its personal significance and biological function, its

> spiritual aspect and its numinous meaning, and thus to explain what Freud was so fascinated by but was unable to grasp.[56]

Jung argues that because Freud rejected the realm of spirit, the numinosity usually associated with spiritual phenomena was displaced upon sexuality and imbued with tremendous meaning and significance. The displacement, actually, is automatic because the two realms happen to be the opposite sides of the same archetypal coin: Eros. For the basic aim of both sexuality and spirituality is a desire for union.

Generally, the object of that desire is someone or something that embodies either the archetype of the self or the archetypes of soul and spirit. For a child, the parents are the first objects of this desire for a union with the core of one's being. The Oedipus complex, in Jung's view, is Freud's literal reading of that longing. With further maturation and psychological differentiation, the archetypes of soul and spirit become the vehicles of Eros, its drive for union sought either in romantic attachments or in spiritual practice. Spiritual ecstasy has a marked sexual component (for example, Song of Songs, the poetry of Rumi, of St John of the Cross and the sculpture "*The Ecstasy of St Theresa*" by Bernini) while romantic sexuality, as every lover knows, has a spiritual aspect associated with it. Consequently, in psychotherapeutic practice, what sometimes appears a sexual neurosis may conceal a spiritual problem, while a spiritual problem, in turn, may mask a sexual one.

Jung, therefore, interpreted Freud's preoccupations with sexuality as a spiritual problem: a conscious rejection and repression of his spiritual impulses. Jung felt he did justice to the topic that so captivated Freud by taking into account the spiritual aspects of sexuality. In a sense he was just as fascinated by the topic of sexuality as Freud, but by its spiritual side. His deliberations concerning the spiritual aspects of Eros make up the contents of *The Psychology of the Transference* and *Mysterium Coniunctionis*.

Imagination and spirit

In his earlier years Jung sought to differentiate his psychology from Freud's and Adler's by insisting that, rather than Eros or the will to power, his basic premise was "the principle of imagination."[57] In contrast to his own positive evaluation of imagination, he thought Freud looked to external reality as the keynote of psychic life and therefore regarded imagination as useless or even reprehensible.[58] Actually, Jung overstated his case, for Freud did not consider the products of fantasy or imagination as reprehensible or of little value. He felt they were therapeutically useful in helping neurotics conceal their irrational motives and desires and in sublimating these impulses into cultural expressions. Adler also thought of fantasy in a heuristic manner: neurotics invent and then believe their "fictions" about themselves and others, and then orient their life and goals around these "guiding fictions," as he referred to them. In this respect, Adler was fond of saying that the essential insight of his psychology could be summed up in the phrase—"all neurosis is vanity."[59]

Therefore, the most Jung could legitimately argue was that Freud and Adler relegated imagination to a supportive role in the pursuit of primary psychological drives or goals. In contrast, Jung thought of imagination in an artistic way, as an autonomous source of creative images and ideas. He also regarded imagination as the source of symbolic images that can heal internal and relational conflicts and further psychological maturation and growth. To point out the differences among himself and his colleagues, Jung even toyed with the synchronistic meaning of their names: *Freud(e)*, "joy" (the pleasure principle); *Adler*, "eagle" (will to power); and *Jung*, "young" (rebirth).[60] By "rebirth" Jung means the child-like capacity for creative renewal based on the infinite play of imagination. (Each of these ostensible characteristics has a shadow side: bitterness and cynicism in Freud; a feeling of weakness and inadequacy in Adler; and rigidity and dogmatism usually associated with the *senex* in the case of Jung.) Jung carved the following inscription on a square block of granite at his retreat in the Bollingen:

> Time is a child—playing like a child—playing a board game—the kingdom of the child. This is Telesphoros, who roams through the dark regions of this cosmos and glows like a star out of the depths. He points the way to the gates of the sun and to the land of dreams.[61]

Based on his own experience, Jung felt that all creative work and ideas derive from imagination, in child-like fantasy whose dynamic principle is play: "Not the artist alone, but every creative individual whatsoever owes all that is greatest in his life to fantasy."[62] On the Bollingen stone, in recognition of the role that fantasy played in his life, Jung personified that dynamic principle in the Kabiric figure of Telesphorus. (Telesphorus was the *familiaris* or daemon of Aesculapius and is said to have inspired his medical prescriptions; the name means "far-carrying" and the dwarf-like phallic figure is a personification of Hermes and of the alchemical Mercurius. See Figure 5.1.)

Figure 5.1 Statuette of Telesphorus with the top section concealing a phallus. Roman, 0–200 Bronze. 10.5 cm. The Thorvaldsens Museum. Photographer Ole Haupt.

Aside from Jung's insistence on the pivotal role and significance of imagination in the life of the psyche, he was the opposite of Freud and Adler in his focus on spirituality. In contrast to both Freud's and Adler's Physis orientation, Jung's consuming interest was spirit. Jung's fascination with Spirit, in the broad and not merely religious sense of the term, set him apart from Freud and led to their inevitable separation. Even at their first meeting, Jung writes, he was perturbed by Freud's attitude toward spirit:

> Wherever, in a person or in a work of art, an expression of spirituality (in the intellectual, not the supernatural sense) came to light, he suspected it, and insinuated that it was repressed sexuality. Anything that could not be directly interpreted as sexuality he referred to as "psychosexuality." I protested that this hypothesis, carried to its logical conclusion, would lead to an annihilating judgment upon culture. Culture would then appear as a mere farce, the morbid consequence of repressed sexuality. "Yes," he assented, "so it is, and that is just a curse of fate against which we are powerless to contend." I was by no means disposed to agree, or to let it go at that, but still I did not feel competent to argue it out with him.[63]

In the end, Jung's temperamental orientation forced him "to argue it out with him" and the two parted company. His interest in the spiritual aspects of the psyche located Jung ahead of his time. Given the materialistic bias of the post-Enlightenment age, Freud's theory gained overwhelming popular acceptance and became an influential school of thought in the psychiatric and academic community. Currently, as spiritual concerns take hold of the popular imagination, Jungian psychology is gaining greater recognition while the psychoanalytical and psychiatric community is forced to come to terms with an area signally disparaged by Freud.

Conclusion

Jung sought to understand the conflict between Freud and Adler as a clash of opposing temperaments. He deliberately set out to formulate a typology to enable him to come to terms with those temperamental differences and their influence on the theoretical perspectives of the two men. Initially, extraversion and introversion were the main categories he used to classify their divergent perspectives towards theoretical and clinical issues. He considered Freud's theory extraverted because it was based on innate objective biological processes that were then subsequently modified by external influences. Adler's approach, in comparison, was introverted because he took the subjective ego position as his starting point and regarded psychological development as the safe-guarding of ego superiority over the objective demands of instinct and environment. Even though, at one point, in *Psychological Types*, Jung argued that "the extraverted theory holds good for the extraverted type, the introverted theory for the introverted type,"[64] he soon realized the formula did not apply to Freud and Adler: for Freud was not an extravert and Adler was not an introvert. Consequently, Jung amended his argument and claimed it was possible for an introvert to create an extraverted theory and for an extravert to devise an introverted theory. That argument, however, required a further appeal to his typological schema and, in the case of Freud, reliance upon a neurotic reversal of a person's original type. In Jung's opinion, Freud shied away from his originally introverted feeling temperament because of an emotional trauma and cultivated, instead, his inferior attitude and function—extraverted thinking, which accounted for his extraverted theory. Jung made no such modification for Adler's typology and we are left to speculate about how the extraverted Adler produced a purportedly introverted theory.

Although Jung developed his typology for the purpose of understanding and potentially resolving the theoretical differences between Freud and Adler and their adherents, the effort essentially failed in its stated intent. The circumstances, however, did impel Jung to formulate a typology based on a comprehensive description of the psyche's conscious apprehension of subjective and objective reality. His model describes in a non-judgmental manner, the differences among individuals based on the extraverted or introverted deployment of their feeling, thinking, intuiting and sensing functions.

Incidentally, both Freud and Adler developed a typology. Many readers are familiar with Freud's oral, anal, phallic and genital character and personality types. Adler felt that "a human being cannot be typified or classified"[65] and emphasized that each individual has his or her unique style of life. Nevertheless, he also formulated a typology: the ruling type; the getting type; the avoiding type; and the socially useful type. Clearly, the categories of Freud's and Adler's typologies reveal the basic temperamental orientations of their founders—the introverted physiological bias of Freud and the extraverted sociological focus of Adler. One cannot discern a similar analogy with Jung and his bias toward spirituality, for his typology makes no reference to soul or to spirit. My typology takes both soul and spirit into account and adds those aspects to a Jungian oriented typology.

The distinction Jung drew between Freud's theory as based on Eros and Adler's on the will to power is more apposite than his attempt to characterize their positions as extraverted and introverted.[66] In this respect, I address the difference between Freud and Adler more directly than Jung, for Power and Eros are core categories of my typology, which together with Physis and Pneuma account for the divergent theoretical standpoints of all three founders of depth psychology. As I will attempt to demonstrate in the following chapters, Freud was an introverted Power Physis type, Adler an extraverted Physis Eros type and Jung an introverted Power Pneuma type.

From my perspective, it was not the opposites of extraversion and introversion but the motivations of Eros and Power that account for the difference between Freud and Adler. Power was Freud's conscious style of functioning, Eros was Adler's. The compensatory archetype for Freud, therefore, was Eros and for Adler, Power. Consequently, as I stated earlier, when Freud analyzed his unconscious, he discovered that it was permeated with erotic fantasies and desires; while Adler found that his unconscious harbored feelings of inferiority together with compensatory fantasies of superiority and Power.

Both men had Physis as their conscious area of interest and this archetypal motivation accounted for Freud's propensity to ground his theories in physiological processes and objective data and for Adler's insistence on the practical application of his theories. In keeping with Freud's introverted nature, his Physis was expressed in an introverted manner with a focus on the individual and the personal. Adler's extraverted temperament, on the other hand, applied Physis in an extraverted communal and socially concerned way. In contrast, Jung's area of interest was Pneuma and in this respect he was radically different from both Freud and Adler. Again, Pneuma can be expressed in either an extraverted or introverted way. As an introvert, Jung pursued Pneuma through careful attention to his fantasies and dreams and in his solitary research and writing. An example of an extraverted Pneuma type is the late John Paul II, who visited 117 countries and logged over 725,000 miles during his pontificate. Incidentally, as with Jung, Power was probably John Paul II's auxiliary archetypal motivation. Jung also shared the motivation of Power with Freud as a style of functioning in his daily life and relations with others.

Since Power and Pneuma were Jung's conscious motivations, Eros and Physis were his unconscious drives. These two shadow drives in all likelihood also account for Jung's attraction to women and for his purported womanizing. But they were also expressed in his preoccupation with the principle of the union of opposites, particularly as found in alchemical fantasies centered on matter. The Physis motivation is clearly present in his predilection for carving in stone and his need for a concrete manifestation of his individuation process by building the tower at Bollingen.[67]

Thus, aside from introducing a new typology that provides insight into basic human motivations, attitudes and behavior, my typology also completes the work begun by Jung when he realized that the theoretical disputes among his colleagues were influenced to a large measure by their conflicting temperaments. Jung's typology alone fails to account for the theoretical differences among them. Archetypal-motivational typology, in expanding Jung's categories, provides appropriate classifications that do justice to the unique perspectives of the three founders of depth psychology. By applying the insights of the depth psychologists themselves concerning the influence of unconscious factors to their own ideas, archetypal-motivational typology completes the circle they themselves began.

However, when I argue that basic temperament and unconscious motivations influence one's theoretical outlook and style of thinking, I do not impugn the validity of the founders' theories. The temperamental biases only define the choice of certain ideas or approaches to reality; they say nothing about their accuracy. The resulting theories must be examined and evaluated in their own terms, or rather, in terms of the fields to which they refer, and not dismissed as mere products of subjective temperamental differences. On the contrary, particularly in the realm of psychology, theoretical perspectives stemming from varied temperaments contribute to a wide-ranging portrayal of the human psyche. For, as Jung states, Nietzsche's observation that every philosophy is but a disguised confession helped him to see that every psychology—his own included—"has the character of a subjective confession".[68]

The varied formulations of Freud, Adler and Jung are actually expressions of different facets of the psyche. An appreciation of the theoretical perspective of all three founders of depth psychology is necessary to form a complete image of the contents and dynamics of the conscious and unconscious mind. Freud tended to focus on the intra-psychic dynamics of the personal unconscious. Adler emphasized the importance of environmental and social adaptation and the value of community feelings. And Jung elaborated upon the transpersonal, mythological and spiritual components of psychic life. In the end, because of their temperamental differences and resulting theoretical biases, the three pioneers of depth psychology, together, provide an initial outline of a comprehensive mythology of the human soul.

6
Sigmund Freud: Introverted Spirited Power Physis Type

Sigmund Freud
6 May 1856–23 September 1939

Jung asked Freud for a picture of himself and this 1906 photograph is the one Freud sent. Photo courtesy of Freud Museum, London.

Introversion

There can be little doubt that the founder of psychoanalysis, a discipline that relies on paying close attention to the interior world of dreams, fantasies and desires, was an introvert. The term, of course, is Jung's, and considering the enmity toward Jung from Freud's major biographers, none of them characterize him in that manner. Also, until recently, the term "introvert" carried a pejorative connotation and was associated with self-indulgent narcissism and deficient social adaptation. Freud's biographers clearly did not want to emphasize this aspect of his personality. One needs to search carefully for references to his introverted temperament and deduce his introversion from descriptions of his personality and way of life. Ernest Jones, Freud's authorized biographer, for example, mentions only in passing that in Freud's university days, "Apart from peace and quiet for reading and the company of like-minded friends, he wanted little else than books"; his chief pleasure was going on solitary walks.[1] Later, as a successful and respected psychoanalyst, Freud did not participate in the lively Viennese café scene, nor did he frequent theaters or the opera. Joan Riviere, who was analyzed by Freud and translated his early essays into English, observes "he appeared somewhat aloof," and "could easily be bored by crowds and gatherings."[2] Close friends, family and select colleagues formed his social circle, which is the norm for introverts.

In his early 20s, Freud wanted to be a laboratory research scientist. He liked to work alone. When he instead turned to medicine, principally because of financial considerations, he established a practice that suited his introverted nature—engaging one person at a time in an exploration of the psyche. The remainder of his professional life was devoted to research and writing. Freud's pioneering work, *The Interpretation of Dreams*, was a supremely introverted enterprise, a painstaking self-analysis conducted over a number of years. Fortunately, his professional practice during this period was, he writes, "hopelessly poor" and he was able to live "only for the 'inner' work."[3] Indeed, Freud was capable of completely immersing himself in his work, so much so that his son Martin recalled that during the writing of *The Interpretation of Dreams* "we saw little of father."[4]

The process of writing engaged Freud: he enjoyed ruminating about his ideas and paid careful attention to style. The impressive corpus of his writings could only come from someone who prized working alone for extended periods of time. Even the manner in which he pursued his writing attests to Freud's introverted nature. First, he read broadly about his chosen subject, but once he felt prepared, he stopped reading and followed his inner impulses. In her biography of Jung, Deirdre Bair writes that Freud criticized Jung about his heavy reliance on outside sources. The references "gave Jung's writing an air of learned authority but detracted from the purity of his thought."[5] Freud's introverted approach to writing allows the reader to follow his thinking process: the qualifications, second thoughts and debates with himself as he proceeds to build an argument. This evident display of Freud's creativity inspires many readers to undertake a similar thinking process and accounts, in some measure, for the writings of his followers.

Spiritedness

In Chapters 3 and 4, I make a distinction among the four archetypal motivations of a personality and the two temperamental qualities of soulfulness and spiritedness that influence the manner in which the motivations are expressed. With respect to the two qualities, I believe Freud was a spirited personality. Spirit is primarily concerned with the "word," with ideas, thoughts, meanings, reason and logic. Freud was fascinated by words and language. He is, after all, the father of the "talking cure." He was also keenly interested in puns and slips of the tongue. He thought dreams have their origins in thoughts which are best expressed through words. In dreams, these thoughts are translated into images that distort or fail to express their logical content. For Freud, dream interpretation consisted of returning the images to their verbal character and conceptual understanding. Freud was also interested in how language is formed in the brain and how linguistic ability developed. His first book, *On the Conception of the Aphasias*, explored the neurology of aphasia and argued that its occurrence should not be attributed solely to brain lesions. And finally, Freud's own self-analysis consisted of writing in his journals and letters to his friend, Wilhelm Fliess. Freud's verbal approach to the psyche and to his self-analysis contrasts sharply with Jung's, which emphasized images and their creative exploration through artistic elaboration and expression.

While soul gravitates toward darkness and depths, spirit prefers light and height. Spirit expresses itself in clarity and brilliance, all the while tending toward abstraction and theory. I believe these attributes are evident in Freud's lucid thinking, writing and love of theory. Freud also demonstrated his affinity with spirit through his heartfelt embrace of the basic principles of the Enlightenment. In the tradition of the *philosophes*, he was a secularist: dismissive of religious beliefs and convinced of the liberating power of reason. Consequently, in his therapeutic method, Freud relied on clarity and understanding to cure or at least ameliorate neuroses. In stark contrast to the empathic and soulful therapeutic approaches of our day, Freud advocated a rational distance from the practitioner's emotions, as well as from those one's patients.

Spirit also manifests as fire, and fire is quick to burn. Freud's sharp, incisive remarks and periodic outbursts of temper characterize this aspect of his nature. Peter Gay writes that Freud concurred with an earlier biographer's description of him as someone with a "volcanic nature."[6] Gay also argues that Freud's analysis of Michelangelo's *Moses*, depicting the prophet subduing his inner rage at seeing the children of Israel worshiping the golden calf, is actually a projection of Freud's own emotional turmoil in 1913, the year he drafted "The Moses of Michelangelo."[7] Two years earlier Adler and his group had defected from Freud's inner circle and, in the meantime, Freud's relationship with Jung, on whom he counted to advance the cause of psychoanalysis into the future, also foundered.

In its positive manifestation "fire" is the enthusiasm and energy a spirited individual brings to an enterprise, a force capable of overcoming seemingly insurmountable difficulties and obstacles. A spirited person, like Freud, will tend to be resolute and decisive, but, at the same time, judgmental, impatient, cutting and not willing to suffer fools lightly. Unchecked by soul and Eros, spirit tends toward dogmatism, fanaticism and authoritarianism, invariably coupled with a demand for loyalty and unswerving adherence to a set of rules or principles. There is ample evidence in the accounts of Freud's attitudes and behavior in the following section on Power that attest to these fiery and spirited traits of his personality.

Power

Narrowing in on Freud's temperament, from the broad characteristics of introversion and spirit to his primary archetypal core of Physis, we next examine Power, his secondary unconscious motivation. The archetype of Power is expressed in a desire to dominate and control all areas of life, whether internal or external, personal or social. I think Freud's power drive was evident in his way of living, in his attempts at self-control and in his theoretical outlook which valued conscious knowledge and command over spontaneous expressions of the psyche. His power drive is also clearly on display in his autocratic rule over the psychoanalytic movement.

In political matters, Peter Gay writes, Freud "was the true politician, more devious than in the rest of his conduct, and his struggles with Adler brought out all his latent gifts for navigating among contending forces and pursuing his program."[8] But as an introvert, Freud preferred to exercise his power in an unobtrusive manner, using loyal adherents to carry out the extraverted responsibilities of leadership. Isidor Sadger, an early recruit to psychoanalysis, observed that Freud

> always refused officially and publicly to play the leader. He presided over the first congress in Salzburg [First Psychoanalytic Congress in 1908] only after Bleuler had refused the chairmanship offered him. Otherwise Freud always promoted others and would always make one of his favorites President of the International Psychoanalytic Association. To all appearances he wanted nothing more than to be merely the chairman of a regional group, at least in name. But in truth, all the strings were held together in his firm hand and none of the others, not even the international president, would have dared to decree anything without first asking Freud.[9]

Sadger also noted that Freud's power drive extended to the need to be the source of all new ideas or discoveries. He was the "primal father" or the "father of all," as he was actually called at the Berlin Psychoanalytic Congresses, and jealously guarded his primacy: "Freud was not pleased," Sadger writes, "when a student went his own way or followed up his own thoughts independently."[10] His authoritarian personality expelled as heretics any who dared to question or alter his doctrines—for that is how he regarded his theories. An affront to his paternal authority, as Freud's treatment of Adler and Jung illustrates, was punished with ostracism, scathing criticism and implacable anger.

Since Power was Freud's auxiliary archetypal motivation, it was partially unconscious or "shadowy"; hence, the emotionally intense and somewhat primitive reactions on his part when his power motivations were thwarted. The opposite of Power is Eros, and Freud knew he lacked the latter attribute, although he could not define it in precise terms: "I regard it as a serious misfortune that Nature did not give me that indefinite something which attracts people. If I think back on my life it is what I have most lacked to make my existence rosy."[11] If a person's public stance is motivated by Power, Eros is then exercised in private life. Nevertheless, it is less differentiated than the superior motivations and tends to have a compulsive quality. In Freud's case that quality can be seen his infatuation with Fliess and later with Adler and Jung. In other Power types, the unconscious nature of Eros is acted out in sexual fixations and addictions, and in religious Power types, in periodic falls from grace. Freud's marked tendency toward hysteria, as we shall see below, is also directly related to his unconscious Eros.

Freud's Power orientation is present in the psychoanalytic method which expresses the power differential between analyst and patient: the analyst is in control, sitting out of sight and at the head of the prone, passive patient. Similar attention to the power equation and an emphasis on domination and control is present in his theories. In the

Oedipal complex, for example, the child seeks to possess the parent of the opposite sex and rid itself of any competition from the same sex parent. The Oedipal complex is resolved by the castration complex in which the boy fears the loss of his penis and the girl discovers her lack of a penis. According to Freud, by virtue of having a penis, men have something women lack and that lack is a source of envy; even women's desire to bear children is an attempt to make up for the lack of a penis. A woman is an incomplete man and, therefore, anatomically at least, men are superior to women. Freud even conceptualizes the experience of love in power terms by making a distinction between loving and being loved: being loved places one in a dependent, submissive position, while loving is active and dominant.

In *Totem and Taboo,* the primal father seeks to retain his sexual monopoly over all available females by making all other males in the horde subservient to his whims. In Freud's view of the dynamics of the psyche, the superego strives to control the ego, while the ego seeks to control the demands of outer reality and the desires of the id. With respect to the values of reality and reason, consciousness is superior to the unconscious and the ego superior to the id. The ideal healthy and well-adjusted human being is in control of the irrational impulses and unrealistic desires of the unconscious. Thus, as the above summary indicates, Freud's power drive is present in almost every one of his major theoretical formulations.

That power motivation is also apparent in Freud's ideas about society. His notion of an ideal civilization is "a community of men who had subordinated their instinctual life to *the dictatorship of reason.*"[12] He admitted that such a community was a utopian expectation and therefore, the next best thing is to "educate an upper strata of men, with independent minds."[13] Freud was an unabashed elitist and considered the majority of mankind "trash."[14] In his view there is an innate inequality among human beings manifesting itself in leaders and followers, with the latter possessing "an extreme passion for authority" and a desire "to be governed by unrestricted force."[15] Like many of his contemporaries who were disillusioned with the institution of monarchy, he became enamored, instead, with the principle of "leadership" and idealized cultural and political leaders. Unfortunately Freud's notion of leadership and the "extreme passion for authority" on the part of the masses turned out to be a premonition of the Nazi era.

Given his elitism, his view of leadership and the "dictatorship of reason," it is easy to imagine how Freud viewed his role in the psychoanalytic movement, as well as how a Freudian society would be organized. Thus he readily acceded to Ernest Jones' scheme of a clandestine committee to ensure psychoanalytic orthodoxy and guard against heresy: "What took hold of my imagination immediately," he wrote to Jones, "is your idea of a secret council composed of the best and most trustworthy among our men to take care of the further development of psychoanalysis and defend the cause against personalities and accidents when I am no more."[16] He had expected Jung to have gathered such a coterie, but after Jung's defection it "had to be formed independently of Jung and of the elected presidents" of the various local associations.[17] The secret committee consisted of Karl Abraham, Max Eitingon, Sandor Ferenczi, Ernest Jones, Otto Rank and Hanns Sachs.

Freud's power drive was already evident in his childhood fantasies of a future career. He did not dream of becoming a writer, a physician, or a scientist. As a young boy, he fantasized becoming a military commander and liked calling himself "conquistador." In his adolescence, these dreams turned to attaining a high government post as cabinet minister. He planned to study jurisprudence at the university and enter politics after graduation. An anecdote is often cited to dramatize Freud's youthful military cast of mind and his dislike of submissiveness. During his self-analysis he remembered that when he was 12, his father told him that once in Freiberg a man knocked off his new fur cap into the mud on the street and shouted: "Jew, get off the pavement!" To the indignant boy's question, "What did you do?" the father replied calmly, "I stepped into the gutter and picked up my hat." His father's subservience and lack of heroism shocked the young Freud, and in his fantasies he contrasted his father's attitude to that of Hamilcar who made his son Hannibal swear on the family altar to take vengeance on the Romans for their sacking of Carthage.[18]

Freud abandoned his adolescent hopes of becoming a cabinet minister only shortly before commencing his university studies. Siegfried Bernfeld, a member of the "second generation" of psychoanalysts in Vienna, who later gathered biographical data on Freud used by Jones, writes:

> After his graduation from High School [*Gymnasium*], Freud suddenly retreats from his search for power over men. He turns to the more sublime power over nature, through science, and he decides to study 'natural history'—biology to us today. Power, prestige, and wealth should come to him only contingent to his being a great scientist.[19]

Thus, instead of conquering empires, Freud shifted his ambitions to conquering nature through knowledge, and instead of wielding political power he hoped to have an enduring and universal influence through discovering the laws of nature. With his close friends he was open about his desire to achieve lasting fame, and constantly sought to make a scientific discovery that would assure his reputation. In his later years, he was pleased to hear his achievement of elucidating the principles of mental life compared with Darwin's discovery of the laws of biological evolution and Newton's elucidation of the forces governing the physical universe. Jones comments that as a young man Freud recognized that "the ultimate secret of power was not force, but understanding."[20] The shift from power over others to power over nature also happened to be consonant with his introverted temperament. But power was still the motivation behind his pursuit of science and he now subscribed to Roger Bacon's dictum, "Knowledge is power." In his "Autobiographical Study" (1925), Freud is dimly aware of the connection between his power drive and his pursuit of knowledge: "I felt no particular partiality for the position and activity of a physician in those early years, nor, by the way, later. Rather I was moved by a sort of greed for knowledge."[21] In this regard, Darwin's discoveries were the source of intense excitement during the 1870s and Freud acknowledged the influence: "the doctrines of Darwin, then topical, powerfully attracted me because they promised an extraordinary advancement in our understanding of the world."[22]

From the above descriptions, one could easily conclude that Freud's basic archetypal motivation was Power. But that was not the case. His primary motivation was Physis, a fascination with natural and physical manifestations of reality. Power was his secondary drive and he used it in the service of his fascination with nature. For Power is a style of being and not limited to a specific sphere; it can be exercised in any area of life. It is no accident, then, that with the combination of Physis and Power as the underlying motivations that ruled the expressions of his conscious life, the young Freud was attracted to the study of nature to satisfy his need for mastery.

Freud's need for power and control extended to his personal life. In his portrait of Freud, Peter Gay writes: he possessed a "commanding air . . . an air of power disciplined. Even Freud's mustache and pointed beard were subdued to order by a barber's daily attention."[23] His "heroic effort at self-mastery in the service of concentrated work . . . chained him to a most precise timetable"; he lived, in his nephew Ernst Waldinger's words, "by the clock."[24] His daily schedule, leisure time and summer vacations were carefully organized and predictable.

Freud's effort at self-mastery was the expression of his power drive and not, as Peter Gay piously suggests, a consciously determined schedule in the service of his work. That might have been Freud's own rationalization or other people's perception of his behavior. Actually, he had little choice in the matter because of the strength of the archetypal motivation. For any drive, to use Freud's own insights and terminology, provides a large measure of libidinal satisfaction and resists conscious interference. Consequently, as he wrote in a 1910 letter to the Zurich pastor Oskar Pfister, he felt that for him "fantasizing and working coincide; I find amusement in nothing else."[25]

In view of Freud's need for outer discipline and personal self-control, one is struck by his admission to Jung that he suffered from an uncontrollable urge to urinate in public places where no toilet was readily available. Jung recounts such an embarrassing incident during their joint 1909 visit to the United States at the invitation of Clark University. They were in New York City, standing on an embankment overlooking the Hudson River, apparently in earnest dispute over some issue, when Freud urinated in his trousers.[26] They quickly took a taxi back to their hotel.

During his September 1908 visit to London, Freud wrote to Jung about the problem asking if he had any ideas about what could cause such a neurosis. In the discussion that ensued in their New York hotel, Jung reiterated his feeling that that symptom had to do with Freud's suppression and devaluation of love. On the surface it is hard to imagine Freud, the author of the sexual theory of neuroses, as someone who suppressed or devalued love. Evidently Jung was referring to Freud's tendency to reduce all expressions of love—spiritual, humanistic or altruistic—to sexual libido. As Jung later recounted the incident, in the previously mentioned 1953 interview with Kurt Eissler, he reiterated his conjecture that the problem occurred because Freud "obviously suppressed and devalued love and thus fell prey to power. The pursuit of power became pathological."[27]

Jung was clearly struck by the intense nature of Freud's power drive, which Freud, at least in this instance, seemed to deny. The conversation, in Jung's reconstruction, went as follows:

> Freud: Why should it be a neurosis? It is a paralysis!
> Jung: Professor, let me tell you with the greatest respect...everyone knows after all that you are extremely ambitious.
> Freud: Me?! . . . Ambitious? Anything but that!
> Jung: Yes, and thus, blind! Terribly blind! This is a psychogenic neurosis because you,—you—you have the wrong attitude! I will get around it, I will analyze you!
> Freud: I would be overjoyed! Good! So, do try it then![28]

They had been analyzing each other's dreams on board ship during their journey to the Unites States, so this was a continuation of their practice. In the above exchange Jung was using Freud's own hypothesis that bed-wetting and urination were related to the character trait of ambition. Freud mentioned that idea in his 1908 essay "Character and Anal Eroticism," the same year that he wrote to Jung about his urge to urinate in public places. [29] In this connection, it is important to note that Freud used to wet his bed when he was two years old and that in his seventh or eighth year he once urinated in his parents' bedroom and in their presence.[30] We can only speculate about the emotional or external conditions which preceded the incident. But Freud did remember his father's reaction, "The boy will come to nothing."[31] In *The Interpretation of Dreams*, Freud comments: "This must have been a frightful blow to my ambition, for references to this scene are still constantly recurring in my dreams and are always linked with an enumerations of my achievements and successes, as though I wanted to say: 'You see, I *have* come to something.'"[32] But if Freud's neurotic urge to urinate was tied to ambition, then certainly power and authority issues were part of the syndrome. Freud knew very well he was ambitious, but in the mores of the day it was considered unseemly to voice such feelings.

Of course, it is striking to hear Freud deflect the issue of neurosis with the idea of paralysis. As the co-author of *Studies in Hysteria* (1895) he described at length the idea of conversion symptoms, yet naively defended himself against Jung's diagnosis. One has to conclude that, as often happens, the focus of a person's psychological research tells us as much about the researcher as about the subject of study. Jung understood the nature of the symptom, but interestingly enough, expanded the cause from sexual repression to a repression of Eros as love. In fact, he reversed Freud's formula and claimed that by reducing all manifestations of Eros to sexual libido, Freud was indulging in a repression of the spiritual aspects of love.

At the time of the incident, however, Jung concentrated on Freud's ambition and power drive, for these were the matters that festered at the heart of their relationship. As they analyzed the incident, while discussing a dream, Freud hesitated in providing appropriate associations. (Years later, Jung implied that these associations had to do with Freud's alleged affair with his sister-in-law.) Sensing Freud's hesitancy, Jung asked Freud whether it was all right to continue in such a personal vein. One must keep in mind that Jung was 35 at the time and Freud almost 20 years his senior. After a long pause, in a barely audible voice,

Freud replied, "my dear boy, I cannot risk my authority."[33] Today, his remark might seem odd, but in the context of early-twentieth-century European formality, to which both men subscribed, it is perfectly legitimate. Nevertheless, Jung concluded that, as far as he was concerned, with that remark Freud had indeed lost his authority. It is a harsh conclusion and probably speaks to Jung's need to withdraw his father projection from Freud and find a suitable reason for the withdrawal.

Also, if Freud's urination symptom was connected to his ambition and power, then Jung, of course, was a threat. Freud was keenly aware of his position of authority and knew that he and Jung were enmeshed in a father and son dynamic. From the beginning of their association, Jung acknowledged that aspect of their relationship and felt a great deal of satisfaction and pride in being anointed by Freud as his heir. The tension of the dynamic surfaced when, prior to their boarding the ship in Bremen, Freud interpreted Jung's interest in the mummified corpses in the Bremen Cathedral as a death wish against him: "What is it with you and these corpses? Wouldn't it better if you admitted that you wish I would drop dead?" And then Freud promptly fainted.[34] This was the first of two incidents when Freud fainted in Jung's presence and each time, according to Jung, Freud blamed the younger man's "resistance against the father" and a "death wish" against him.[35]

Although Freud genuinely liked Jung and admired his fearless spirit and intellectual acumen, in the grip of the archetypal dynamics between them as father and son, he was also ambivalent about his heir apparent. I think the reemergence of his urination neurosis, while in on unfamiliar grounds in New York and in the presence of the energetic Jung, who responded enthusiastically to the American experience, was prompted by Freud's feelings of inferiority and inadequacy. Hence, he regressed to an unconscious mode of expressing his power drive. In this context, the issue of authority was already in the air. However, I think Jung's assertion that for him, Freud lost his authority when he refused to provide personal associations to a dream, was somewhat disingenuous. Had Jung been more conscious of his own ambitions, perhaps Freud would not have fallen victim to the regressive neurotic symptom. But then, of course, the two men would have parted, which in 1909 neither was yet ready to do.

When reflecting on the incident many years later, Jung expanded his original analysis of Freud's neurosis from a repression of the spiritual aspects of sexuality to a "systematic devaluation of the unconscious."[36] The statement reveals Jung's view of the unconscious as a source of creative and spiritual impulses and not only of unbridled libidinal drives and repressed contents. In Jung's opinion, because Freud had a one-sided and dismissive attitude toward the unconscious, it stopped cooperating with him and began to work against him, humiliating him in an analogous manner.

Elaborating on Jung's somewhat general statement, I would add that in dreams, urination is a symbol not only of self-assertion, or ambition in Freud's terms, but also of self-expression, of being true to one's nature. The analogy the symptom and symbol of urination seek to draw is that striving for self-expression—or in Jungian terms, the drive for individuation—is as uncontrollable and as insistent as the need to urinate. Other basic drives, such as hunger, sleep and even defecation can be postponed and are somewhat amenable to conscious control; urination is a much more pressing urge and less yielding to control.

According to Jung, Freud's neurotic inability to control his urination was a symptom of a wrong attitude toward the unconscious. Consequently, the unconscious responded in a compensatory manner, saying in effect: "Now, Dr Freud, here is something that with all your discipline, insight and self-mastery, even you cannot control." But had the symptom been correctly understood at the time, it indicated that in his power oriented attitude, Freud was being disloyal to his true nature, a nature that evidently called for a more Eros related attitude and way of life. For, as Jung argues, the opposite of Power is Eros and because Freud's ego identified with the will to Power, his Eros was repressed. Perhaps his one-sided theoretical emphasis on sexuality and even his affair with Minna, his sister-in-law, if true, were attempts to bring Eros into his life. But evidently these attempts missed their aim, for they did not satisfy his innate urge for wholeness. In that sense, Jung may have made the correct diagnosis: Freud's systematic devaluation of the creative and spiritual aspects of the unconscious, his reduction of Eros to the sexual instincts and consequent fall into the arms of the power anima, was the cause of his embarrassing and humiliating neurotic symptom. Nevertheless, it is also impossible to dismiss the power struggle between the two men and the role it played in Freud's neurotic reactions while in Jung's presence.

Physis

Power, as we have seen, was certainly an important part of Freud's personality, but his overriding archetypal motivation was Physis. The primacy of that motivation accounts for Freud's fascination with the natural, material, concrete and physical manifestations of reality. As a university student, his first love was laboratory research in physiology and he initially intended to pursue a strictly academic career as a research scientist. His appreciation of sensate detail is evident in the precise sketches he executed during the course of his seven years as a laboratory assistant in marine biology. (See Figure 6.1.) Because Physis was his dominant conscious motivation, his dreams did not emphasize sense data (for the unconscious is compensatory to consciousness): "my dreams," he observed, "are in general less rich in sensory elements than I am led to suppose in the case of other people."[37] They did, however, contain a good number of Power oriented and erotic allusions.

Freud's love of material objects was also evident in his extensive collection of books and antiquities. But aside from its Physis aspects, collecting is also a form of possessiveness that satisfies a certain Power need—a

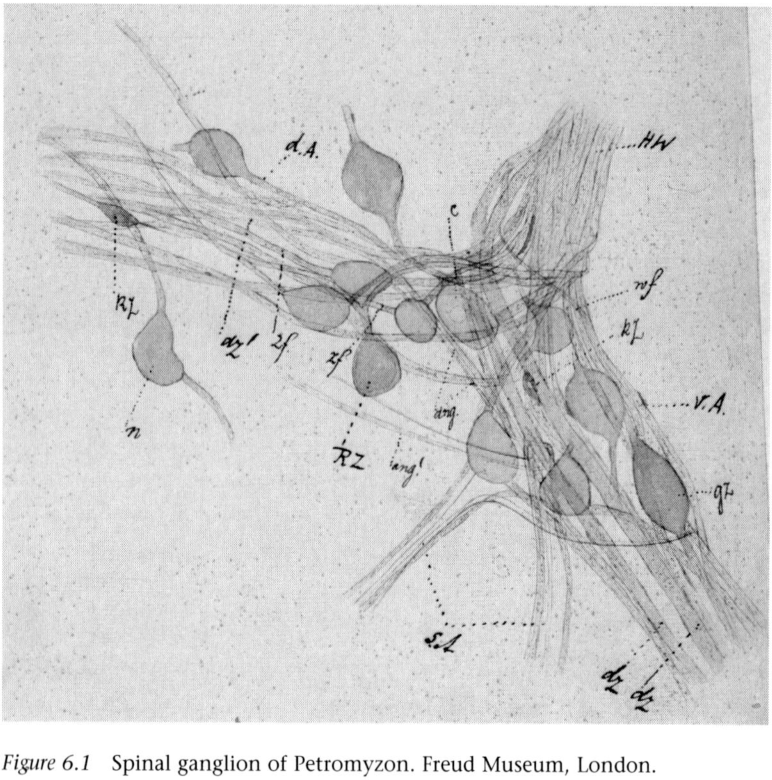

Figure 6.1 Spinal ganglion of Petromyzon. Freud Museum, London.

symbolic or miniature form of empire building. The antiquities especially provided Freud with a sensuous connection to civilizations thousands of years in the past: for him, merely reading about them was too abstract. "His antique objects," Peter Gay writes, "gave him sheer visual and tactile pleasure; Freud caressed them with his eyes or fondled them as he sat at his desk."[38] The pleasure apparently was both sensual and aesthetic.

Then there was the matter of his eyes. Peter Gay writes that "all of Freud's acquaintances, however widely they might differ in the rest of their description, would comment on Freud's keen, probing eyes."[39] For example, one of his close friends described Freud's eyes as "brown and lustrous" with a "scrutinizing expression."[40] In my experience, many introverted Physis types tend to have such lustrous probing eyes; they take in every detail of the external world and connect to it primarily with their eyes. In *Totem and Taboo*, Freud acknowledges that looking is actually a form of touching; and touching, in his view, "is the first step towards obtaining any sort of control over, of attempting to make use of, a person or object."[41]

The Physis type is at home in the world and is therefore, an epicurean at heart. Freud approved of Horace's maxim *carpe diem* and thought that "each of us has had hours and times in which he has admitted the rightness of this philosophy of life."[42] He was a sensuous man, a characteristic seen in his love of food and addiction to smoking. These qualities were probably also linked to his Eros motivation. On the other hand, his fastidious attention to toilette and dress and his love of regularity and order probably satisfied both his need for control and for concreteness. I will refer, only in passing, to the anal roots of these characteristics: in Freud's typology, the anal personality is described as orderly, miserly and stubborn.

In spite of his intellectual and cultural pursuits, in his everyday life Freud had, as Peter Gay writes, "a practical cast of mind" and his "tastes ran to the conventional. The things he chose to live with were uncompromising in their conservatism"; he was a stolid bourgeois and, by his own admission, somewhat of a philistine.[43] Surprisingly, for a man so original and creative in his own right, he was dismissive of the fascinating early-twentieth-century innovations in literature, theater, painting and music—innovations often inspired by his theories! As creative as he himself was, the artist's sensibility seemed beyond his ken: "Meaning is but little with these men," he wrote to Ernest Jones, "all they care about is line, shape, agreement of contours. They are given up to the *Lustprinzip*," that is, ruled by the "pleasure principle".[44] There is an element of projection in Freud's critical remark, for as sensuous and pleasure-seeking as he was in his personal life, he considered being governed by the pleasure principle as regressive or infantile. Actually, by subordinating pleasure to reality in his developmental theory he was paying homage to Physis, his dominant ruling principle.

In keeping with his Physis orientation, Freud had no interest in metaphysical speculations about the nature of the universe or the meaning of life. In later years, reflecting on his work, he wrote that since he lacked a "talent for philosophy by nature," he made a virtue of necessity" and trained himself to be objective: to "'convert the facts that revealed themselves to me' in as 'undisguised, unprejudiced, and unprepared' form as possible."[45] From my perspective, however, his lack of talent for philosophy and corresponding interest in objective reality was a consequence of his Physis temperament and not just a matter of training.

While Freud himself was not philosophically inclined, his approach to reality reflected nineteenth-century positivism, which sought to apply scientific principles and methods to the study of human thought and behavior. Although he created a revolution in the psychiatric canon of his day by placing the primacy of mental illness in the mind rather than in the body, in the final analysis Freud believed that all neuroses and all psychic life must have a somatic side. In *The Interpretation of Dreams* he argues that there is a "causal connection between the somatic and the mental. Even when investigation shows that the primary exciting cause of a phenomenon is psychical, deeper research will one day trace the path further and discover an organic basis for the mental event."[46] His concept of libido, for example, is based on a "special chemistry of the sexual function," which is not limited to the sexual organs; the "sexual excitation" caused by this special chemistry is present in all bodily organs.[47]

The consequence of the primacy of organic chemistry in psychic life means that, for Freud, causal determinism was the only reasonable explanatory principle for neuroses, character and behavior. Chance may certainly play a role and even choice is possible, but neither is spontaneous, arbitrary or random. Freud's basic theoretical and hermeneutic premise is that there are no accidents in the conscious and unconscious operations of the psyche. Physiological and psychological determinism characterize the life of human beings and philosophical or religious advocacy of free will is based on illusion.[48]

Telling evidence of Freud's Physis orientation was his adulation of Wilhelm Fliess, his onetime alter ego and mentor. When Fliess and Freud met in the fall of 1887, Freud was retreating from his enthusiastic advocacy of the curative effects of cocaine. Fliess advocated two ideas that later became integral parts of Freud's theories: the role of bisexuality and of infantile sexuality in neuroses. Fliess published his speculations about infantile sexuality in the mid-1890s, ten years before Freud elaborated the thesis in *Three Essays on the Theory of Sexuality*.

Not surprisingly, for an ear, nose and throat specialist, Fliess came to regard the nose as the central organ of the body and argued that it influenced and reflected the general course of health and illness. He hypothesized a relationship between the mucous membrane of the nose and the genital organs: the membranes swelled with genital excitation and during menstruation. No doubt, for Freud, the symbolic analogy between the nose and the penis and the common phenomena of periodic nose bleeds made the connection feasible. Fliess claimed to have discovered a general biorhythmic cycle of 28 days for women and 23 days for men. Consequently, he used the sex and date of birth of a child to account for stages of development, periodic illnesses and even the date of death.

Fliess termed the psychological disturbances attributed to the nose "nasal reflex neuroses." The wide-ranging symptoms consisted of headache, opportunistic neurological pains and problems with circulation, respiration and digestion. These symptoms could be relieved by the application of cocaine to the nose or by surgery on the nose. Freud's famous Irma dream in *The Interpretation of Dreams* actually concerns a woman he referred to Fliess, who subjected her to one of his nasal surgeries for the relief of neurotic symptoms and carelessly left a half meter of gauze packing in her nasal cavity. In any case, Freud's initial fascination with Fliess was in a large measure influenced by the fact that Fliess advocated a theory of neurosis based on physiology.

Freud's archetypal shadow

At this point, having completed a description of Freud in terms of archetypal-motivational typology, we may conjecture about the shadow aspects of his personality. As an "introverted spirited Power Physis" type, his unconscious and less developed side consisted of "extraverted soulful Eros and Pneuma". These unconscious and undeveloped archetypal contents are usually seen as inimical to one's conscious orientation and are therefore devalued. Thus, receptivity and emptiness, the archetypal qualities of Soul, for instance, were regarded by Freud as passivity and the absence of something, for example, the lack of a penis producing penis envy in women. Consciously identified with spirit, he projected soul onto women and concretized its attributes in devalued terms onto feminine physiology. The archetype of Eros with its drive for connection or union was also projected onto women and characterized in a negative form as possessiveness. With men, Eros again referred to the feminine side of men, evident in latent homosexuality, repressed homoerotic tendencies and incomplete sexual maturation. Through a series of elaborate theoretical arguments involving, among other things, a regression to primary narcissism and restructuring of the world in a negative light, Freud argued that these homoerotic impulses turned into feelings of paranoia.[49]

With that conclusion Freud knew that he was hitting close to home because he tended to idealize his male friends and when the relationships soured, to hate them, turn them into enemies and label them paranoid. Because of the dynamic interplay between his repressed Eros and his active Power drive and the need for a balance between them, we can now understand why, as he himself admits, "an intimate friend and a hated enemy have always been necessary requirements of my emotional life . . . I always knew how to provide myself with both over and over."[50] It is possible to chart the pattern Freud describes in his associations with colleagues, beginning with Bleuler and Fliess and later with Adler and Jung. Since these men reciprocated Freud's affection, once Freud withdrew his idealization, he decided that both Fliess and Adler were paranoid. "My erstwhile friend Fliess," Freud wrote, "developed a beautiful paranoia after he had disposed of his inclination, certainly not slight, toward me."[51] He added, "Adler is a little Fliess redivivus, just as paranoid."[52] As for himself, having completed his essay on Leonardo, which had "obsessed" him, he felt that he had overcome his own unconscious homoerotic feelings: "A piece of homosexual charge has been withdrawn and utilized for the enlargement of my own ego. I have succeeded where the paranoiac fails."[53] With Jung, the issue of paranoia did not arise because Jung openly stated that he thought of Freud as a father and himself as his son. Freud gladly accepted that deferential familial designation. When difficulties arose between them, he interpreted the problem in Oedipal terms, accusing the son of desiring to murder the father.

In my opinion, the connection between homosexuality and paranoia is tenuous at best, but Freud's labeling his former friends as paranoid certainly carries an element of projection on his part. Freud inaugurated and modeled the unfortunate practice on the part of many psychoanalysts to append ostensibly objective psychopathic diagnostic labels onto their critics and opponents.

In the previous chapter I mentioned Freud's negative attitude toward Pneuma, his inferior and most unconscious archetypal motivation.

During their first meeting, Jung observed that Freud sought to reduce all expressions of Spirit, whether cultural or religious, to one of the permutations of sexual repression or displacement: wish-fulfillment, delusion, projection, sublimation. His reductive tendency in this area was the consequence of his dominant Physis orientation, for anyone with that orientation will seek to ground all fantasies and concepts in empirical data, in Freud's case, the sexual drive.

The situation becomes more complicated. Freud's secondary consciously deployed motivation was Power, which meant that Eros, as the tertiary motivation was partly unconscious. The result was that his two shadow motivations, Eros and Pneuma merged in Freud's unconscious. His spiritual tendencies attached themselves to the unconscious aspects of Eros and imbued them with religious significance. This merger accounts for Jung's thesis that Freud's fascination with sexuality was a displaced form of spirituality.

In a more attenuated manner, Freud's inferior Pneuma was also evident in his superstitions, which focused on number symbolism. In the Jewish tradition, the 52nd year is considered critical in the life of a man and for years Freud thought he would die at 51; when that year passed, he expected to die at 61 or 62. He would study the telephone numbers and the hotel room numbers he was assigned to confirm his expectation. Psychoanalytically, he regarded superstitions as expressions of concealed murderous impulses and concluded that his own superstitions in this regard harbored an unconscious desire for immortality. But even that self-analysis did not free him from the obsession, which, as he informed Jung, was an expression of "the specifically Jewish nature of my mysticism."[54]

Freud's Jewish heritage came up in another context. Many readers are familiar with his subversion of overt Jewish beliefs and traditions in *Moses and Monotheism*. Freud depicted Moses, the founding prophet of Judaism, as an Egyptian prince who imposed a monotheistic religion on the enslaved Hebrews after the demise of the monotheistic heresy of the pharaoh Akhenaton. Replaying the scenario of patricide in *Totem and Taboo*, the band of Hebrews murdered this Egyptian Moses, repressed his teachings and took up the worship of Yahve, who Freud argues was a primitive volcanic god of the Arabic tribe of Midianites. Sixty years later, the "repressed returned" through the initiative of another leader of the Hebrew tribes, who borrowed the name of the first Moses, and succeeded in effecting a theological compromise between the archaic tribal Yahve and the spiritually superior god of Akhenaton.

Freud knew he was on shaky ground in his speculations and considered adding a subtitle to the book, *A Historical Novel*. In my view, he resisted the urge to do so because, in keeping with his Physis orientation, he sought to divest the story of Moses and the exodus of its spiritual underpinning and turn these events, in spite of the lack of any historical evidence, into concrete fact. If he could not achieve that then he preferred to see the events as fiction. In either case, he refused to give any credence to the possibility that spiritual forces were responsible for these events.

It is astounding that Freud insisted on having the book published in 1938, after fleeing Austria and arriving safely in London. He was unmoved by entreaties and protests of his Jewish friends and colleagues and by his personal experience of the brutal anti-Semitism raging in Vienna after the *Anschluss*. His daughter Anna was questioned by the Gestapo and he spend a harrowing day waiting for her return. He also told the novelist Arnold Zweig about a letter he received from a Jewish American writer imploring him not to deprive his fellow Jews of the sole consolation of their faith in the midst of their misery.[55] Freud admitted he did not enjoy offending his compatriots, but remained adamant: "What can I do about it? I have occupied my whole long life with standing up for what I considered to be the scientific truth, even when it was uncomfortable and disagreeable to my fellow men. I cannot close it with an act of disavowal."[56] The fact is that no one asked him to disavow anything, but merely to postpone publishing an anti-religious and anti-Judaic tract in the midst of the horrendous, officially sanctioned anti-Semitism raging in the heart of Europe. Moreover, two chapters of the three chapter book, outlining his basic thesis, had already appeared in the journal *Imago*. Also, while he was in Vienna, he did withhold publication of the third chapter so as not to offend the hierarchy of the Catholic Church in Austria, which he hoped would protect the country from the Nazi menace. Furthermore, *Moses and Monotheism* was not one of his "scientific" works, but a speculative account of history and mythology. Evidently, in this instance, Freud was as empathically obtuse and politically naïve as Jung was when the latter insisted on speaking about "the differences between Germanic and the Jewish psychology" in 1933.[57]

Freud's callousness in this context can only be explained by his inferior Eros and by his dominant Physis orientation which adhered to facts as he understood them. His dedication to Physis and resulting antipathy toward anything relating to Pneuma easily overrode his Eros, even under the dangerous circumstances of 1938. Clearly, his power drive also played a role in the decision to oppose advice that conflicted with his personal goals: for, unfortunately, to reprise Jung's observation, "where the will to power is paramount, love is lacking."[58]

That absence of love toward his fellow Jews must have extended to himself as a Jew. The rationale he gave for undertaking the study of Moses was twofold: an attempt to understand "the origin of the special character of the Jewish people, a character which is probably what has made their survival to the present day possible"; and, at the same time, to grasp the reasons for centuries of entrenched anti-Semitism.[59] He concluded that Moses was responsible for both by giving the Hebrews "a religion which heightened their self-confidence to such a degree that they believed themselves to be superior to all other peoples."[60] Freud regarded this sense of superiority as responsible for the survival of the Jews as well as for the antipathy such an attitude evoked in others. He alluded to other reasons for anti-Semitism: the Christian notion that Jews killed their God; animosity against minorities by the majority to consolidate its feelings of solidarity; the weakness of a minority inviting oppression; intolerance for anyone who is different from the majority; and, interestingly enough, displaced hatred of Christianity. Freud argued that the religious and cultural anti-Semitism of Europeans is fueled by unconscious resentment of being forced to give up their emotionally and ethically less demanding pagan ways and then projecting that resentment onto the ethnic group that gave birth to Christianity. Nevertheless, he concluded that the Mosaic vision of Jews as the "chosen people" accounted for both their survival and for the anti-Semitism that has plagued them throughout the ages in various cultures.

Given the events of his day, it is understandable why Freud sought to examine the roots and causes of anti-Semitism. He began the study in 1934, after the Nazis gained power in Germany and, as he told Arnold Zweig, "'in view of the new persecutions,' he had asked himself just 'how the Jew came to be and why he had drawn this immortal hatred on himself.'"[61] But aside from the notion of displaced hatred of Christianity, none of the other reasons for anti-Semitism he cites are particularly new or insightful. From that perspective, the book hardly warranted publication. On the other hand, the fact that Freud initiated an examination of the "peculiar character of the Jewish people" at a time when the difference between Jews and non-Jews was used as a justification for official discrimination and mass terror requires a psychoanalytic explanation.

Under the circumstances it is difficult to avoid asking the question whether Freud was not identifying with the oppressor and blaming the victim, but, most of all, whether an element of self-loathing did not enter into his attack on the very foundation of Jewish identity with his portrayal of Moses as an Egyptian? There was little historical basis for that portrayal. The notion was essentially a product of his fantasy, and an obsessive one at that, for, as he complained to Arnold Zweig, "'Moses will not let my imagination go'....the project 'has become a fixation for me.'"[62] Why, then, would his unconscious move in a direction that he consciously recognized as an attack on the source of his people's self-confidence? Freud acknowledged that the Jews' belief in themselves as God's chosen people was responsible for their survival throughout history and, therefore, for his own survival. The lack of Eros and plain common sense in his decision to publish the book is startling. Perhaps his psychological state of mind was influenced by his deteriorating health and the emergence of the death drive.

The most generous interpretation of his undertaking the study at the time, and his insistence on publishing the book in 1938, is to consider *Moses and Monotheism* as an attempt on Freud's part to provide a psychoanalytic cure for anti-Semitism and to end the suffering caused by it. His implicit agenda was to eradicate anti-Semitism by subjecting the myth of the chosen people to an historical analysis. The process is analogous to the psychoanalysis of a neurotic symptom whose origins derive from the Oedipal period. The idea was to liberate Jews from the cause of their neurotic belief and behavior, and the source of their suffering, by demonstrating that that concept of the chosen people was not inherent to the original Hebrew tribes, but was foisted upon them and made part of their collective superego by a powerful foreign father figure. Freud expected that by demonstrating the historical, as opposed to the supernatural, origin of the idea of the chosen people, contemporary Jews will divest themselves of that false belief—a belief that has separated them from others, provided a major motivation for anti-Semitism and caused untold suffering through the ages. Their view of themselves as the chosen people may have been responsible for their survival in the past, but in the modern era, that perspective is no longer useful and, in fact, counterproductive. In this respect Freud, giving free reign to his archetypal power fantasies, sees himself as the new Moses, perhaps even as the long-awaited Messiah, who will finally liberate the Jews from their Egyptian bondage! This is not a far-fetched thought, for as a secular Enlightenment thinker, with Pneuma as his archetypal shadow, Freud had no difficulty envisioning a brotherhood of man based on the universality of reason and the demise of all religious and other superstitions responsible for racial prejudices and ethnic rivalries.

Freud's anti-spirit vision is evident in the other book of his old age, *Future of an Illusion* (1927), in which he made a concerted attack on religion and affirmed his Enlightenment faith in reason and science. He offered the discoveries of psychoanalysis as a contribution to the Enlightenment critique of religion. From the psychoanalytic perspective, he averred, religion is a collective neurosis built on childish illusions. Religious ideas are not the result of thinking: "they are illusions, fulfillments of the oldest, strongest and most urgent wishes of mankind": the desire for paternal love and protection and the satisfaction of narcissistic needs.[63] Freud acknowledged that these childhood wishes have a valid basis in the helplessness and dependence of the child on parents, who are both feared and trusted. The child's experience is replicated in the experience of human beings when confronted with the irrational and immense powers of nature: hence the allure of religion and its pervasiveness in human history. The tremendous power of the illusion lies in the strength of the childhood desires and wishes for love, protection and search for gratification. Freud concluded that, as with the illusions of neurotics, human beings would be better served by their disillusionment in this regard and by their acceptance of adult responsibility for the realities of existence.

Freud did not live to see the full extent of Nazi barbarism. That horror would have certainly destroyed any of his own remaining Enlightenment illusions, which were already undermined by World War I. Generally, biographers view his rationalistic and anti-religious stance as following in the tradition of earlier Enlightenment thinkers and not as expressions of his personal temperamental bias. I think it is the other way around. Freud's dominant archetypal motivation of Physis was responsible for his attraction to the rational scientific worldview of the Enlightenment and for the formation of his materialistically oriented theories. His attitude toward religion and his attempt to reduce religious phenomena to the realm of material reality is a temperamental bias and not the result of the secular, materialistic standpoint of his age, or the logical consequence of his theories.

7
Alfred Adler: Extraverted Soulful Physis Eros Type

Alfred Adler
7 February 1870–28 May 1937

Photo courtesy of Margot Adler.

Adler and Freud

Before I proceed with a description of Adler's typology I think it is important to outline the circumstances that led Adler to separate from Freud and to note the role that their temperaments played in the dispute. Freud was an introverted spirited type with Physis as his primary motivation and Power as his secondary drive. If one compares the archetypal motivations of Freud and Adler, Physis is the only feature they had in common, even though for Adler, Physis was his secondary motivation, while for Freud it was dominant. I wonder, therefore, whether Freud's temperamental tendency to connect psychological phenomena to the physiological development of children did not inspire Adler to undertake the seminal work, *A Study of Organ Inferiority*, that marked the beginning of his career as a depth psychologist and his brief collaboration with Freud. The monograph of 92 pages was published in 1907, but Adler summarized its contents in a talk, "On the Organic Bases of Neuroses," during a November 1905 meeting of the Wednesday Psychological Society, the precursor of the Vienna Psychoanalytic Society. He argued that the majority of neuroses derive from a congenital weakness in one or several bodily organs. Certainly, with Freud in mind, he added that these physiological inferiorities invariably entail a sexual inferiority, particularly if the deficient organ is an erogenous zone or located near one. But, the chief psychological component of his thesis was that people struggle to overcome their particular organ inferiorities and concomitant feelings of weakness and inadequacy (*Minderwertigkeitsgefühl*, lit., "feeling of lesser value") with compensatory activities in their personal and social life; in fact, the tendency is not merely to compensate, but to over-compensate.

The meeting at which Adler presented his study was a gathering of Viennese physicians sympathetic to Freud's ideas. Indeed, Adler was one of the four physicians Freud initially invited to assemble at his home every Wednesday evening, beginning in the fall of 1902, for informal discussions. In 1908, as the group grew in size, it was reorganized and renamed the Vienna Psychoanalytic Society. At Freud's suggestion, Adler served as the society's chairperson and was appointed co-editor of the newly inaugurated monthly journal, *Zentralblatt für Psychoanalyse*.

During this period, Adler attempted to integrate Freud's ideas with his own creative elaboration of psychoanalytic theory. For example, in a 1904 article, "The Physician as Educator," he credited Freud with highlighting the importance of "infantile impressions, experiences, and developments in normal and neurotic individuals."[1] It was also in this essay that he first used the term "organ inferiority." The concept was based on the medical observation that in each individual there are certain organs that tend to be more susceptible to disease and appear to offer less resistance to general infection; the weakness of the specific organs are visible at birth or disclosed over time. Adler's originality consisted of developing a psychological theory based on that clinical notion.

As partial evidence for his theory of organ inferiority and its compensation, he cited a study that disclosed that 70 percent of German art students had visual anomalies. He also referred to well-known anecdotal instances of over-compensation: the great Athenian orator, Demosthenes, who overcame a congenital speech defect; Beethoven, who became deaf; and Mozart, who is said to have had deformed ears. Napoleon's diminutive size and overarching ambition is another example of compensation.

Freud was appreciative of Adler's contribution; it seemed to provide a theoretical underpinning for his assumption that neuroses developed on the basis of a congenital predisposition. Freud was especially drawn to the idea of compensation and volunteered additional anecdotal evidence, citing a contemporary German painter who was blind in one eye. He also thought that great chefs tend to be emotionally unstable. His own cook, he noted, invariably cooked better just before the onset of an illness. It is not clear what organ inferiority was involved in the case of the emotional instability of chefs, but one hears an echo of Fliess and his biorhythms in Freud's observation.

Freud's and Adler's meeting of minds on the basis of their similarity of a Physis orientation towards reality was short-lived. In 1908, just as he was promoted by Freud to leading positions in the Psychoanalytic Society, Adler published an essay that questioned the thesis of sexual libido as the sole determinant of psychic life and neuroses. In a bold challenge to Freud's theory, he proposed that there was not one but two dominant drives, sexuality and aggression, and, what is more, he argued that frustrated aggression rather than suppressed sexuality was the primary cause of anxiety. Freud could not let that pass; in an essay appearing the following year he responded:

> Alfred Adler, in a suggestive paper, has recently developed the view that anxiety arises from the suppression of what he calls the "aggressive instinct," and by a very sweeping synthetic process he ascribes to that instinct the chief part in human events, "in real life and in the neuroses" . . . I am unable to assent to this view, and indeed I regard it as a misleading generalization. I cannot bring myself to assume the existence of a special aggressive instinct alongside the familiar instincts of self-preservation and of sex, and on an equal footing with them.[2]

It took the carnage of World War I for Freud to acknowledge the aggressive instinct. In his book, *Beyond the Pleasure Principle* (1920), Freud unsettled his psychoanalytic colleagues by changing his mind and proposing a dual classification of instincts somewhat similar to Adler's original formulation

Unlike so many of the early adherents of Freud, Adler evidently did not look upon him as an authority figure and fearlessly pursued his own creative ideas. In a 1910 essay on "Psychic Hermaphroditism in Life and in the Neuroses," he elaborated upon Fliess' idea of the bisexuality of human beings and claimed that, together with organ inferiorities, there are feminine (i.e., submissive) characteristics present in a male neurotic and masculine (i.e., aggressive) ones in a female neurotic. He also extended the feelings of inferiority, previously caused by various organ inferiorities, to the weakness and dependence every child experiences in the face of the superiority of adults:

> The starting point for the feminine tendencies of the [male] neurotic is the child's feeling of weakness in the face of adults. From this arises a need for support, a demand for affection, a physiological and psychological dependency and submission. In cases of early and subjectively felt organ inferiority, these traits are intensified. Increased dependency and the intensified feeling of our own littleness and weakness lead to inhibition of aggression and thereby to the phenomenon of anxiety. Uncertainty regarding our own ability arouses doubt and inaugurates vacillation between the feminine tendencies of anxiety and related phenomena and the masculine tendencies of aggression and compulsion phenomena.[3]

Instead of the "aggressive instinct," Adler now called the dynamic force behind neuroses "masculine protest"—an unfortunate and confusing term. The idea it sought to convey was that both men and women strive to overcome their feelings of weakness—which in keeping with the cultural prejudice of his day was equated with femininity—with a compensatory aggressive, or masculine response.

By 1910 Adler had articulated a psychoanalytic theory that diverged radically from Freud's cardinal premises. Both the 1908 and 1910 essays appeared in a foremost German-language medical journal and Freud felt that Adler was undermining the theoretical foundations of psychoanalysis. In addition, given Adler's growing prestige and social skills, he posed a threat to Freud's control of the Vienna Psychoanalytic Society. In what can only be called a projection stemming from Freud's thwarted Power drive, he labeled Adler "paranoid." Deeply disturbed, Freud complained to Jung that "it is getting really bad with Adler:"

> The crux of the matter—and that is what really alarms me—is that he minimizes the sexual drive and our opponents will soon be able to speak of an experienced psychoanalyst whose conclusions are radically different from ours. Naturally in my attitude towards him I am torn between my conviction that all this is lopsided and harmful and my fear of being regarded as an intolerant old man who holds the young men down.[4]

In contrast, Adler, with his extraverted Eros and its principle of inclusiveness, saw no difficulty with having come to different conclusions than Freud. Either naively or disingenuously, he assumed that the Psychoanalytic Society was engaged in scientific research and that, along the way, various perspectives would emerge and help advance the newly emerging field of psychoanalysis. For instance, in the Preface to the society's *Symposium on Suicide*, he wrote:

> For about seven years, a circle of medical men and psychologists interested in the study of psychoanalysis have been meeting every week to discuss their experiences. This circle, which arose out of the work of Freud and Breuer, is primarily responsible for the development of psychoanalytic methods and [ideas].[5]

Evidently Adler failed to recognize that Freud, with Power as his dominant style of functioning, was not about to let "a hundred flowers bloom" for, as opposed to the inclusiveness of Eros, Power aims at dominance and control. Besides, Freud had spent too many years carefully formulating his hypotheses and was not about to abandon them in the face of two essays by a member of the society over which he presided. In this respect, Adler, whose theory rests on the premise of a universal striving for superiority, seemed oblivious to the possibility that in developing a theory opposed to Freud's he may have been motivated by his own struggle for superiority. In contrast, Freud was aware of the threat to his dominant position, both as the chief theorist of psychoanalysis and as the *eminance gris* of the Psychoanalytic Society. In keeping with his introverted Power orientation, Freud sidestepped a direct confrontation and worked behind the scenes to reassert his control. The situation was delicate because Adler was chairperson of the Psychoanalytic Society and had recruited into its fold a significant number of his friends and colleagues.

In January 1911 Freud had one of his associates call for a series of meetings of the Psychoanalytic Society to discuss Adler's views. Invited to explain his ideas, at what must have felt like an inquisition, Adler continued to argue that the drive for assertion and superiority was the guiding principle of psychic life and feelings of inferiority were at the bottom of all neuroses. Freud responded that by denying sexuality as the primary psychological drive, Adler's "entire doctrine has a reactionary and retrogressive character."[6] Other Freud loyalists pursued the attack in the same vein. Freud made it clear that the two views were incompatible and could not be reconciled, as some of Adler's adherents proposed. Consequently, Adler resigned as chair of the society and Freud was elected in his stead.

Next, Freud engineered Adler's resignation from the editorship of the *Zentralblatt*. "I must avenge the offended goddess Libido," he wrote to Jung and make certain that "heresy does not occupy too much space in the *Zentralblatt*."[7] Continuing his invective, he wrote to Ernest Jones that Adler's dissension is "the revolt of an abnormal individual driven mad by ambition, his influence upon others depending on his strong terrorism and sadismus."[8] Anyone acquainted with Adler could hardly square that description with his personality and behavior; rather it reveals just how threatened Freud felt. It is also somewhat ironic that Freud's behavior and tone provide ample evidence for the existence of the very same aggressive instinct that he was arguing against.

In view of Freud's persistent antagonism, Adler, together with three other members, resigned from the Psychoanalytic Society and organized a Society for Free Psychoanalytic Study. Freud then insisted that the remaining members of Adler's circle choose between the two groups; five more members resigned to join Adler. In 1913, distinguishing itself further from Freud, Adler's group changed its name to the Society for Individual Psychology.

In later life, Adler sought to understand the differences between himself and Freud in typological terms. He described Freud's senex-like demeanor and authoritative character as typical of the first-born child, who as an adult "likes to take part in the exercise of authority and exaggerates the importance of rules and laws. Everything should be done by rule, and no rule should be changed; power should always be preserved in the hands of those entitled to it."[9] He thought his own rebellious and easy-going nature was typical of the second child.

In my opinion, even though birth order may have some influence on the development of personality, it will not override the essentially inborn motivational tendencies of a child. The first-born child with a temperamental inclination towards domination and control may use the external circumstance of birth order to further those Power considerations. The second-born child with a tendency for Eros will use that position to express his dominant disposition. Even Adler admits that the second child is highly motivated by power considerations and strives to catch up with or surpass the first born. This is an empirical matter given to statistical study; but I am inclined to think that the correlation between archetypal Power and the first born, and Eros and the second born, will not be statistically significant. From my perspective, birth order notwithstanding, the difference in personality and attitudes between Adler and Freud stems from their different archetypal style of relating to the world: Freud's style was defined by the dominating, controlling characteristics of Power, Adler's by the tolerant, egalitarian feeling of Eros.

Physis

I have outlined the dispute between Freud and Adler as a matter of historical interest and now turn to a description of Adler's archetypal typology. Since I have alluded to Physis as the one archetypal character feature Adler shared with Freud, I will continue to outline their similarities and differences concerning Physis and subsequently describe Adler's extraversion, soulfulness and Eros. Adler's Physis orientation is attested to by his materialistic and empirical outlook. Like Freud, he distrusted all ideas not amenable to conventional scientific verification. For example, he broke "with his German protégé Fritz Kunkel for espousing Jungian-like ideas about a "higher" unconscious.[10] Probably with tongue in cheek, Adler referred to belief in God as "a gift of faith."[11] But he was more tolerant of religion than Freud and valued its ideals of charity, compassion and altruism. He even co-authored a book with a Lutheran minister, Ernest Jahn, on *Religion and Individual Psychology* (1933). Adler later wrote, "I regard it as no mean commendation when Jahn emphasizes that Individual Psychology has rediscovered many a lost position of Christian guidance. I have always endeavored to show that Individual Psychology is the heir to all great movements whose aim is the welfare of mankind."[12] His interest in religion, however, remained focused on its social contributions; he had no interest in its metaphysical postulates or purely spiritual concerns.

Like Freud, Adler sought to ground his psychological theories in physiology. That tendency is evident in his theory of organ inferiority and in his initial description of the aggressive drive originating in the child's struggle to satisfy the demands of its various organs.[13] For Adler, even the abstract notion of "drive" refers to "a sum of elementary functions of the corresponding organ and its nerve tracts . . . . The goal of the drive is determined by the satisfaction of the organic needs [for example, eating to satisfy hunger] and by the gaining of pleasure from the environment."[14] Because, in the early period of his career, Adler sought to link all psychic manifestations to physiology, Freud could rightly argue that Adler's psychology is "in large part, biology."[15]

Adler's Physis orientation is also evident in the practical cast of his mind. "He was always more interested in the concrete fact than in any theory," Phyllis Bottome, his friend and biographer, observed.[16] Although he was a creative theoretician, he always sought to apply his theories in practice. For instance, several years before he met Freud, Adler published a monograph, *Health Book for the Tailor Trade* (1898), in which he described the typical diseases that afflict tailors and the working conditions that contributed to these illnesses. He then called for remedial governmental action with a series of progressive proposals, among them: mandatory retirement and unemployment insurance; maximum weekly working hours; prohibition of piece work.[17] He also "criticized contemporary academic medicine for ignoring the very existence of social diseases," advocated a "new social medicine," in which the physician acted as social reformer and proposed the establishment of an Academic Chair for Social Medicine dedicated to the study of public hygiene.[18]

Another example of Adler's application of theory to practice was his creation of child guidance clinics for the school district of Vienna. These clinics functioned from 1921 until 1934, when they were abolished by the Nazis. They provided psychological assessment and counseling for children with learning difficulties, emotional afflictions and behavioral problems. The clinics consisted of "treatment teams," chaired by Adler or one of his protégés, and involved psychologists, teachers and social workers. The teams met with the parents and the child and after due consideration proposed appropriate intervention or treatment.

Adler established these child counseling centers because he was convinced children's emotional and behavioral difficulties stemmed from disturbed attempts to overcome feelings of inferiority or from the frustration of their need for affection. In the same year that Adler wrote his essay on the aggressive drive, he also published, in an educational journal, a brief article on a child's innate need for affection:

> Children want to be fondled, loved, and praised. They have a tendency to cuddle up, always to remain close to loved persons, and

> to want to be to be taken into bed with them. Later this desire aims at loving relationships from which originate love of relatives, friendships, social feelings [*Gemeinschaftsgefühl*], and love.[19]

He was addressing educators in this regard, because he felt that effective education depended on the enlightened management of this tremendously valuable drive:

> A large part of the child's development depends on the proper guidance of this drive complex . . . Before attaining satisfaction, the impulse should be forced to detour in order to furnish the drive for the cultural behavior of the child. Thus the way and goal of the need for affection are raised to a higher cultural level . . . . If the child . . . attains only satisfactions of a primitive kind without delay, his wishes will remain directed toward immediate, sensual pleasure.[20]

Furthermore, he went on to argue, if the need for affection is not sublimated to a social level and, at the same time, immediate sensual gratification is denied, the energy and frustration of the drive is funneled into anger and hostility against the immediate environment. If the aggressive drive is turned inward, it leads to various forms of self-abuse (for example, self-mutilation or addiction), or even to suicide. Adler thought that "every unsatisfied drive ultimately orients the organism toward aggression against the environment. The rough characters and the unbridled, incorrigible children can instruct us in the way the continuously unsatisfied drive for affection stimulates the paths of aggression."[21] Adler was probably the first to provide a depth psychological understanding of childhood feelings of alienation, juvenile delinquency and teenage suicide. Eventually, Adler abandoned the notion of an independent, innate aggressive drive and subsumed it under the broader category of *striving for superiority*. Aggression then becomes a symptom of a failure to develop social feelings or of an unsatisfied longing for loving relationships. Phyllis Bottome writes that Adler used to say to his friends with a grim smile: "I enriched psychoanalysis by the aggressive drive. I gladly make them a present of it."[22] On the other hand, she notes, he was proud to call himself "the legitimate father of the Inferiority Complex."[23]

With his interest in applying theory to practice, Adler sought to train teachers, clinicians and parents to understand a child's emotional needs. In 1924 he was appointed professor at the Pedagogical Institute in Vienna and gave courses on such topics as "The Difficult Child" and "Problem Children in School." In the first three years over 600 teachers took his courses. His pioneering work gained him an international reputation and scores of foreign professional educators came to Vienna to hear him lecture and to observe the operation of the child guidance clinics.

Adler's penchant for applying psychological knowledge to practical concerns of life, whether personal, educational or social, was a leitmotif in his life. Phyllis Bottome writes:

> He was always more interested in the concrete fact than in any theory. There was for this biologist intent on the laws of life itself, a dubious flavour of personality about a "theory" divorced from instant practice. Not "*what*" do people think but "*why*" do they think it; and if they think it—why do they not practice it—were the questions oftenest on the tip of Adler's tongue.[24]

Seeking to characterize Adler's unique contribution to psychology, Henri Ellenberger, in *The Discovery of the Unconscious*, writes:

> Adlerian psychology belongs neither to the traditional academic psychology not to experimental psychology, and it radically differs from Freudian psychoanalysis. It is unfair to Adler to evaluate his system with the yardstick of academic, experimental, or Freudian psychology. The term *Menschenkenntnis* [i.e., knowledge of man] designates the particular psychological trend to which Adler's Individual Psychology belongs. This kind of pragmatic psychology, sometimes called concrete psychology, does not pretend to go into matters very deeply, but to provide principles and methods that enable one to acquire a practical knowledge of oneself and others.[25]

Menschenkenntnis happens to be the German title of Adler's book, *Understanding Human Nature* (1927). The book is a popular exposition of his theory of personality development based on a series of lectures delivered in 1913; it sold over a 100,000 copies within six months of publication and would eventually sell over a million copies in the English-speaking world. In contrast, through the 1920s and early 1930s Freud's most popular book, *The Interpretation of Dreams*, sold approximately 16,000 copies in Great Britain and the United States. Clearly resentful of Adler's popularity in the United States, Freud explained the phenomenon, as previously noted, by the "general tendency in America to shorten study and preparation and to proceed as fast as possible to practical application."[26] To the extent that Freud's observation is valid,

Adler, with his tendency to apply theory to practice, found a ready response in the pragmatic outlook of Americans.

Eros

Physis and the resulting orientation toward concrete reality was Adler's auxiliary motivation. His chief archetypal motivation was Eros. Thus, while Freud, in the aftermath of World War I altered his theory to incorporate the aggressive instinct, Adler surprised his colleagues by proclaiming that "what the world chiefly wants today is *Gemeinschaftsgefühl*."[27]

Gemeinschaftsgefühl translates as "community feeling," but has come to be known as "social interest," which unfortunately does not convey the feeling tone or even the meaning of the German term. The idea was not new to Adler. He had referred to it in his 1908 essay, "The Child's Need of Affection"; it also was a basic tenet of the 12-point outline of individual psychology drawn up by Adler and his colleagues in 1913: for example, the neurotic individual is self-centered, lusts for power and leaves no room for community feeling to develop.[28] What changed was the weight Adler now imputed to the idea and the urgency he felt in the need to convey it to others.

Having abandoned the notion of an innate aggressive drive and espousing instead as a central principle the inherent capacity for community feeling, Adler was convinced that future wars could be avoided if children were raised in an atmosphere that fostered the development of such feelings. Cooperation and respect for one's neighbor, he argued, need to become as natural to human beings as breathing or walking upright.[29] He did not believe that reason, noble intentions, revulsion to violence, pacifism or ethical evolution would solve the problem of violence and war. Only concrete efforts to alter the manner in which children are reared and educated could effectively address the issue.

World War I, therefore, motivated Adler to take his psychology out of the consulting room and promote its use as a social and educational tool. There were consequences, however. With his emphasis on community feeling and social reform, he lost first the Nietzscheans, and later the professionally oriented psychologists of his group. As I reported in an earlier chapter, one of them later confessed:

> this sudden missionary idea of *Gemeinschaftsgefühl*—how could we deal with it? The medical profession must keep its science above the crowd! Adler should, as a scientist, have known this, and he should have

> known that if he insisted on spreading this sort of religious science through the laity we, as a profession could not support him.[30]

But Adler's emphasis on community feeling was not the result of a logical or political decision. The war had simply brought to the surface his own innate Eros, now combined with his extraverted attitude. His conclusion that all human beings have a desire for affection and relationship and that a mature individual embodies a well-developed community feeling is a direct reflection of his own Eros nature. His temperamental bias was also disclosed a 1904 article "The Physician as Educator," where he wrote: "the most important aid in education is love" and "the child's love . . . is the surest guaranty of educability."[31] His definition of love, incidentally, was empathy and desire for relationship and not, as with Freud, an urge for narcissistic pleasure and mirroring.

A recent study that compared the altruistic behavior of toddlers and chimpanzees seems to confirm Adler's idea that human beings have an inborn tendency to cooperate with and help others. The chimpanzees in the study worked together when they profited from the mutual effort. Eighteen-month-old toddlers, on the other hand, helped an adult trying to perform ordinary tasks, such as reaching for a marker or stacking books, even when no help was needed; and they did so without prompting and with no benefit gained, not even praise.[32]

Already as a medical student, as much as he appreciated facts, Adler was put off by the emphasis on diagnosis and research that was the ruling ethos of the medical school at the University of Vienna. The objective clinical approach of his professors ran counter to Adler's temperamental bias for compassionate patient care. He saw his role as a physician in humanitarian and altruistic terms.

Here, he differed from Freud, who used his practice as laboratory research for the elaboration of his theories and was only mildly interested in the humanitarian aspects of his analytic practice. Freud's approach to his patients, which he institutionalized as a technique, was impersonal, objective and clinical. Adler, on the other hand, engaged his patients personally: in fact many of them remained his life-long friends. Also as an extravert, he did not care to spend most of his time in the consulting room or at his desk writing, which was the penchant of the introverted Freud. Instead he preferred teaching and lecturing, or, as in the case of the Vienna child clinics, working as a member of a treatment team.

In his later years, reflecting on the origins of individual psychology, Adler mused:

> As far as I can look back, I was always surrounded by friends and comrades, and for the most part, I was a well-loved playmate. This development began early and has never ceased. It is probably [from] this feeling of solidarity with others that my understanding of the need for cooperation arose, a motive which has become the key to Individual Psychology.[33]

Several stories from his childhood illustrate Adler's inborn feelings of empathy, an aspect of Eros. When he was three years old, his parents left him and his siblings in the care of a governess who apparently took the children to a local cabaret. When the parents returned, they found Alfred standing on top of the dining room table singing a popular song about a woman who was so sensitive and gentle that she even cried to see a chicken's neck wrung.[34]

The other episode had to do with the death of his younger brother, Rudolf, from diphtheria. Again, Adler was about three. He remembers riding back home from the funeral and seeing his mother crying uncontrollably. His grandfather tried to console her and said something that made her smile. Adler was horrified and the thought clearly crossed his mind: "How could a mother smile on her child's burial day!" He notes that he remembered her reaction for years with incomprehension and resentment.[35]

Adler's Eros nature is also attested to by his striving for harmony in his encounters with others and his lack of professional airs and social snobbery. He enjoyed lecturing to the general public and wrote for the popular press, for example, in the United States, *McCall's*, *Cosmopolitan* and *Esquire*. During his lectures he defused tensions with humor and fenced off debate by expressing warm agreement with the spirit of the question. He showered the speaker with praise and compliments, and only after a genial atmosphere was established, proceeded to respond and defend his point of view.

Adler genuinely liked people and made friends easily; his favorite pastime was socializing and talking late into the night in Viennese cafés. His lack of discrimination among those whom he befriended and tolerated was notorious:

> His friends, who loved Adler's company, did not always care to share it with an increasing circle of half-cured neurotics, out-at-elbow tramps, or other strange persons. It was disconcerting to look forward to a scientific discussion, on a long Sunday excursion, and find sixty other persons without scientific attainments on the railway station prepared to join in.[36]

Adler is generally described by those who knew him as outgoing, warm and friendly. Freud, on the other hand, was formal and reserved in public and disclosed the affectionate side of his personality only with his immediate family and close friends. He drew a sharp distinction between his friends and his enemies. Freud especially despised Adler and considered him a traitor who undermined psychoanalysis by pandering to a public uncomfortable with Freud's sexual theories. Freud also had little tolerance for Adler's theoretical emphasis on *Gemeinschaftsgefühl* or community feeling.

Freud addressed the issue of Eros as a guiding social principle in *Civilization and Its Discontents*. In the book he subjected the Christian injunction to "love one's neighbor as oneself" to both a logical and a psychological critique. His conclusion was that not only is the neighbor—not to speak of one's enemy—"unworthy of my love; [but] I must honestly confess that he has more claim to my hostility and even my hatred."[37] Adler could not have been far from Freud's mind when he wrote these words, for his critique of Christian love was at the same time an attack on Adler's *Gemeinschaftsgefühl*.

In response, Adler felt that Freud's psychology was without moral or communal standards and, in fact, promoted the formation of anti-social types. "It is a spoilt child psychology," he averred, "but what can be expected from a man who asks, 'Why should I love my neighbor?'"[38] Adler had outlined this thesis in a brief description of the pampered child:

> In pampered children the degree of social feeling, their interest in others, despite an occasional thin varnish, is so slight that even the casual observer become aware of it. Their entire behavior expresses either openly or covered by a flourish, the surprised, even indignant question: "Why should I love my neighbor?" Not even the mother remains spared from their lovelessness. She becomes a subservient object, and object of their lust.[39]

As the last sentences imply, Adler had a radically different view of the Oedipus complex than Freud. He did not regard it as universal and considered the expression of sexual feelings of children towards their parents as preparations for future adult relationships. Adler thought that the typical feelings associated with the Oedipus complex are the result of flawed upbringing and encountered primarily in spoiled children: "what Freud has designated as the Oedipus complex, which appears to him the natural foundation of psychological development, is nothing but one of the many phenomena in the life of a pampered child who is the unresisting plaything of his intensified wishes."[40] If, in later life, these wishes result in a neurosis, it merely proves "how difficult it is to increase social interest after the fifth year of life."[41] In contrast to Freud's thesis that a healthy individual has solved the problems of love and work, Adler asserted that without community feeling, no individual is healthy and mature. In one instance, he added a fourth element: the appreciation of art and culture, but unfortunately he did not elaborate upon the idea.

Both Freud and Adler, however, looked to Eros as the central tenet of their respective psychologies, although each defined Eros in his own way: Freud as sexual libido, Adler as community feeling. In accord with his introverted bias, Freud focused on the permutations of libido within the individual and in the immediate family. Adler the extravert, never lost sight of the social component of childhood development: organ inferiority involved a dynamic relationship between the individual's biological inheritance and the demands of the surrounding social environment. The striving for superiority also took place in a social context. For Adler, Eros was the basis of all social reform and a solution to the problem of personal and collective violence. In the closing paragraph of *Civilization and Its Discontents*, Freud, too, acknowledged the importance of transpersonal love, expecting "eternal Eros" to assert itself against that other heavenly power, Thanatos, which seemed to be threatening humankind with total annihilation. But Freud's appeal to transpersonal Eros at the end of the book seems almost like an afterthought, or a pious wish.

By contrast, Adler's emphasis on community feeling is a manifestation of his guiding principle, Eros, and probably accounts for his conversion to Christianity at the age of 34. Adler's followers are at a loss to explain the conversion; apparently, it was not motivated by spiritual or religious concerns. Even anti-Semitic or professional considerations seem not to have played a major role for, at the time, Adler had completed his education, was well established in his medical practice and had no civil service ambitions. He did not seem to feel that his Jewish background was an obstacle in his personal or professional life. Nevertheless, on 17 October 1904, together with his two young daughters Valentine and Alexandra, he was baptized into the Protestant faith. Later, his infant son Kurt was also baptized. As far as we know, Adler and his children did not attend church and were not practicing Christians. Phyllis Bottome's proposed explanation for the conversion is the one that makes the most sense, because it accords with the ruling archetype of Adler's life: it was "a protest against the isolation that he felt was a spiritual danger in the Orthodox Jewish faith"[42] and a desire to "share a common deity with the universal faith of man."[43] In other words, his *Gemeinschaftsgefühl* rebelled against the conception of a deity limited to one ethnic group. Christianity, at least ideally, proclaimed a universal deity whose principle attribute was love and whose followers were encouraged to develop love of neighbor. Also, Christianity was the dominant religion of his surrounding culture, and, as an extravert, he longed to be part of his social milieu.

Once, during a discussion with a theosophist about the Hindu doctrine of transmigration of souls, Adler asked those present to say what they would like to be in their next life. As for himself, he wanted to come back as a rose because "it is beautiful to look at, and it grows on a bush with many others."[44] The rose, of course, is a symbol of love!

Given his overt commitment to Eros, it is interesting to observe the vicissitudes of love in his personal life. In his mid-20s, Adler fell in love with Raissa Epstein, a daughter of Russian-Jewish parents, who came to study abroad, first in Zurich and then in Vienna. Most likely they met at a socialist gathering, for both were attracted to the progressive ideas of the day. After a brief courtship they were married in a traditional Jewish ceremony in Smolensk, Russia, on 23 December 1897.

Early in the marriage they shared the same enthusiasm for political and social reform, but, as time went on, their temperamental differences asserted themselves and difficulties arose in the personal relationship. The course of their union demonstrates that the outward contents of marital conflict are usually surface manifestations of an underlying divergence in the ruling principles motivating each personality.

Raissa was an emancipated, fiercely independent woman who, at best, tolerated the demands of domesticity and motherhood. She was an ardent feminist and political revolutionary most of her life. Unlike Adler, whose interest in socialism stemmed from his humanistic concerns, Raissa was interested in the political aspects of socialism and supportive of a proletarian revolution. In other words, Adler married his Power anima.

The Adlers befriended Leon Trotsky and his wife Natalia during the couple's five year (1905–10) sojourn in Vienna. Raissa remained a life-long friend and partisan of Trotsky and his international brand of revolutionary socialism. By 1930, when Adler was severing his ties with Austria and making plans to move permanently to the United States, Raissa had no intention of joining him. They had been estranged for years and essentially lived separate lives. Once in the United States, Adler continued to write to her even though she seldom or never responded.

Undaunted, he would not let her go. Once the Nazi menace was all too evident, Raissa finally did join him and they were reconciled.

Yet, while Adler was enthusiastic about his life in the United States and cultivating wealthy supporters, such as the New England businessmen Charles Henry Davies and Edward L. Filene, Raissa was still caught up in the throes of revolutionary fervor. In response to an accusation by the Central Committee of the Austrian Communist Party, of which she was a respected member, that her support of Trotsky was counter-revolutionary, she penned a fiery rejoinder in the hyperbolic rhetoric of militant revolutionaries of her day:

> There is an acute revolutionary situation in Austria, [and] the order of the day is the establishment of the Soviets . . . The Party, and especially the Central Committee, could learn a lot from the writings of General Trotsky, particularly from his brochure on the "Austrian Crisis" . . . Indeed, comrades, I am for cleansing the Party of all opportunistic, bureaucratic elements, from top to bottom, and because I am in earnest about this, I associate myself fully and completely with the leftist [Trotskyite] opposition. For it is in the position to lead the Communist Internationale [Komintern] out of the rotten swamp of opportunism and set them on the great, historic way of the fight of the proletarian revolution.[45]

The rhetoric alone demonstrates the gulf between Raissa and her husband. Adler's Eros motivated character could never speak in such harsh terms, nor contemplate the purges and revolutionary activity she envisioned. Though a socialist in his political leanings, he was oremost a psychologist who believed that society could be improved only through changes in individuals. Raissa, in stark contrast, was convinced that society, as well as human nature, could be improved through changes in the political system. It is remarkable and attests to Adler's common sense and emotional maturity that he never became infected by the psycho-political epidemics sweeping the Continent during the decades following World War I. Not only Raissa, but many of his closest friends and loyal followers were swept away by the political maelstrom, either on the Left or the Right, and tried to convince him to join them. He steadfastly refused and consequently lost not only the approbation of his wife, but the loyalty of powerful friends who may have helped advance the cause of his work. Stubbornly and, in hindsight, astutely, he insisted that individual psychology was a science that had nothing to do with politics and that needed to be kept apart from every form of ideology and political movement.

The differences between Raissa and Alfred Adler, although played out in the political and cultural terms of their day, can be found among many couples. The conflict has to do with a difference in temperament and in the fact is that opposites both attract and repel. There is a tendency for individuals to be attracted to, and to marry, not just their parental imagoes, but their opposite types. Generally, the more extreme a person's identification with a type, the greater the need for a counterbalance and the stronger the attraction to an extreme opposite type of personality. This tendency for a balanced union of opposites, or a *coniunctio,* as the alchemists referred to this psychological dynamic, seems to indicate a propensity on the part of the psyche for wholeness. Marriage is the external manifestation of that archetypal drive.

On the other hand, there is an equally strong tendency for opposites to repel each other, balancing the drive for union with a drive for individuation and separation. One can observe this side of the equation in marital conflict and divorce. Love and war, Venus and Mars, are the opposite sides of the same archetypal coin, and marriage is the crucible in which these two great daemons interact. Jung's magnum opus, *Mysterium Coniunctionis: An Inquiry into the Separation and Synthesis of Psychic Opposites in Alchemy*, explores this dynamic with the help of the alchemical metaphor which imagined the conflict and its resolution in these paradoxical terms: "a warring peace, a sweet wound, a mild evil."[46]

In terms of human temperament, the problem of attraction and repulsion of opposites is played out in typology. Introverts are attracted to extraverts, soulful types to their spirited counterparts, Pneuma to Physis, and Eros to Power types. Since an individual's typology includes all four archetypes in various combinations, the fascination usually entails more than one of these aspects of the personality. Sometimes a couple may share one or two attributes; rarely, all four will be opposed.

From what we know of Adler, he was an extraverted soulful Physis Eros type. Raissa was probably an introverted spirited Physis Power type. The only attribute they had in common was Physis. (Interestingly, she has the same typological profile as Freud.) Their dominant motivations, Eros and Power respectively, were opposed and consequently the source of conflict between them. But they remained true to their basic natures and refused to subsume their personality or repress their individuality for the sake of the other. Fortunately, because of time and circumstance, they were eventually able to achieve a "warring peace" between their opposed natures. I should however point out that it was Adler's Eros that maintained the connection and, ultimately, achieved their reconciliation.

Extraversion

Given Adler's extraverted temperament, it must have been particularly difficult, and contrary to his natural inclination, to resist the political blandishments of his wife, friends and colleagues. For as we have seen, there was nothing that Adler liked better than to be part of a congenial group of people dedicated to the improvement of society. In my summary of Adler's work, I frequently alluded to his extraversion; it was evident in how he expressed his Eros, his concern about patient care, his love of socializing, his work in setting up child guidance clinics and in his practical and theoretical emphasis on the importance of community feeling. His theory of organ inferiority and the attendant feelings of inferiority and compensatory strivings for superiority never lose sight of the social context. The importance he placed on birth order as a determinant of character and his view of the Oedipus complex as a spoiled child syndrome further attest to his extraverted bias.

It appears, however, that at the beginning of his career he did go through an intense introverted period. Sophie, the Adler family's cook for 20 years, reported that when she first came, "the Herr Doktor was never without a book or a pen in his hand. When he came in from his rounds, he would sit up to all hours in the morning, writing and reading. It was not so later, for people came to the house all day long—and far into the night—but when he was a young man, he did not talk very much."[47] Clearly, these early years of his career served as a gestation period during which he formulated the original ideas he would later elaborate and then expand upon for the rest of his life. Once that creative period was over, Adler seems to have never returned to such an intense introverted withdrawal. At heart he was a social creature, outgoing and buoyant with a talent for finding instant rapport with people from all walks of life. "He rarely felt drawn to solitude", Edward Hoffman writes, "even when intellectually excited, he never seems to have kept a diary or journal."[48] Writing bored him and he was not good at it. His preference was "to discuss ideas, whether philosophical or social, amidst friendly company in a relaxed public setting. In coming decades as Adler became an increasingly well-known figure in Vienna and abroad, such activity would be his hallmark."[49]

His growing reputation allowed Adler to satisfy his penchant for social contact with a busy schedule of teaching and lecturing. In the United States, during the mid-1930s, he became one of the most sought after and highly compensated public speakers. After one such lecture in Boston, where he spent the night with a family, his host inquired about his dreams. "I *never* dream!" Adler retorted.[50] I think the remark, even if an exaggeration, indicates how far he was removed from an inner life. One of the pioneers of depth psychology, he never experienced a proper analysis, unlike Freud and Jung who pursued a thorough self-analysis. Adler apparently had little inclination for introspection.

In the end, he paid for his extraversion with his life. In April 1937, at the age of 67, he undertook the most demanding lecture tour of his professional career: ten weeks of lectures in France, Belgium, the Netherlands and Great Britain. In a postcard to a friend, Adler boasted, "Tomorrow I finish my 42nd lecture. It has been very easy for me."[51] Well into the tour, in The Hague, he experienced chest pains; a medical colleague and a cardiologist strongly advised a cardiological examination and complete rest. Instead, he left for England the next day. After three days of lectures at the University of Aberdeen, Scotland, he breakfasted alone, went out for a walk and collapsed. He died of a heart attack on the way to hospital. When Freud was told about his death, he remarked: "For a Jewish boy from a Viennese suburb, a death in Aberdeen, Scotland, is an unprecedented career and proof of how far he had come. Truly, his contemporaries have richly rewarded him for his service in having contradicted psychoanalysis."[52] Freud's response once again demonstrates the temperamental primacy of his own ambitions and power drive.

Soulfulness

Photographs of Adler openly portray him as a soulful man. In contrast to what one would expect to see in an extraverted personality, the portraits disclose a gentle, sensitive human being. Looking at these images, however, one can also discern another side, that of a brooding man who could easily turn surly. Ernest Jones experienced this shadow side of Adler's personality and described him as "a morose and cantankerous person whose behavior oscillated between contentiousness and sulkiness."[53] Of course, Jones is speaking of the period when Adler was separating from Freud. But there are other reported instances when Adler's usual genial persona was in abeyance and he turned uncharacteristically argumentative and aggressive.

His soulful and sensitive nature had its liabilities: he nurtured slights for a long time, particularly when feelings of inferiority were involved. For example, he never got over the rejection of his application for an academic position at the University of Vienna; it remained, Phyllis Bottome writes, "an unstaunched wound for the rest of his life."[54]

A similar situation developed years later at Columbia University in New York, where Adler was visiting professor at the College of Physicians and Surgeons. Without consulting him, one of Adler's friends proposed his name for a permanent chair of psychology at the school. The proposal was voted down, and even though he had not initiated the request, when he learned of the rejection, Adler resigned his position at Columbia in a pique.

Adler became especially incensed when anyone considered him a student or a disciple of Freud. His opponents, particularly, were aware of his touchiness in this regard. Phyllis Bottome writes that when he was made an honorary citizen of Vienna, someone maliciously informed the mayor that if he wanted to please Adler, he should mention that the honor was bestowed on him in recognition of his work as a student of Freud. In his response Adler maintained his composure, but "said with quiet sarcasm that . . . he could not lay claim of ever having been a pupil of Freud, since he was merely the founder of 'Individual Psychology.'"[55]

The more positive aspects of Adler's soulful temperament were evident in his love of music and his appreciation of nature. He said that as a boy he had tunes running though his head instead of thoughts. He studied the piano, tried composing and enjoyed singing Schubert *lieder* and German folk songs. He loved flowers and enjoyed gardening, devoting time and effort to cultivate plants brought from countries he visited hoping they would flourish at his country home outside Vienna.

I believe Adler's soulful qualities were also evident in the calming effect he had upon people and, apparently, even upon animals. A doctor at a mental hospital reported that the most dangerous and agitated patients would relax in his presence. And Phyllis Bottome writes that she once saw "a highly nervous Alsatian, who barked himself hoarse at the approach of any stranger, welcome Adler's first visit without so much as a premonitory sniff, instantly laying his head upon the strange but friendly knee."[56]

A glimpse of Adler's touchiness about to his association with Freud and his defensiveness with respect to his own theories is evident in two encounters he had with the American psychologist Abraham Maslow. Maslow wrote a Ph.D. dissertation contrasting Freud's and Adler's theories and was therefore pleased to be introduced to Adler during the mid-1930s in New York City. As a graduate student in psychology at the University of Wisconsin, Maslow was interested in researching human sexuality. His psychology department, however, allowed only animal research, and consequently Maslow devised an experiment that involved the sexual behavior of monkeys. The conclusion of his study was that the more dominant the monkey, whether male or female, in the social hierarchy of the group, the more sexually active it was: social dominance determined their sexual behavior. Maslow also observed that the frequent heterosexual and homosexual mountings among the primates were motivated by power considerations rather than sexual desire and therefore concluded that among monkeys, "Sexual behavior is used as an aggressive weapon often, instead of bullying or fighting, and is to a large extent interchangeable with these later power weapons."[57] He wanted to apply these insights to human sexuality and suggested that Adler's view of power take into account the results of his primate research.

Adler was pleased by Maslow's interest. He thought the young psychologist's research provided empirical evidence for his theories and published one of his articles in the *International Journal for Individual Psychology*. After his graduation Maslow shifted his attention to human sexuality. He published several research papers on the relationship between college women's sexual feelings and experiences and their personality, particularly their *dominance-feeling*, or self-esteem, in contemporary terms. His conclusion paralleled the one he proposed in his dissertation: women with a strong dominance-feeling were more active sexually than women with lower dominance-feelings. His findings again seemed to confirm Adler's thesis that issues of superiority take precedence over, and even determine, the expression of sexuality.

Adler befriended the young psychologist and once, during a casual dinner conversation, Maslow said something that implied Adler was initially Freud's follower. The usually polite and composed older man flew into a rage and, with the restaurant patrons looking on, almost shouted that that was a "lie and a swindle" concocted by Freud: he was never Freud's student or disciple! Freud had invited him to join his inner circle and from the beginning, Adler insisted, he always retained his independence and pursued his own research.[58]

The friendship and collaboration between Adler and Maslow came to a sudden halt when, during one of the informal Friday evening meetings held at Adler's Gramercy Park Hotel residence, Maslow said something critical of Adler. Soon Maslow found himself herded into a corner by his mentor and challenged: "Well, are you for me or against me?"[59] Shaken and offended, Maslow stopped attending the meetings. To Maslow's life-long regret, that incident turned out to be their final interaction, for Adler died a year later. Shortly before he himself died in 1970, in the

Journal of Individual Psychology's tribute to Adler on the 100th anniversary of his birth, Maslow acknowledged Adler's vision: "For me, Alfred Adler becomes more and more correct year by year. As the facts come in, they give stronger and stronger support to his image of man . . . especially . . . to his holistic emphasis."[60]

The holistic emphasis is an aspect of Adler's Eros, which is an archetypal drive that seeks union and connection in contrast to analysis and differentiation. This holistic feature of Adler's temperament was supported by his intuition. As we have seen, in his unconscious motivations, he was an extraverted Physis Eros type. In terms of Jung's typology, Adler was also an intuitive feeling type with inferior sensation. The inferior sensation indicates that his dominant conscious function was intuition.

Adler relied upon his highly developed intuition in his clinical work. When confronted with "a new patient, about whom he knew nothing," Ellenberger writes, "he would look at him a moment, ask a few questions, and then get a complete picture of the subject's difficulties, clinical disturbances, and life problems".[61] He displayed the same ability at public case presentations. He would listen to the case history and then predict what the patient would say and how he or she would behave when introduced to the group of psychologists or educators.

Adler also used his intuition to evaluate coming political events. As early as 1918, he wrote that the Bolshevik reliance on violence would provoke counter-violence on a scale that could lead to the conquest and subjugation of Europe.[62] In the spring of 1937, during his final lecture tour, he met one of his friends in London who was planning to return to Austria. "Are you crazy?" Adler said. "Take your family out immediately and go to the United States. Number one: the Nazis will soon be in Vienna. Number two: war will come. And number three: the United States is the best place not only to live, but also to work."[63]

Like many intuitives, Adler hated being pinned down in his theoretical formulations and "disliked precise definitions or 'prescriptions' as he used to call them; when he was asked to explain his exact meaning, he would say, 'But now you want to milk the life out of the cow!'"[64] Intuitive types just see too many possibilities, qualifications and exceptions to feel comfortable with any unequivocal definition. As Adler's colorful response indicates, they feel that precision does violence to their sense of truth and vitiates living reality. To force intuitives to respond to a question in simple yes or no terms is to subject them to mental torture.

In keeping with the compensatory dynamics of the psyche, the price of a highly evolved intuition is inferior sensation. Adler's inattention to detail and poor administrative skills, in the end, probably hurt his cause, for he was incapable of systematically establishing an organization that would further his teachings and ideas. He never even managed to find consistent secretarial help, so that important papers were mislaid and correspondence would go missing or remain unanswered. Phyllis Bottome thought that a good secretary might have prolonged his life by ten years.[65]

Conclusion

Adler's temperament combined with the historical circumstances of the day account for the fact that he is remembered chiefly as an historical figure who played a prominent role during the founding years of depth psychology. Fascist social policy obliterated decades of Adler's pioneering work with child guidance clinics along with his growing influence on educational and developmental psychology in Austria and Germany. His death in 1937, the Nazi persecution of his Jewish and socialist colleagues and the devastation and social upheaval caused by World War II effectively put an end to Adlerian communities in Central Europe, Great Britain and the United States. By the end of the war, his most ardent supporters had aged or died. *The Journal of Individual Psychology* ceased publication and his books went out of print.

Aside from these historical developments, Adler's personality also played a role in his waning influence after the war. Biographer Edward Hoffman writes that Adler fell into "the 'trap of personality,' a trap largely of his own making."[66] In Hoffman's opinion, Adler failed to see that his popular success was largely the result of his genial charismatic personality. The popularity of his books, the favorable media coverage and the worldwide speaking engagements did little to establish his school of thought on a firm institutional foundation. "After his death," Hoffman continues, "it became obvious how much of individual psychology as an intellectual movement outside Austria had been dependent upon its energetic creator to attract and hold interest."[67]

Similarly, the failure to place his psychology on a solid organizational basis was largely the result of his temperament. As an extraverted Eros type, Adler's primary motivation was constant activity and contact with others. His personal emphasis on Eros rather than Power and his poor sensation meant that he had little interest in the practical effort required to establish an organization to carry on his work. While his Austrian followers and colleagues did create such institutions, in spite of his almost decade-long residence in the United States, no significant American Adlerian institutions were founded. Also, the combination of his Eros orientation and his socialist convictions meant that Adler sought to share his knowledge freely with the world at large and utilize it for social betterment. He was more interested in educational and social policy rather than in establishing programs to train Adlerian analysts. By contrast Freud, with his awareness of power considerations, his elitist attitudes and dogmatic stance, sought to restrict and control the dissemination of psychoanalytic thought among a select group of loyal adherents who employed it primarily in fee-based work with individual patients.

The temperamental contrast between Adler and Freud also accounts for the fact that so many of Adler's theoretical innovations and concepts have been taken over by Freud and others with no acknowledgement of Adler's contribution. The absence of an Adlerian voice in popular depth psychology discourse is starkly evident in the common misattribution of the inferiority complex to either Freud or Jung. In its obituary of Freud *The Times* of London ascribed it to Freud. After Jung's death in 1961, *The New York Times* listed it among the terms, such as extravert and introvert, coined by Jung. Henri Ellenberger in his classic history of depth psychology, *The Discovery of the Unconscious*, observes that "there is the puzzling phenomenon of a collective denial of Adler's work and the systematic attribution of anything coined by him to other authors."[68] It would be difficult to find another author, Ellenberger writes, from whom

> so much has been borrowed from all sides without acknowledgement than Alfred Adler. His teaching has become, to use a French idiom, an "open quarry" (*une carrière publique*), that is, a place where anyone and all may come and draw anything without compunction. An author will meticulously quote the source of any sentence he takes from elsewhere, but it does not occur to him to do the same whenever the source is individual psychology; it is as if nothing original could ever come from Adler.[69]

The reality is other than it appears, for Adler was the equal of Freud and Jung in his penetrating exploration of the psyche, his original exposition of its dynamics and his innovative psychotherapeutic aims and methods. Ironically, as the extraverted representative of the three, his work and its influence are the least recognized and acknowledged. It lies hidden in Freud's belated adoption of the aggressive drive and in other notions first articulated by Adler: the confluence of drives; their displacement; the transformation of a drive into its opposite; and the internalization of external demands (which Anna Freud eventually expanded into the concept of "identification with the aggressor"). At the onset of their dispute, Freud set the tone for later dismissals of Adler, claiming that Adler took credit for discoveries implicit in his own work by giving them different names: psychic hermaphroditism, for instance, for the bisexuality of human beings (actually an idea first proposed by Freud's mentor, Wilhelm Fliess); and masculine protest, for the aggressive component of the sexual instincts. Later Freudians claimed that Adler merely developed these implicit and other neglected aspects of Freud's thinking: in other words, nothing original stemmed from Adler; all his ideas came from Freud.

On the other hand, Freud also recognized that "all these teachings of Adler's are . . . not without importance" and argued that Adler's rejection of the sexual basis of libido would harm the cause of psychoanalysis.[70] Freud further acknowledged that "a significant intellect with a great gift for presentation is at work on these matters" and summarized Adler's approach:

> Instead of psychology, it presents, in large part, biology; instead of the psychology of the unconscious, it presents surface ego psychology. Lastly, instead of the psychology of the libido, of sexuality, it offers general psychology. It will, therefore, make use of the latent resistances that are alive in every psychoanalyst, in order to make its influence felt....This is ego psychology, deepened by the knowledge of the psychology of the unconscious.[71]

Freud's assessment was incisive and astute. He correctly identified Adler's Physis and extraverted orientations with the biological and "surface" ego psychology emphasis. He was also aware of the resistance to his sexually based theories and correctly predicted that at the beginning, at least, Adler's more general approach to the psyche would gain ready adherents. He even acknowledged Adler's gift for popularizing psychological ideas. In the end, however, Freud would have been pleased and most likely surprised by the professional as well as the popular acceptance of psychoanalytic theory and the eclipse of Adler's individual psychology.

Adler's disappearance from popular discourse notwithstanding, his influence permeated future developments in psychoanalysis. Harry Stack Sullivan, Karen Horney, Erich Fromm and other prominent psychoanalysts followed Adler in their rejection of Freud's basic theories. Like him they expanded the concept of libido, reduced the role of sexuality in childhood development and reinterpreted the Oedipus complex. They also counter-balanced innate instincts or drives with social and interpersonal relationships or, following Adler, with self-assertive and competitive drives. Like Adler, they considered neurosis the result of a faulty life style rather than the product of conflicts between ego, id and superego. Unlike Freud, they did not conceive of human nature as inherently anxious and destructive. And they moved the focus of therapy from past events to present conflicts, with less attention to the analysis of dreams and symbols.[72]

Ellenberger provides numerous instances in the writings of these neo-psychoanalysts in which Adler's ideas appear with apparently no awareness or deliberate disregard of his seminal work. Even Jean-Paul Sartre and Ludwig Binswanger, who formulated the principles of existential psychoanalysis, failed to mention that it was Adler who first proposed the notion of a "fundamental project" that is, a guiding fiction that informs a person's life and accounts for her or his convictions and behavior. Binswanger's dual mode, plural mode and singular mode of being-with-others is, Ellenberger writes, identical with Adler's descriptions of community feeling, striving for superiority and striving for isolation.[73]

By contrast, Viktor Frankl, who founded a form of existential psychoanalysis called *logotherapy*, always acknowledged his debt to Adler. In a tribute to Adler on the 100th anniversary of his birth, Frankl declared that Adler was "the first creatively to oppose Sigmund Freud. What he, in so doing, achieved and accomplished is no less than a Copernican switch. No longer could man be considered as the product, pawn and victim of drives and instincts."[74]

The list of contributions by Adler that have been assimilated by other theorists and that are now part of the psychological mainstream is long and impressive. Aside from the ideas already mentioned, others include: the uniqueness of the individual; the importance of early memories; the influence of birth order on the formation of personality; issues of power in parenting and marriage; psycho-social explanation of the causes of adolescent maladjustment and juvenile delinquency; and the importance of cultivating social interest or feeling. His contribution to treatment modalities include: school guidance and counseling; community involvement and team approach in psychiatry; group psychotherapy; parent and teacher training in developmental psychology; and disseminating psychological knowledge to the general public. The importance of the father–child bond emphasized by Adler is only now gaining recognition. Remarkably for a socialist, Adler did not consider marriage a bourgeois institution, but saw monogamy as the highest and most challenging form of human social feeling. His egalitarianism is evinced in the conviction that marriage is a "task for two" based on mutual cooperation, respect and the sharing of power.

In addition to the historical circumstances and issues of personality responsible for the decline of Adler's visible influence, there may be other reasons for the eclipse of individual psychology. Freud and Jung relied primarily upon their writings to carry their message forward and devoted a great deal of time to a careful and even stylistic revision of their work. Adler, on the other hand, hated to write and was not good at it. Until recently, there was no edition of the collected works of Alfred Adler: only two posthumously published anthologies edited by Heinz L. and Rowena R. Ansbacher.[75]

Additionally, both Freud and Jung sought to connect their theoretical concepts with mythological and literary antecedents; hence their ideas resonate with the imagination and have a living presence in the psyche. Adler's pragmatic, ordinary and reasonable approach to psychology provided little for imaginative play or theoretical speculation. True, his personal Eros and charisma made an immediate impression on his colleagues and the public, but ultimately had no lasting effect. Nevertheless, Adler's contribution to the study of unconscious dynamics equals that of Freud and Jung. His extraverted Physis Eros personality added a point of view that extended and complemented those of the other two pioneers of depth psychology.

8
C. G. Jung: Introverted Soulful Power Pneuma Type: Part I

C. G. Jung
26 July 1876–6 June 1961

Photo courtesy of Andreas Jung.

Jung and Adler

Adler's influence on the development of depth psychology extends to Jung. A number of basic concepts and ideas usually associated with Jungian psychology were first introduced by Adler. These ideas include: wholeness and individuation; an emphasis on the individual that is balanced with a vision of the interdependence of all life; the theory of compensation; an extension of the concept of libido beyond its Freudian confines; and the hypothesis of the teleological, or goal-oriented flow of psychic libido. Another significant similarity between Adler and Jung, and difference from Freud, is their therapeutic method. In Adlerian and Jungian therapy patient and therapist sit facing each other. Sessions usually take place once or twice a week as opposed to four or five times a week. The "frame," or the rules governing treatment, is less rigid than in the Freudian model, while transference and the vagaries of childhood development are not considered central aspects of the treatment. Both Jung and Adler thought that the current reality of the patient established a context for treatment and must be taken into account: for example, the avoidance of life tasks, such as marriage or the necessity of earning a living, may also cause neurotic symptoms. Similarly, Jung and Adler regarded the failure to accept the limitations imposed by one's nature or by the unalterable circumstances of a person's life as another possible source of neuroses.

Jungians might be surprised to learn that it was Adler and not Jung who first spoke of an innate "urge towards an integration of personality."[1] and who insisted on the indivisibility of the individual. Adler would also readily recognize his contribution to Jung's description of individuation as "the process by which a person becomes a psychological 'in-dividual,' that is, a separate indivisible unity or 'whole.'"[2] Moreover, a person's "wholeness," Adler argued, was key to his or her symptoms.[3] In other words, a neurotic symptom is not an alien, split-off psychic content, but must be seen in the context of the underlying coherence or unity of the personality. For example, paranoid symptoms disclose a personality motivated by issues of domination and power.

The emphasis on the individual is also evident in Adler's and Jung's insistence, in the face of the popular fascination with collective movements in their day, that individuals, rather than groups or movements, inspire cultural, social and political changes. Phyllis Bottome writes that Adler's "fundamental belief was that only a better individual can make a better system."[4] Jung wrote, the individual is "the sole carrier of mind and life"[5] and the nature of a community "depends on the spiritual and moral stature of the individuals composing it."[6] For both Adler and Jung, I think it fair to say, communal improvement or change entailed, above all, the withdrawal of negative shadow projections onto the "other" and the recognition of the interdependence of all life.

The two men shared and championed the Romantic view of the subjective uniqueness of the individual in contrast to the objective egalitarianism of Enlightenment thought, which they held to be responsible for mass movements and collectivism. However, they tempered their Romantic view of the individual with a vision of cosmic unity, which provides a basis for social cohesion. Adler, who unlike Jung, has never been accused of mysticism in his theoretical formulations, stated that "an individual cannot be conceived isolated from the cosmos that influences him in a thousand ways."[7] Even "*community feeling*," he writes, "is a reflection of the general interdependence of the cosmos, which lives within us, from which we cannot abstract ourselves completely, and endows us with the faculty to feel into, that is to empathize with other beings."[8] One gets the sense that if Adler were a traditionally religious person he would be comfortable with the definition of God as love.

For Jung, the interdependence of the cosmos is found in the archetype of the self. That archetype is often personified as a cosmic being, like Jehovah, or the Egyptian Atum, the Hindu Purusha, the Persian Gayomart, the Chinese P'an Ku, the Gnostic Anthropos, which contains within itself the entire universe. The archetype of the self lies at the core of each individual's psyche and accounts for the spiritual and cultural bonds among people from diverse sociological and educational backgrounds. In relationships informed by the archetype of the self, personal differences and egoistic interests are generally overcome or subordinated to the common interests and values of the group.

Jung was cognizant of the above similarities between his ideas and Adler's. He acknowledged Adler's insights and contributions to the psychology of the unconscious, particularly Adler's idea of the power drive as a central feature of personality development equal to that of the sex drive: the one giving rise to the inferiority complex, the other to the Oedipus complex. But Jung felt most indebted to Adler for the theory of compensation. According to the Jungian analyst Liliane Frey-Rohn, Jung frequently referred to Adler as "the creator of the theory of compensation."[9] Like all creative individuals, Jung freely incorporated ideas from others and reformulated them in his own unique manner to construct a new vision of reality. He was aware of that and made no qualms about it: "I constantly borrow knowledge from others. What I have done in alchemy and in psychiatry is partly original work. Apart from that, I depend on taking the forming material from the outside.[10]

As we have seen, Adler proposed the theory of compensation first with respect to physiological inferiority and later with reference to psychological feelings of inadequacy. In the context of Adler's and Jung's belief in the indivisibility and wholeness of the individual, it was natural for Jung to extend the idea of compensation from feelings of inferiority to a general theory that applied to dreams and to all psychic life. He subsequently expanded Adler's use of the term to the principle of homeostasis, and argued that homeostasis applies not just to physiology but also psychology. For Jung, both the body and the psyche seek an equilibrium based on a balance of organic functions and chemical composition in the case of the body, and psychic functions and libido in the case of the psyche. This broadened theory of compensation provided a basis for Jung's understanding of the origin and formation of symptoms; it also became the explanatory principle for dreams, replacing Freud's idea of dreams as wish-fulfillment. Jung considered compensation a basic law of the psyche, and one that was not limited to pathological phenomena, but that characterized all of psychic life. Furthermore, he contrasted compensation with complementation, which "designates a relationship in which two things supplement one another more or less mechanically."[11] Compensation, on the other hand, is a psychological refinement of complementarity and means "balancing and comparing different data or points of view so as to produce an adjustment or a rectification."[12]

Almost from their first encounter with Freud both Adler and Jung, in the course of formulating their own ideas about the nature of the psyche, expressed strong reservations about the exclusively sexually-based concept of libido. Adler, presenting his theories to the Vienna Psychoanalytic Society in 1911, clearly stated his position: "Biologically speaking it would not be possible to maintain that every drive has a sexual component, including the drive to eat, the drive to see, and the drive to touch."[13] Each of these drives is the result of a separate "differentiation of originally present potentialities of the cell. Thus a nutritive organ has followed the will and need of assimilation; touch, auditory, and visual organs followed the will and necessity to feel, hear, and see; a procreative organ followed the will and necessity for progeny."[14] According to Adler, the organic sensation of pleasure and pain, and later the brain, as the organ of prudence and thinking, were introduced in the course of human biological development as means of safeguarding and protecting the various organs and are not attributes or products of the sexual instinct. Sexuality is not unique in influencing a person's life and therefore cannot be considered the only source of neuroses. Adler concluded: "If sexuality enters relations with the *total drive life* and its causes, the same is true of any other drive. Before the sex drive has reached a degree worth mentioning, approximately at the end of the first year, the psychological life of the child is already richly developed."[15] Not surprisingly, after his presentation, Adler was drummed out of the Vienna Psychoanalytic Society and forced to go his own way. Later, he would refer to Freud's libido theory as a "sexual myth."[16]

In September 1912, Jung delivered a series of lectures at the medical school of Fordham University in New York. The content of these lectures was a critical summary of psychoanalytic theory to date and an exposition of his diverging views, a number of which coincided with Adler's: the expansion of the concept of libido to a general life force; a non-sexual theory of neurosis; the importance of social adaptation; and the teleological significance of neurotic fantasies and symptoms. Someone must have pointed out the similarities and consequently, in the Foreword to the first published edition of his lectures, Jung noted that apparently he and Adler had reached similar conclusions concerning the above matters independently of each other.[17] Jung's statement is somewhat disingenuous, for Adler's theories were well known in the small psychoanalytic community of the day and clearly influenced Jung's thinking. Evidently, at this early point in his life, Jung was not willing to acknowledge that many of his ideas were first articulated by Adler.

With regard to the notion of libido, Jung, like Adler, argued that the first manifestations of the life-process, both intra- and extra-uterine, are characterized by the dominance of nutrition, growth and "*by the absence of any sexual function.*"[18] Jung, however, extended the pre-sexual stage to between three and five years of age. Instead of speaking of "libido" or, awkwardly, of a "total drive life," he adopted the term "psychic energy."[19] Although he recognized that there must be a link between physiology and psyche, Jung thought the nature of that link was not clear. He argued that the "'psychophysical' hypothesis...[with] its epiphenomenalist point of view is simply a legacy from the old-fashioned scientific materialism" with its "belief that the psyche is secreted by the brain as the gall is by the liver.[20] He continued: "A psychology that treats the psyche as an epiphenomenon would better call itself *brain-psychology*, and remain satisfied with the meager results that such a psycho-physiology can yield."[21] Jung's words are germane to the current brain-imaging studies. Aside from identifying the areas of the brain that are involved in various psychological functions, such as logic, emotion or memory, these studies offer no insight into psychological processes and dynamics. They are hardly helpful prognostically or diagnostically. Scientists engaged in these studies, more often than not, subscribe to the materialistic notion that the psyche is simply a by-product of the neurological operations of the brain. For example, in his book, *The Astonishing Hypothesis: The Scientific Search for the Soul*, Francis Crick, one of the discoverers of the double-helical structure of DNA, writes: "your joys and your sorrows, your memories and your ambitions, your sense of personal identity and free will, are in fact no more than the behavior of a vast assembly of nerve cells and their associated molecules."[22] Similarly, Jerome M. Siegel, director of the UCLA Center for Sleep Research concludes, "dreams are a kind of epiphenomenon . . . an extraneous by-product, like foam on beer."[23]

Jung acknowledges that the psyche may be dependent on the functioning of the brain, but insists there are no grounds for seeing it as a mere secondary phenomenon. From that perspective, he argues, one might as well view the varied manifestation of life—animal, vegetable and mineral—which clearly operate within their own laws and principles, as mere elaborations of the chemistry of carbon compounds.[24] Instead, Jung contends that there are internal causal connections between psychic phenomena, for instance, the disruptive effect complexes have on conscious functioning. From Jung's perspective, the psyche needs to be regarded as a "*relatively* closed system" with its own separate area of operation and field of energy.[25]

In *Transformations and Symbols of Libido* (later called *Symbols of Transformation*), the book that marks his separation from Freud, Jung even reverses the notion that instincts, or a general life energy, are the source of psychic energy and argues that psychic energy can activate and then make use of instinctive energy to further its own purposes. This transformation of instinctive energy is achieved through what he calls the *canalization of libido* "into an *analogue of the object of instinct.*"[26] By "analogue," Jung means symbol. In other words, he is arguing that the psyche is able to take a specific instinctive drive, for instance, the drive for procreation, which is that instinct's object, and through analogous symbolic action, such as thrusting spears into a hole in the ground, seek to ensure the fertility of the land.[27]

Later, when Jung elaborates his model of the psyche, he proposes the hypothesis that psychic energy is a combination of material and archetypal energy, that is, energy streaming in from the material and non-material realms of existence. Jung proposes that at their core, material and archetypal energy are indistinguishable from each other, like matter and energy in quantum physics. Following the sixteenth-century alchemist Gerard Dorn, he calls this unified field of energy the *unus mundus* and regards it as the source of synchronistic and parapsychological phenomena, such as telekinesis and poltergeist. Jung notes that Adler coined the term *iunctim*, (from the Latin, "joined together") for such phenomena.[28]

In contrast to Freud's causal and reductive orientation toward the understanding and treatment of neuroses, both Adler and Jung espouse a teleological and synthetic approach. For Adler, "every single life phenomenon" is an expression of a "self-ideal or fictional goal that serves as the unifying principle of personality."[29] The flow of libido is toward a future construct that compensates for feelings of inferiority and advances feelings of self-esteem or superiority. Each person, therefore, seeks competence in some area of life to bolster a sense of self-worth or dominance. Psychic life, as much as it may have been influenced by the past, is essentially future oriented and not retrospective in character.

Jung also speaks of the progressive movement of the libido aimed at "a continuous process of adaptation to environmental conditions."[30] Neurotic difficulties arise when there is a blockage or a disturbance of that natural flow. Combining the notions of the teleological and progressive flow of psychic energy, Jung writes:

> Life is teleology *par excellence*; it is the intrinsic striving towards a goal. . . .Youthful longing for the world and for life, for the attainment of high hopes and distant goals, is life's obvious teleological urge which at once changes into fear of life, neurotic resistances, depressions, and phobias if at some point it remains caught in the past, or shrinks from risks without which the unseen goal cannot be attained.[31]

This neurotic avoidance of life's tasks is not the same as the introvert's hesitant response to the stimulus of sensations and demands of the outer world.

Introversion

With their theoretical similarities, it is remarkable that Adler and Jung were opposite in introversion and extraversion. Adler, as we have seen, was highly extraverted, while Jung was deeply introverted. Only an introvert could assert, as Jung does in the Preface to his autobiography, that all his memories of people, travels, outer surroundings and circumstances pale in comparison to his inner experiences. He enjoyed an outwardly abundant and varied life, full of professional and personal encounters with engrossing patients and significant thinkers and personalities of his time. He traveled to India, to Africa, throughout Europe and the United States and was actively engaged in the historical events of the first half of the twentieth century. But, his introverted bias is so pronounced that Jung concludes his "life has been singularly poor in outward happenings. I cannot tell much about them, for it would strike me as hollow and insubstantial. I can understand myself only in the light of inner happenings. It is these that make up the singularity of my life, and with these my autobiography deals."[32]

He then proceeds to recall early events from his life that seem to indicate a lonely and isolated childhood. Many of Jung's biographers argue that those circumstances reinforced his introverted tendencies and consolidated his reliance on the inner world. It seems to me, however, that one should not point to outer events as explanations for an introvert's cultivation of solitude and fascination with inner experience. Already as a four-year-old, Jung would hide in a closed off parlor of his father's parish house, a room filled with old paintings, and "sit for hours in front of the pictures, gazing at all this beauty."[33] On visits to the estate of his maternal uncle and his wife who, at the time, had nine children—six more were to come—and where other relatives with similarly large families tended to congregate, "Carl was often a silent and disapproving observer who wandered alone about the grounds."[34] A disapproving stance, of course, was a way of keeping his distance from the noisy and bustling household. Like all children, he played secret fantasy games. One of his fantasy games was to sit on a large projecting stone, imagine that he was the stone, and then wonder who was sitting on whom. Another game involved a carved manikin which he placed inside a pencil box and hid on top of a rafter in the attic. He would bring presents to the manikin, write letters to it in a secret language and consider these letters the manikin's private library.

Carl had other secrets. One was the earliest dream he could remember, that of an enormous phallus upright on a golden throne in an underground chamber with a single eye gazing upward and an aura of brightness above its head. The boy was paralyzed with terror at the sight and heard his mother's voice, "Yes, just look at him. That is the man-eater!"[35] The dream haunted him for years, but he told it to no one until his mid-60s.[36] Another secret that he would not share with anyone, also for long time, was a vision he had in his 12th year.

> One fine summer day ...I came out of school at noon and went to the cathedral square [in Basel]. The sky was gloriously blue, the day one of radiant sunshine. The roof of the cathedral glittered, the sun sparkling from the new, brightly glazed tiles. I was overwhelmed by the beauty of the sight, and thought: "The world is beautiful and the church is beautiful, and God made all this and sits above far away in the blue sky on a golden throne and..."[37]

Here, he felt himself go numb. He dared not think the next thought. For three long days he struggled with himself, trying to avoid thinking the forbidden thought and erase the entire incident from his mind. After endless philosophical and theological debates with himself, he finally decided he would risk it and then throw himself on the mercy of God:

> I gathered all my courage, as though I were about to leap forthwith into hell-fire, and let the thought come. I saw before me the cathedral, the blue sky. God sits on His golden throne, high above the world—and from under the throne an enormous turd falls upon the sparkling new roof, shatters it, and breaks the walls of the cathedral asunder.[38]

With that, instead of feeling damned, he was overwhelmed by an incomparable state of bliss and wept with happiness and gratitude. The experience, in his view, revealed a living and omnipotent God who was not limited by traditional views of Him based on the Bible or Church doctrine. But at the same time, the vision increased Jung's sense of loneliness and made him feel he was "a devil or a swine…[and] infinitely depraved."[39] In later life he concluded:

> My one great achievement during those years was that I resisted the temptation to talk about it to anyone. Thus the pattern of my relationship to the world was already prefigured: today as then I am a solitary, because I know things and must hint at things which other people do not know, and usually do not even want to know.[40]

Had he given in to the temptation and talked about his vision in all likelihood it would have been dismissed as a disturbed fantasy and lost its numinous power. Actually, the dream of the phallus and the vision of God on his throne are complementary—they portray subterranean and celestial images of God, a long forgotten and repressed ancient image and a contemporary Christian one. Note the golden throne in each dream. The phallus and the turd also embody tremendous potential for creativity, generativity and destruction, parallel to the attributes of Lord Shiva as creator, destroyer and maintainer. I think the two experiences account for Jung's later interest in the shadow side of God.

There is one other dream that belongs with the two above which, unfortunately, was omitted from *Memories, Dreams, Reflections*, but is found in the more extensive *Protocols* that served as the background material for his autobiography. There, when speaking about why he became interested in the "black art" of alchemy, Jung recounted a dream that occurred during the same period when he was struggling with the nature of God:

> I was very insecure at the time and I always had the wish, if I only had a direct experience of the eternal, of a sighting of God. And then I had the dream in which I thought: now it is coming, now I will finally experience it! There was a door, and I understood that if I opened this door, the experience would happen and I would see. I opened this door and what was behind it—a big manure heap and on top of it there lay a big sow.
>
> Can you imagine what an awful impression that was for me. Not quite as bad as the experience at the Basler Münster, [Basel Cathedral] but still almost as bad.[41]

The sow is representation of the great mother; in ancient Greece it was the favored sacrifice to Demeter, the mother goddess of the earth. Both the sow and the pile of manure emphasize the chthonic side of creation and fertility, the *physis* and feminine side of the divine that had been repressed by Judaism and Christianity. Jung's vision and dream, in hindsight, indicate that toward the end of the second Christian millennium, the Western collective unconscious was pressing to right the balance. The turd and the manure represent the *prima materia* of alchemy, the source of the philosophers' gold or stone, a symbol of salvation and immortality. Jung's vision of the turd destroying the Basel Cathedral, therefore, must be seen not only as an act of destruction but also as an act of grace: it depicts an interest on the part of the Godhead, at least as envisioned by Jung, for a new incarnation and a rebirth of the Christian myth.

At age 11, about a year before the above dream and vision, Carl was playfully shoved by a boy. He hit his head on the curbstone and fainted. As he felt the blow, he remembered thinking, "Now you won't have to go to school any more."[42] Carl was happy to stay at home and whenever his parents tried to get him to do schoolwork he fainted. When he did return to school, he would again faint, for some reason precisely between 11 and noon every morning, and was finally asked to stay at home. His enforced vacation lasted for more than half a year and he loved it:

> I was free, could dream for hours, be anywhere I liked, in the woods or by the water, or draw. I resumed my battle pictures and furious scenes of war, of old castles that were being assaulted or burned, or drew page upon page of caricatures. . . . Above all, I was able to plunge

> into the world of the mysterious. To that realm belonged trees, a pool, the swamp and animals, and my father's library.[43]

His parents hoped that a stay with his paternal uncle in Winterthur might do the boy some good. But again, in spite of the presence of his cousins and many other playmates free from school during the summer, Carl preferred to go to the train station, sit quietly on a bench and observe the hustle and bustle.[44] Like many introverts, he enjoyed being an anonymous, silent observer of others, for such passive observation is another form of fantasy. In the fall, there were consultations with various doctors. Carl was still deemed unfit to return to school and was sent instead to a farming valley in the Bernese Oberland where he boarded with a Catholic priest and was under the supervision of a doctor.

One day during this period Carl overheard his father talking with a friend about his son's future, worrying that he could not provide for an adult unable to earn a living. That glimpse of reality had an effect on Carl and he resolved to come out of his adolescent stupor. He resolved to overcome his fainting spells, which still occurred whenever he began to study, and found it was not that easy. Through persistent effort, he succeeded and returned to school. He felt guilty and ashamed of his previous behavior, but also knew that his passion for being alone and his delight in solitude was what had led him astray. In those early adolescent years, he recalls, nature "seemed to me full of wonders, and I wanted to steep myself in them. Every stone, every plant, every single thing seemed alive and indescribably marvelous. I immersed myself in nature, crawled, as it were, into the very essence of nature and away from the whole human world."[45] But after overhearing his father's concerns, he became serious about his studies, rising at five every day, some days even earlier, to do his work. He gave up his solitary ways and joined in the usual pranks and games of school boys.[46]

In his 13th year, Jung had an experience which, in his view, marked the end of his childhood. One morning on his way to school he felt as if he emerged from a dense cloud and suddenly realized, "now I am *myself*."[47] Before this moment, he mused, things just happened to him, but "now I happened to myself. . . . Previously I had been willed to do this and that; now *I* willed. This experience seemed to me tremendously important and new: there was 'authority' in me."[48] In his autobiography he writes that at this time, and all during his neurotic fainting spells, he had forgotten about the little manikin in the attic: "Otherwise, I would probably have realized even then the analogy between my feeling of authority and the feeling of value which the treasure inspired in me. But that was not so;

all memory of the pencil case had vanished."[49] What he is saying here is that the manikin carried an intimation of his sense of self that had now risen to consciousness. With that increased sense of autonomy and of his responsibilities with respect to the external world, his former intensely one-sided connection with the inner world came to an end.[50]

Nevertheless, the end of his childhood did not alter Jung's essentially introverted disposition. As an adult he periodically retreated to his country house on the upper Zurich lake near the village of Bollingen. There he spent days and weeks in isolation and solitary preoccupations, much as in childhood. Jung regretted having sold a parcel next to his property to a colleague, so to assure his privacy the neighbors agreed upon a signal: Jung raised a flag on his tower whenever he did not want to be disturbed.

In *Psychological Types*, Jung comes to terms with his introversion in an analytical and objective way. When he describes the introvert as shy and hesitant in social relations and even fearful and mistrustful of the human world, Jung was speaking of himself. His dominant function was thinking and his portrayal of the introverted thinking type also applies to him. I quote and paraphrase him at some length in what follows, for these are self-revelatory passages.

The introvert's thinking, Jung writes, whether directed toward abstract ideas or concrete data, always begins with and returns to the subject, that is, to the person doing the thinking. Ideas and theories are the focus rather than knowledge of facts; the aim is subjective intensity and depth rather than objective extensity and breadth. To illustrate the difference, Jung mentions Kant as an example of an introverted thinker and Darwin as his extraverted counterpart. The introverted thinker collects facts to buttress a theory; he is never interested in facts for their own sake or for discovering their inherent meaning or content. Jung explains,

> Facts are of secondary importance to this kind of thinking; what seems to it of paramount importance is the development and presentation of the subjective idea, of the initial symbolic image hovering darkly before the mind's eye. Its aim is never an intellectual reconstruction of the concrete fact, but a shaping of that dark image into a luminous idea.[51]

The above statement describes the nature of Jung's thinking, but I believe it also applies to Freud and demonstrates that Freud was indeed an introvert and not an extravert. Neither Jung nor Freud were primarily oriented toward the outer world nor were they interested in first gathering data and then formulating a hypothesis. Like Einstein and all intuitive thinkers, they first formulated a hypothesis and then sought its verification through experiments or facts. Given the scientific bias of his era, Freud presented his ideas as derived from objective data. But anyone familiar with his work knows that Freud used and even manipulated facts to suit his theories. When scientific data did not support his ideas—for example, the lack of evidence for Lamarck's theory of acquired characteristics—he simply ignored the lack of evidence and stuck to his Lamarckian hypothesis of cultural transmission. Thus, both Jung's and Freud's theories are never intellectual reconstructions of concrete facts; they are, in Jung's evocative words, a shaping of symbolic images hovering darkly before the mind's eye into luminous ideas.

In its extreme form, extraverted thinking becomes paralyzed by the sheer data it tends to observe and accumulate. Similarly, introverted thinking carried to an extreme will force the facts to serve the inner image or ignore them completely to give the subjective fantasy free play. This type of thinking, Jung writes, "will have a mythological streak which one is apt to interpret as 'originality' or, in more pronounced cases, as mere whimsicality, since its archaic character is not immediately apparent to specialists unfamiliar with mythological motifs."[52] Although the introverted thinker may feel that the facts on which the idea is based are responsible for its validity, actually, the idea "derives its convincing power from the unconscious archetype, which, as such, is eternally valid and true," and consequently, "the subjective power of conviction exerted by an idea of this kind is usually very great."[53] Again, Jung is speaking of himself, but the statement applies to Freud as well: for example, Freud's conviction of the rightness of his sexual theory.[54]

After outlining the characteristics of an introvert's thinking, Jung proceeds to describe the introverted thinker's personality, particularly as it affects others. The introverted thinker appears somewhat enigmatic because his relation to others wavers between indifference and aversion. She or he "may be polite, amiable, and kind, but one is constantly aware of a certain uneasiness," which stems from a defensive posture: the other may prove to be a nuisance by doubting or disputing the introverted thinker's ideas.[55] Thus, "in his personal relations he is taciturn, or else throws himself on people who cannot understand him, and for him this is one more proof of the abysmal stupidity of man."[56] Moreover, "his judgment appears cold, inflexible, arbitrary, and ruthless, because it relates far less to the object than to the subject."[57] He "never shrinks from thinking a thought because it might prove to be dangerous, subversive, heretical, or wounding to other people's feelings . . . [and] in the pursuit of his ideas he is generally stubborn, headstrong, and quite unamenable to influence."[58] One is reminded of Freud's fearless proposal of his sexual theories and of his anti-religious writings, particularly the book on Moses, which he insisted on publishing in the midst of the Nazi persecution of German Jews. Jung was equally obtuse by raising the question of racial and ethnic differences between Jews and other Europeans during the same period.

An intensification of the above traits, Jung continues, leads to a lack of flexibility and the shutting off of all outside influences. Here again, and in what follows, Jung must have had Freud in mind, although he is at the same time describing his own tendencies.

> His tone becomes personal and surly. . . . He begins to confuse his subjective truth with his own personality. Although he will not try to press his convictions on anyone personally, he will burst out with vicious, personal retorts against every criticism, however unjust. Thus his isolation gradually increases. His originally fertilizing ideas become destructive, poisoned by the sediment of bitterness.[59]

"Bitterness" is the term Jung used in his later life to describe the emotional condition in which Freud found himself as a result of his dogmatism. But Jung must have struggled with that feeling as well. Jung's own vicious outbursts and personal retorts against every criticism are amply documented and account for his inability to maintain intellectual friendships, particularly with male colleagues and associates. In his description of the introverted thinking type, Jung acknowledges that this type tends to have bad experiences with colleagues and rivals, for he is clumsy about currying their favor and as a rule only "succeeds in showing them how entirely superfluous they are to him."[60] Still, while outsiders may experience the thinking introvert as distant, inconsiderate, arrogant and domineering, "his closest friends value his intimacy very highly."[61] The loyalty of many close friends of Freud and Jung certainly attest to the validity of this statement.

As a teacher, the introverted thinking type is limited because he is not interested in his students or in their intellectual development. Teaching is a forum in which he can present his own ideas or work out a theoretical problem that concerns him. He may be a poor teacher as his thought is occupied with the subject and not with its presentation or with the students' assimilation of the material. In addition, although the inner structure of his thoughts may be clear to him, "he is not in the least clear where or how they link up with the world or reality."[62] Consequently, he has a difficult time conveying his idea to others, and at the same time finds it difficult to grasp that "what is clear to him may not be equally clear to everyone."[63] As for his written work, his style is "cluttered with all sorts of adjuncts, accessories, qualifications, retractions, saving clauses, doubts, etc., which all come from his scrupulosity. His work goes slowly and with difficulty."[64] When it comes to sending his ideas out into the world,

> he never introduces them like a mother solicitous for her children, but simply dumps them there and gets extremely annoyed if they fail to thrive on their own account. . . . If in his eyes his product appears correct and true, then it must be so in practice, and others have got to bow to its truth. Hardly ever will he go out of his way to win anyone's appreciation of it, especially anyone of influence.[65]

Obviously, although the above may have been the natural tendency of both Freud and Jung, each worked against his grain and deliberately cultivated people of influence to publicize and disseminate his views. And certainly their power drive also played a role in helping them overcome these tendencies.

In practical matters the introverted thinker is often gauche, remarkably unconcerned or childishly naïve; "ambitious women," Jung adds, "have only to know how to take advantage of his cluelessness in practical matters to make an easy prey of him."[66] Additionally, the introverted thinker's feeling is undeveloped and unconscious, resulting in its "primitive extraverted character."[67] This accounts for many of his troublesome encounters with both men and women.

As deeply introverted as Jung may have been by temperament, the drive toward maturation forcefully engaged him in the usual extraverted requirements of the first half of life—education, career, marriage. Jung's break with Freud occurred in his 38th year, a midpoint in life that often announces itself through an internal or external crisis, or a combination of both. Jung, like Adler before him, used Freud as a *Gegenspieler*. The term is Adler's and means an "opposing player," someone to work against in order to define oneself. But for Jung, Freud also carried the projection of an archetypal father figure, much more so than his own father, whom Jung experienced as weak and ineffective. For example, even in matters of religion, Jung's father, a Protestant minister, had essentially lost his faith and was simply holding on to it for lack of anything better. Freud, on the other hand, was firmly convinced of the truth of his theoretical premises and insisted on a personal commitment to them on the part of his followers. Freud therefore played a vital role in Jung's individuation, for Freud had no difficulty in taking a stand and asserting his authority. Jung sorely needed the encounter of opposing Freud to discover his own standpoint and his own authority. In a telling remark, when asked why his most talented disciples had broken away from him, Freud replied: "Precisely because they, too, wanted to be Popes."[68]

After their breaks with Freud, Adler and Jung went their separate ways. In keeping with their temperamental dispositions, Adler proceeded to engage in extraverted organizational activities, lecturing and teaching, while Jung retreated into his inner world. He resigned his position as lecturer at the University of Zurich, where he had every expectation of a professorship: a position which in Switzerland, to this day, carries significant power and prestige. He also stopped reading professional books and journals. He observed, "I found myself utterly incapable of reading a scientific book. This went on for three years. I felt I could no longer keep up with the world of intellect."[69]

Confrontation with the unconscious

After parting with Freud, Jung writes, "a period of inner uncertainty began for me. It would be no exaggeration to call it a state of disorientation. I felt totally suspended in mid-air, for I had not yet found my own footing."[70] The old question of faith that had bedeviled his father now afflicted him. He realized that in spite of having written a book on the myths with which human beings have always lived, he himself had no myth to live by: for the Christian myth was no longer alive for him and he always had difficulties with Freud's theories as a compass with which to orient his personal and professional life. With his patients, therefore, he resolved "not to bring any theoretical premises to bear upon them, but to wait and see what they would tell of their own accord."[71] Jung soon discovered that, at least with dreams, the suspension of a theoretical point of view proved to be fruitful; for the "interpretations seemed to follow of their own accord from the patient's replies and associations."[72] That was a startling discovery and opened the way for an approach to dreams which relied on sticking closely to the images and contents of a dream, rather than forcing it into a preconceived theory based on ideas of wish-fulfillment, displacement and repression.

The 1913 break with Freud and subsequent withdrawal from the outer world activated Jung's inner life. An incessant stream of vivid dreams, fantasies and powerful emotions assaulted him: "I stood helpless before an alien world; everything in it seemed difficult and incomprehensible.

I was living in a constant state of tension; often I felt as if gigantic blocks of stone were tumbling down upon me. One thunderstorm followed another. My enduring these storms was a question of brute strength."[73] As with his childhood dreams and visions, he found that he could not talk about these unsettling inner events now totally preoccuping him. Jung does not mention in his autobiography, or perhaps the fact was excised, that it was during this trying time that he became intimate with Toni Wolff. She served as his psychological and intellectual confidant who supported him through this critical period of his life.

Jung knew that Nietzsche, Hölderlin and many others had been shattered by similar inundations of unconscious contents. He did yoga exercises to calm himself and to hold his emotions in check. But as soon as he regained a sense of balance, he again opened himself up to the onslaught. He found that if he "managed to translate the emotions into images—that is to say, to find the images which were concealed in the emotions—I was inwardly calmed and reassured."[74] Jung began to illustrate his dreams and engage his emotions in dialogue, or give them other visible means of expression. At first, in keeping with psychoanalytic expectations, he thought the psychic pressures may have had to do with past traumas. He reviewed the events of his life at least twice, but came up with nothing that offered a satisfactory explanation. In the end, he decided to undergo the process as a scientific experiment:

> I . . . conceived my voluntary confrontation with the unconscious as a scientific experiment which I myself was conducting and in whose outcome I was vitally interested. Today I might equally well say that it was an experiment which was being conducted on *me*. One of the greatest difficulties for me lay in dealing with my negative feelings. I was voluntarily submitting myself to emotions of which I could not really approve, and I was writing down fantasies which often struck me as nonsense, and toward which I had strong resistances. For as long as we do not understand their meaning, such fantasies are a diabolical mixture of the sublime and the ridiculous. It cost me a great deal to undergo them, but I had been challenged by fate. Only by extreme effort was I finally able to escape from the labyrinth.[75]

The record of his voluntary psychosis and his loving attention to the contents that threatened to overwhelm him is now available in the recently published *Red Book*. I should point out that Jung was well prepared for the confrontation. He had spent nearly ten years working closely with schizophrenic patients at the Burghölzli psychiatric hospital in Zurich. Also, in 1912, he completed a detailed mythological analysis of the schizophrenic fantasies of a young American woman, pseudonymously known as Frank Miller. The study was published in two parts in a German language journal under the title of *Wandlungen und Symbole der Libido* ("Transformations and Symbols of the Libido") and precipitated his break with Freud. Nevertheless, it took enormous courage to risk the possibility of a psychosis from which he might never emerge; and he was aware of the fact. It came to pass that by paying close attention to the contents assailing his conscious mind and trying to grasp their meaning and import—as he had done with his schizophrenic patients and with the Miller fantasies—he was able to retain a modicum of sanity and, in time, heal himself. Looking back, we can now regard his experience as a shamanistic initiation, a creative illness that broadened the scope of his personality, restored his balance and made it possible for him to heal others.

Jung began to emerge out of this emotional crisis toward the end of World War I. He was aware of the synchronicity between his personal struggles and the war. He knew that the personal psyche is contained within the collective psyche and may, therefore, be disturbed by events not of its own making. In such cases, he observed, the problem seems personal, for the personal psyche is actually troubled, but at least part of the cause must be sought in the disturbance in the social atmosphere or the overall collective situation.[76] One sees the possibility in the case of Jung, particularly since in October 1913, he had the following vision:

> I saw a monstrous flood covering all the northern and low-lying lands between the North Sea and the Alps. When it came up to Switzerland I saw that the mountains grew higher and higher to protect our country. I realized that a frightful catastrophe was in progress. I saw the mighty yellow waves, the floating rubble of civilization, and the drowned bodies of uncounted thousands. Then the whole sea turned to blood. This vision lasted about one hour. I was perplexed and nauseated, and ashamed of my weakness.[77]

Two weeks later the vision returned even more vividly and with greater emphasis on the blood. A voice said: "Look at it well; it is wholly real and it will be so. You cannot doubt it."[78] That winter someone asked his opinion about the unfolding political events; he replied he had no thoughts about the matter, but only saw rivers of blood. At first he thought the vision might portend a political revolution, but in the winter of 1913 that seemed inconceivable, and so he concluded that the visions had to do with his psychic state, that he was on the verge of an impending psychosis. When war broke out in August 1914, he was able to put the visions in a proper context: "Now my task was clear: I had to try to understand what had happened and to what extent my own experience coincided with that of mankind in general."[79]

As the war was winding down in the winter of 1918–19, Jung, too, began to emerge from his private hell. He was on military duty at Château d'Oex as *Commandant de la Région Anglaise des Internés de Guerre* and began the practice of drawing a small circular representation of his inner state of mind. He did not really understand what he was doing, but these cryptograms of the state of his self seemed highly significant and he "guarded them like precious pearls."[80] Much later, he learned that these circular drawings resembled mandalas and represented the self, the mid-point or center of one's personality. It was during these years, he writes, that he began to understand that the self is the goal of psychological development:

> There is no linear evolution; there is only a circumambulation of the self. Uniform development exists, at most, only at the beginning; later, everything points toward the center. This insight gave me stability, and gradually my inner peace returned. I knew that in finding the mandala as an expression of the self I had attained what was for the ultimate. Perhaps someone else knows more, but not I.[81]

Soulfulness

As we shall see in the following chapter, Jung was not a mild-mannered person. In his outward demeanor, particularly as a young man, he was arrogant, obstinate and authoritarian. These are not qualities generally associated with a soulful temperament and in Jung's case, I believe they were essentially persona and ego traits. Jung's inner life, as we have seen from a description of his childhood, was deeply connected to soul. In his Introduction to *Man and His Symbols*, Jung provides a summary of attributes characteristic of soul: fantasy, dreams, vague feelings, moods, memories, prophetic hunches, imagination, reflection, receptiveness to the irrational, a relationship with the unconscious, feeling for beauty and a love of nature. (Three of these aspects found their way to the title to his autobiography, *Memories, Dreams, Reflections*.) But, as with every major symbol and archetypal image, the opposite balancing qualities are also present. In addition to its imaginal and other-worldly orientation, soul is also connected to material reality, present in everyday life experience and enamored of intimate connections with people, ideas and things. Thus, Jung's repeated insistence that he was an empiricist in theory and practice was motivated by his soulful nature; for it was his soul that compensated his highly intuitive, pneumatic nature and kept him grounded in reality and everyday experience. It is important to keep in mind that empirical reality is the product of an interaction between imagination and sense data, with soul or psyche serving as mediator between *intellectus*, intellectual concepts, and *res*, sensually perceived objects. All forms of reality or being, Jung argues, are therefore either derived from or indirectly experienced within the psyche, and *esse in anima*, that is, "being in soul," is the only reality or form of being that we can experience directly.[82] Consequently, as we saw earlier, in contrast to Freud's "Eros" and Adler's "will to power", Jung based his psychology on the "principle of imagination,"[83] which is founded on the primacy of soul and its imaginal language.

In his seminal book, *Re-Visioning Psychology*, James Hillman, who devoted his life's work to an elaboration of this imaginal principle of Jungian psychology, argues that if one examines the nature of soul, it turns out to be related primarily to depth, to the underworld and to death.[84] Depth psychology, in his reading, is soul psychology. It is no surprise, therefore, that Jung plumbed the depths of the psyche. In the course of that exploration he discovered the soul of humanity. To differentiate this deeper level of the soul from the personal unconscious or subjective psyche, he called it the "collective unconscious" or the objective psyche. He sought to demonstrate the existence of this universal soul of humanity and define its characteristics through the study of anthropology, religion and mythology.

Penetrating still deeper, with his investigation of alchemy, Jung encountered the soul of the world, the *anima mundi*. A central alchemical myth states that the world soul has fallen into *physis* and needs to be liberated through the redemptive work of the alchemist. Jung's psychological reading of the alchemical myth and opus led him to conclude that the ancient alchemists, through intuitive knowledge and unconscious projection, surmised that matter is not inert, but animated by its own aims and capable of interacting with the human psyche. The ancient science of astrology, which informed the alchemists' work, is based on a similar principle. These ruminations about the connection between matter and psyche inspired Jung to formulate the hypothesis of the *unus mundus* and the principle of synchronicity.

Jungian psychology, as it peers into the depths of the psyche, encounters matter, while contemporary physics, as it explores the subatomic realm of matter, encounters the psyche. Marie-Louise von Franz notes, "Every physicist today is aware that everything we know about matter in the external world is mental," or more precisely, is a form of psychic mirroring of external reality.[85] The physicist knows that "he devises hypothetical images in the form of mathematical structures that he hopes will coincide with the behavior of the material phenomena observed in the experiment."[86] The modern physicist also knows an "objective" observation of the nature and behavior of subatomic phenomena is impossible; for the very process of observation alters that behavior. This same principle applies to attempts at "objective" observation of inner psychic phenomena, our emotions and fantasies for instance.

Jung was excited by the hypothesis of an inherent connection between matter and psyche; for not only did that possibility bring together two apparently disparate fields of study, physics and psychology, it also carried the prospect of an outside perspective on the workings of the psyche. He writes:

> The strange encounter between atomic physics and psychology has the inestimable advantage of giving us at least a faint idea of a possible Archimedean point for psychology. The microphysical world of the atom exhibits certain features whose affinities with the psychic have impressed themselves even on the physicists. Here, it would seem, is at least a suggestion of how the psychic process could be "reconstructed" in another medium, in that, namely, of the microphysics of matter. Certainly no one at present could give the remotest indication of what such a "reconstruction" would look like. Obviously it can only be undertaken by nature herself, or rather, we may suppose it to be happening continuously, all the time the psyche perceives the physical world.[87]

If I understand Jung correctly, in this early formulation he is proposing that the synchronistic process between matter and psyche is not just limited to unique or parapsychological events, but is the normal manner in which psyche and matter interact *all the time*. Later, Jung evidently refined his thesis and argued that "synchronicity is a relatively rare phenomenon."[88] In contrast, his colleague C. A. Meier continued to argue for synchronicity as a general law and pointed to the relation between body and psyche as an example of ongoing synchronicity.

Meier referred to his idea as the "general theory" and Jung's as the "special theory" of synchronicity, analogous to Einstein's general and special theories of relativity.[89] In the above statement, incidentally, Jung is not arguing for the primacy of either matter or psyche, but for a fluid interaction between the two, similar to the modern conception of the relation between matter and energy.[90]

Aside from the theoretical pursuit of soul in matter, Jung's soulful temperament is evident in his personal life and his generally conservative attitude; for soul ties one to concrete reality, to earth, country, community and family. Jung recognized and honored traditional associations. For example, it was important to him that he was able to use his grandfather's tobacco pouch. He willingly fulfilled his annual Swiss army service well into his 40s and took seriously all other obligations of a Swiss citizen. As much as he was thrilled by travel, by new experiences and ideas, he loved having a stable and concrete connection to the earth. Buying the land on which Emma and he built their house in Küsnacht was an "unforgettable event," he writes.[91] When it came to building a home, Jung wanted a solid traditional house and charged the architect "to create a fortress that transcended time."[92] Shortly before his death, he was still thrilled by the idea of being rooted in the earth: "To think that this was my earth!. . . . This was the earth where I will stay, my earth in which I am standing like a tree!"[93] In spite of prestigious offers from universities in Europe and the United States, he never wavered: "I could not be separated from my earth. And that was that."[94] Obviously he was not only referring to his private plot of land, but to Switzerland as well.

Jung's retreat in Bollingen was another structure built to withstand the ravages of time. It was also the place where he sought to live close to nature. A man from the sixteenth century, he was proud to say, would find only the kerosene lamps and matches new, everything else in the house would be familiar. "I have done without electricity, and tend the fireplace and stove myself. Evenings, I light the old lamps. There is no running water and I pump the water from the well. I chop the wood and cook the food."[95] He was not indulging an eccentricity or pursuing a "back to nature" ideology, but simply trying to make a place where his soul would feel at home. "Body and soul," he insists, ". . . have an intensely historical character and find no proper place in what is new, in things that have just come into being."[96] No doubt with Freud's *Civilization and Its Discontents* in mind, Jung went on to say that it is not the repression of our libidinal nature, but "the loss of connection with the past, our uprootedness, which has given rise to the 'discontents' of civilization."[97] In a similar vein, I think he would argue that the contemporary high incidence of attention deficit disorder among children and adults is the result of over-stimulation by mass media, internet technology and loss of connection with the innate rhythms of nature. A group of teachers once consulted Jung complaining that with children born after World War I they were not able to cover the same amount of material as with previous generations. Jung replied that there were simply fewer external distractions to contend with when he and they were students.

In Bollingen, surrounded by nature and silence, his ancestral soul found a home. Mysteriously, it rose to the surface of his consciousness, and he felt impelled to deal with the questions and issues—which he does not specify—left unanswered by the lives of his ancestors. "I carve out rough answers as best as I can. I have even drawn them on the walls. It is as if a silent, greater family, stretching down the centuries, were peopling the house."[98]

Jung had had an earlier, and much more dramatic, experience with the unanswered questions of the dead in 1916 when he was working on the flood of unconscious material unleashed after his break with Freud. The experience began with a fantasy of his soul having flown away from him. Years later, he understood that such "loss of soul" means that the person's anima has retreated into the collective unconscious, the layer of the transpersonal psyche that corresponds to the mythical land of the dead. There, the soul activates the collective ancestral traces and, like a medium, allows the "dead" to manifest.

In Jung's case, that manifestation took the usual form of haunting and poltergeist phenomena. One of his daughters saw a white figure pass through her room. Another daughter had her blanket twice snatched away during the night. His son had a nightmare so intense that both his parents were required to calm him down. And then, at five o'clock in the afternoon, the front door bell began ringing frantically, with no one there. "The atmosphere was thick....The whole house was filled as if there were a crowd present, crammed full of spirits."[99] Jung "was all a-quiver with the question: 'For God's sake, what in the world is this?'" Suddenly, a chorus cried out: "We have come back from Jerusalem where we found not what we sought."[100] In response, Jung began to compose what has come to be known as the *Septem Sermones ad Mortuos* (The Seven Sermons to the Dead). As soon as he began writing the atmosphere cleared and the haunting was over. "From that time on," however, Jung writes, "the dead have become ever more distinct for me as the voices of the Unanswered, Unresolved, and Unredeemed."[101]

In describing the above phenomena Jung is not implying an actual connection with the dead, as, for instance, the spiritualists would claim. (In this regard I think contemporary psychics who claim to receive messages from the dead are actually reading the information stored in the personal unconscious of the people who consult them about their deceased relatives and friends.) He is simply recognizing that the collective unconscious contains transpersonal contents that are not limited by our present time and space and that the energy contained in those contents can cause synchronistic events in which matter and psyche intertwine.

Adding to its connection with psychic depth, with the underworld, with nature, earth, history and ancestors, soul is also the carrier of our religious function. Jung's careful attention to the promptings of his ancestral soul is an expression of the religious nature of the psyche. Jung liked to define religion as the careful consideration or observation of the archetypal forces that underlie one's daily life: "by 'religion,'. . . I mean a kind of attitude which takes careful and conscientious account of certain numinous feelings, ideas, and events and reflects upon them."[102] Religion in his view, does not rest solely upon tradition and faith, but has its roots in the archetypes. These are the gods, the powers-that-be and "they are continuously present and active; as such they need no believing in, but only an intuition of their meaning and a certain sapient awe, . . . which never loses sight of their import."[103] In recognition of this fact, Jung had carved over the entry to the Küsnacht house the Delphic oracle's pronouncement *Vocatus atque non vocatus, Deus aderit* ("Called or not called, God will be present"). His definition of God, too, had an earthy and not at all a spiritual or theological quality. In an interview a few days before his death he was asked about his idea of God, he replied: "To this day God is the name by which I designate all things which cross my willful path violently and recklessly, all things which upset my subjective views, plans and intentions and change the course of my life for better or worse."[104]

Soul is also in love with beauty. Most men, as can be seen from their fascination with images of beautiful women and with the pursuit of beauty in music, art, design and literature—not to speak of the culinary arts—are seduced by beauty and, if poetically or artistically inclined, devote their lives to it. John Keats' famous verse is really the soul's motto: "'Beauty is truth, truth beauty,' that is all ye know on earth and all ye need to know." For the soul, beauty is the ultimate value, a principle acknowledged by Plato, apparently another soulful man, who equated the archetype of beauty and its beatific vision with the supreme deity.[105]

Jung paid his obeisance to beauty in the aesthetic manner in which he recorded and illustrated his significant dreams, fantasies and visions. As a university student, he was in love with Holbein and the Old Dutch Masters. During his trip to Paris as a young physician, he spent days in the Louvre and other art museums, "to the point of exhaustion," and even tried his hand at painting landscapes of northern France.[106] His writing, although no match for the elegant style of Freud, favors imagery and forms of expression that border on the poetic. Also, unlike Freud's precise formulations, Jung favored a circular mode of expression that reflected his soulful temperament. He realized the style caused confusion and made him difficult to read and he frequently offered apologies:

> I am sorry that I repeat certain things. I always did that in my books. I regarded certain things again and again, and always from a new "angle" because my thinking is circular. I circle around the same question again and again. That is the method that appeals to me. In a way it's a new kind of peripatetic [word missing]. It just works best for me to write this way.[107]

Even his apology is couched in the same circularity of expression. His style resembles the progress of a butterfly flitting about a garden and is true to the nature of the soul, which loves to linger and dwell on things over and over again.

Jung's resolve to keep track of his dreams and fantasies in 1913 as a scientific experiment performed on himself was also a way for him to remain grounded in reality. As he recorded his fantasies, however, a doubt emerged: "What am I really doing? Certainly this has nothing to do with science. But then what is it?" In response, an inner feminine voice answered with authority, "It is art."[108] Jung protested that what he was doing had nothing at all to do with art. The voice again insisted that is was art. This time he responded, "No, it is not art! On the contrary, it is nature." He prepared himself for an argument but there was no response.[109] So he began to think that the "woman within" had no speech centers and suggested she use his. She then came through with a long statement, which Jung unfortunately does not record. He was intrigued that an inner feminine figure should interfere with his conscious aims and have her own opinion about them. He surmised that she must be a "soul" in the primitive sense of the term, and wondered why the designation "anima" was given to the soul and why it was thought of as feminine. In time, he concluded that "this inner feminine figure plays a typical, or archetypal, role in the unconscious of a man, and I called her the 'anima.' The corresponding figure in the unconscious of woman I called the 'animus.'"[110]

He continued writing his fantasies, but now saw them as "letters" to a part of himself that had a different standpoint than his conscious one and that responded with unexpected remarks and observations. "I was like a patient in analysis with a ghost and a woman!"[111] He studied her reactions and attitudes and came to see that she was not an entirely positive figure, but wily and cunning. He felt she could have easily seduced him into believing that he was a "misunderstood artist, and that my so-called artistic nature gave me the right to neglect reality."[112] In other words, if Jung had taken his unconscious fantasies and turned them into artistic representations, he might have been satisfied with that and "felt no moral obligation toward them."[113] He would then miss the fact that the fantasies required some kind of psychological understanding and practical application. "If I had followed her voice," he writes, "she would in all probability have said to me one day, 'Do you imagine the nonsense you're engaged in is really art? Not a bit.'"[114] Thus, he drew the conclusion that "the insinuations of the anima, the mouthpiece of the unconscious, can utterly destroy a man. In the final analysis the decisive factor is always consciousness, which can understand the manifestations of the unconscious and take up a position towards them."[115]

I describe the entire incident and Jung's conclusion because this is his psychological account of the discovery of the anima and because of his emphasis on maintaining a conscious and moral standpoint with respect to the soul's promptings. Many artists, for example, feel their essential task is simply to give expression to their artistic nature. But Jung argues their work is not complete and their personality is certainly not whole or integrated unless they also reflect about the form and content of their creative output.

In the above account of his encounter with the anima, Jung does not disclose that the feminine figure whose voice he heard and to whom he wrote his nightly "letters," appeared in the guise of Maria Moltzer. She was a Dutch physician whom he had met while he was an assistant psychiatrist at the Burghölzli clinic. He was an intensely physically attracted to her, and since she came to represent his anima, it is worthwhile to note that she was "reed-thin," usually called "Sister Moltzer" and "described as nunlike, ascetic, virginal, and pure."[116] The description, to a large extent, also applies to Jung's mistress, Toni Wolff, with whom he began a relationship at the time of his encounters with the anima. We can conclude, therefore, there was something "nunlike, ascetic, virginal, and pure" about Jung's anima. But that was only one side. Emma Jung, his wife, represented the other side. By contrast, she was an earthy woman, a handsome, dignified mother of five children; intelligent, self-contained and practically-minded. The two women clearly corresponded to the complementary sides of Jung's anima. Incidentally, Emma was also Jung's opposite in typology: his dominant functions were thinking and intuition; hers were feeling and sensation. Such direct opposition, with no function in common, does not make for a harmonious relationship.

The two sides of his anima, represented by Toni Wolff and Emma, illustrate the Jungian clinical notion of a split anima. The idea is based on the fact that the anima, like every archetype, is composed of opposites. We see these opposites in the virgin/whore and the virgin/mother dichotomy. With the animus it is the devil/saint and puer/senex pairing. Jung's insistence on keeping both Emma and Toni in his life was an attempt to hold these opposing attributes of his soul together and to avoid splitting off or repressing one side in favor of the other. I do not know whether, at the start, he was conscious of what he was doing, but his actions were certainly in keeping with his later insistence on maintaining the union and tension of opposites; in hindsight, he might have eventually realized the impulse behind his behavior. I also think it notable that Marie-Louise von Franz, who was only 18 when she met Jung and replaced Toni Wolff as his intellectual confidant, developed a personality that was a combination of Emma and Toni, both earthy and virginal.

Jung's soulful temperament was also evident through his interest in the feminine aspects of the psyche and in his appreciation of women. His essay "Women in Europe" argues that "women are far more 'psychological' than men."[117] Men are "usually satisfied with 'logic' alone" or "interested in things, in facts, and not in the feelings and fantasies that cluster round" these facts and which, as far as they are concerned, have nothing to do with them.[118] Men tend to ignore and even deem repugnant everything they consider "psychic," "emotional" or "unconscious."[119] On the other hand, these are exactly the things that interest women: "So it is naturally woman who is the most direct exponent of psychology and gives it its richest content."[120] What modern psychology "owes to the direct influence of women," Jung writes, "is a theme that would fill a large volume."[121] As far as I know, that volume still remains to be written and will have to include the efforts of the notable women associated with Freud, Adler and Jung and of others who came after to critique or develop their theories.

Because Jung felt that women are more psychological and more connected to Eros than men, it falls to them to unify the psyche, which men, with their emphasis on logos and spirit, have sundered by treating it as an impersonal and objective phenomenon. This "tremendous cultural task," he concludes, might signal "the dawn of a new era," namely, the beginning of a psychological relationship between men and women and the healing of the patriarchal split between logos and Eros, between body and soul, spirit and matter.[122]

Jung's soulfulness appears in his connection with alchemy where the feminine principle plays at least an equal, if not a superior role, to that of the masculine. Alchemy is concerned with all the soul issues that the spirit oriented Christian ethos ignores or represses: matter, the feminine and the problem of evil. The alchemical opus consists of an attempt to unite all opposites, often represented by various chemical, theriomorphic and anthropomorphic masculine and feminine images. The union of good and evil, for instance, is personified by the alchemical image of Mercurius, who is dual in nature. As the *prima materia* with which the opus begins and ends, Mercurius, can grant life or death, salvation or damnation, depending upon the inner condition or attitude of the person who encounters it. The goal of the opus is represented as a paradoxical union of the amalgamated opposites and described variously as the philosophers' stone, the squared circle or the hermaphroditic emperor or empress. This union of all opposites is also referred to as *Deus terrestris* or *Salvator* ("terrestrial God" or "Savior"), designations that refer to the incarnation of Christ.

The alchemical notion of a divine image consisting of a union of matter and spirit, good and evil, feminine and masculine influenced Jung's thinking in his book, *Answer to Job*, where he argued for the inclusion of the feminine principle in the Western image of God. Historically, he thought the process began with the entry of the feminine personification of wisdom in the Old Testament book of Proverbs in the fifth century B.C. About two and a half centuries later the "Wisdom of Jesus ben Sirach" or *Ecclesiasticus* depicted wisdom as coeternal with the creator. She was described as the creative breath or "word," or as the spirit (actually, "soul" is the more precise term) of God that brooded over the waters at the beginning of creation.

> I came forth from the mouth of the Most High,
> and I covered the earth like a mist.

I had my tent in the heights,
and my throne was a pillar of cloud.
Alone, I have made the circuit of the heavens,
and walked through the depths of the abyss.
Over the waves of the sea and over the whole earth,
and over every people and nation I have held sway.

(*Ecclesiasticus* 24:3–10)[123]

Note the connection of this feminine manifestation of the creator with the earth and its inhabitants. Similarly in the Proverbs, Wisdom says of herself:

when he traced the foundations of the earth,
I was beside the master craftsman,
delighting him day after day,
ever at play in his presence,
at play everywhere on his earth,
delighting to be with the children of men.

(Proverbs 8:29–31.)[124]

The incarnation of Christ, the appearance of the Holy Spirit in the form of a dove at his baptism in the Jordan River, and his gospel of love were the next historical events that indicated a growing evolution of the feminine manifestation of the Western God image. Then, throughout the Christian era, the veneration of the human Mary as the Mother of God strengthened this connection of the earthly feminine with the heavenly masculine deity. This pressure from "below" eventually resulted in the 1950 papal promulgation of the new doctrine of the Assumption of the Blessed Virgin Mary into Heaven. The dogma states that Mary is united with the Father, and as bride, with the Son. The arrangement moves the heavenly court from a trinity, which is a masculine number, to a quaternity, which has feminine connotations. For Jung, this doctrinal event and its symbolism was welcome confirmation of the changes taking place in the archetypal dominants from the masculine to the feminine. It was also an acknowledgement that "the feminine, like the masculine, demands an equally personal representation" in the Western image of God and that, in turn, points "to the equality of women."[125]

In addition to his recognition of the implications of the papal proclamation of the Assumption of Mary, Jung was keenly aware of the increasing number of visions of Mary throughout the Christian world.

He took the matter further and asserted that when the "longing for the exaltation of the Mother of God passes through the people, this tendency, if thought to its logical conclusion, means the desire for the birth" of a new savior. Here, he is positing that modern Western culture longs for a new myth to address the disorientation of our day. But this time, he thinks, the new savior will not be a religious or cultural hero. On the contrary, the new savior, or in Christian terms the child Jesus, is to be born within the soul of every individual. Jung outlines a startling version of that myth:

> The motive and content of the popular movement which contributed to the Pope's decision solemnly to declare the new dogma consist not in the birth of a new god, but in the continuing incarnation of God which began with Christ. . . . [and] brings about a Christification of many.[126]

The "Christification of many", Jung adds, is a consequence of the descent of the Holy Ghost, the third person of the Trinity who, as symbolized by the dove, is essentially feminine in nature and therefore identical with Sophia or wisdom.

The "Christification of many" is essentially the ensoulment of every individual, a grounding in this life, in this world, and not in the life and the world to come. With this vision of the future, Jung is elevating the principle of soul over spirit. Although the events taking place in the spiritual and cultural life of the West seem to be bearing out his hypothesis, it remains to be seen whether his vision is a pious wish, based on his own soulful tendencies, or whether it will, in fact, become the new archetypal pattern that informs the *Weltanschauung* of the West. Edward Edinger has elaborated this theme in *The Creation of Consciousness: Jung's Myth for Modern Man* and *The New God-Image: A Study of Jung's Key Letters Concerning the Evolution of the Western God-Image.*

9
C. G. Jung: Introverted Soulful Power Pneuma Type: Part II

Power

Lest anyone think that because of his preoccupation with matters of soul and spirit Jung was a saintly man, the account of his relationship to power, his secondary unconscious motivation, will quickly dispel any such notion. Compensatory to his sensitive, soulful nature, Jung had an aggressive and domineering side. As we saw above, once he resolved to overcome his resistance to school, Jung suppressed his introverted nature and "became a hearty fellow who joined in his school mates' games and pranks."[1] A sturdy young man, at age 14 almost six feet tall, Jung was not shy about asserting his physical prowess; he enjoyed roughhousing and was frequently "scolded or punished for aggressive behavior" at school.[2] At the university, his fraternity brothers dubbed him "the Barrel," while his friend Albert Oeri called him "the Steam Roller." His bull-like nature was not merely physical, for later in life Oeri recalled how Jung was able to "keep everyone under his intellectual thumb" as well.[3]

As husband and father, Jung exercised the culturally sanctioned Swiss patriarchal authority: he assumed that his wife's role was to provide a home, look after the children, and offer emotional support for his professional career. There was never any question that her intellectual interests or emotional concerns should receive equal attention. Her role was to serve. These cultural prerogatives coincided with Jung's unconscious power needs and were hardly subjected to scrutiny.

The power relationship between Bleuler and Jung

The account of Jung's formative years at the Burghözli psychiatric hospital and his tempestuous relations with the director, Eugen Bleuler, deserves a separate and lengthy treatment. A number of vignettes illustrate Jung's power drive in that situation. When he began work as "second level assistant physician" in December 1900, the Burghötzli was already a world-renowned center of mental health research and, thanks to its director, Bleuler, it was a remarkably humane and progressive institution.[4] The doctors lived on the premises, usually with their families, and interacted closely and personally with the patients. The patients, whenever possible, participated in their own treatment plans and in the daily operation of the hospital. There was no segregation between the sexes or between doctors and supporting staff. The therapeutic emphasis was on establishing a personal relationship between doctors and patients and it was made clear to everyone on staff that his or her role was to serve the needs of the patients. Moreover, Bleuler asked nothing of his staff that he was not willing to do himself.

When Jung arrived at Burghölzli he was shocked to see Bleuler greet him at the entrance of the clinic and then insist on carrying his suitcase to his room. Jung had come from Basel, the political and cultural center of Switzerland, where formality was *de rigueur* and differences in social class and professional status were strictly acknowledged. His discomfiture increased when the director immediately took him on a tour of the premises, introducing him to doctors and patients having tea together. That evening, Bleuler sat next to him at dinner, alongside patients, doctors and support staff members.

The clinical and social egalitarianism that prevailed at Burghölzli did not offset the ingrained elitist attitudes of the newly arrived physician. In the coming months Jung's authoritarian "Steam Roller" personality asserted itself, so much so that when Auguste Forel, the former director, visited, he is said to have remarked, "Who is the boss in this hospital? . . . Dr Bleuler or Herr Jung?"[5] The "Herr" was a calculated insult and meant to clip the young man's wings. Whether true or not the story gained currency and was repeated for the benefit of new doctors joining the staff. Evidently Forel's rebuke had little effect; Jung may have even savored the implied message of the anecdote. In time, as his scientific reputation grew, Jung's attitude and behavior hardly changed. Colleagues considered him an "opportunistic bully," brash, vain and self-centered.[6] Bleuler found his authority at the hospital constantly challenged and toward the end of Jung's ten year stay, it was clear Jung sought to oust Bleuler from the prestigious chair of psychiatry at the University of Zurich.

Jung's attitude toward Bleuler was condescending, evidently because of the director's modest family background; he spoke of Bleuler disdainfully as the product of "the cross-breeding of a peasant and a school-teacher."[7] Jung considered himself an aristocrat. His maternal grandfather had been president of the association of Basel pastors of the Swiss Reformed Church, and his paternal grandfather served as dean of Basel's University Faculty of Medicine. Later in life, Jung acknowledged that because of his family heritage in Basel, he had a "terribly snooty" attitude: "There I belonged, so to speak, to the aristocracy, and also [the aristocracy] of the mind." In Basel, he remarked, an intellectual tradition was nurtured which one could sense in conversations with people: "With Bleuler all that was missing."[8]

What Bleuler lacked in social position and worldliness did not impede his contributions to the treatment and theory of mental illness, which were innovative and significant. He put an end to the practice of warehousing patients and refined the diagnosis of mental illness, coining the terms *schizophrenia, autism* and *ambivalence*. Jung learned a great deal from Bleuler and acknowledged his reputation as a psychiatrist. But during his apprenticeship, the most positive estimate of Bleuler that he could muster was to say that his supervisor was "motivated solely by a truly Christian ambition not to stand in the way of others," and characterized by "a youthful eagerness to learn."[9] Jung's self-involved attitude caused him to misjudge Bleuler. Behind his egalitarian and easy-going manner, Bleuler had his pride and his own quiet way of asserting authority.

Bleuler, who was Freud's contemporary, was appreciative of Freud's work on hysteria and dreams and had corresponded with Freud for several years. As the association between Jung and Freud deepened, Jung reported enthusiastically to Freud that he had managed to convert Bleuler to Freud's point of view. Freud, during the first decade of the twentieth century, felt professionally ostracized and isolated, and considered Jung's success in recruiting the highly regarded director of Burghölzli a tremendous coup. Bleuler's international reputation in the field of psychiatry provided an umbrella of legitimacy for Freud's fledging movement. An advocate of innovation in the treatment of mental illness, Bleuler went along with the two men. He agreed to serve as co-director with Freud—Jung was the editor—of the first psychoanalytic periodical, *Jahrbuch für psychoanalytische und psychopathologische Forschungen*. In keeping with his own liberal attitude, Bleuler assumed that the journal would provide an open forum for scientific discussion. By 1911, however, he resigned from the International Psychoanalytic Association, citing objections to the unquestioning loyalty demanded by Freud and his inner circle. (This was also the year Adler was forced out of the Vienna Psychoanalytic Society.) Bleuler noted that there might be some value in such an attitude for religious or political institutions, but considered it harmful for science.[10] His resignation may have also been influenced by the fact that during the previous year Jung, his junior colleague and assistant, was elected as the first president of the newly formed association.

As Jung's ambition and self-confidence soared on the wings of his growing reputation and his designation by Freud as the "crown prince" of the psychoanalytic movement, the two men's relationship became more and more strained. Bleuler, the *Jahrbuch's* co-director, was never consulted by Jung, the editor, who made every decision and conferred only with Freud. At the hospital, Bleuler felt that his assistant ignored him; Jung acted "as if he owned the place," and "let no opportunity pass without mocking him."[11] Upon his appointment as editor of the *Jahrbuch*, Bleuler sarcastically called Jung a "scientific giant" and his "triumphant rival."[12] Jung's arrogance had already surfaced in 1907, immediately after his first visit with Freud in Vienna, when he proposed to Bleuler the formation of a private laboratory of psychology with himself as director. The clinic was to be loosely affiliated with Burghölzli, but essentially independent. His second proposal was "that the chair of psychiatry at Zurich University be given to a researcher other than the director of the hospital."[13] It hardly needs saying who that researcher might be. Bleuler, apparently too shocked to respond, simply muttered that he would have to think about it.

What finally brought things to a head between Jung and Bleuler was a four day visit by Freud to Burghölzli in September 1908. Freud spent all his time with Jung and, incredibly, never saw Bleuler, either at his arrival or departure. Neither Freud nor Jung saw fit, simply as a matter of courtesy, to pay a visit to the director of the hospital. The overt snub was too much even for the tolerant Bleuler and within two weeks of Freud's visit he asked for Jung's resignation. Jung's blindness regarding his power struggles with Bleuler is evidenced by his stunned and confused reaction to Bleuler's request.

Both men wanted a graceful departure: Jung did not wish to enhance his reputation as an inconsiderate, disrespectful bully; and Bleuler did not want to be perceived as an embittered and weak administrator. They agreed that Jung would officially resign in the spring of 1909, when classes ended at the University of Zurich, as Jung lectured at the university in connection with his appointment at Burghölzli. Jung was to announce that the desire to pursue his own research was the reason for his resignation and Bleuler would accept the resignation with public expressions of regret. But Bleuler did get the last word: in January 1909 he bypassed Jung, for the second time apparently, and appointed one of Jung's colleagues, Franz Riklin Sr, to a permanent lectureship position at the university.

Again, Jung was shocked. Still full of himself, he simply assumed he would continue to teach even after his resignation. Jung's lectures were extremely popular and were held in the largest room in the building. Jung reasoned that his ascendant scientific reputation would assure a continuing lectureship and in time, a professorship at the university. Even before his proposal to take over the chair of psychiatry from Bleuler, Jung entertained the notion that the university might create another chair of psychology that would focus primarily on theoretical rather than clinical matters, the latter being Bleuler's province. But Bleuler, a respected faculty member, found a number of allies at the university with serious reservations about Jung, both because of his public advocacy of Freud's theories and his growing reputation as a womanizer. Looking at the entire relationship between Bleuler and Jung, one observes a struggle between two strong-willed men with different ways of asserting power. Alphonse Maeder, an assistant physician at Burghölzli who witnessed the final stages of the battle, commented that it was a conflict of "'two masters,' locked in mortal combat, 'fighting to the death.'"[14] To the extent that Jung perceived Bleuler as a father figure, it was also a struggle between a father and son, almost a rehearsal for his fateful conflict with Freud.

Jung's lectures at the university became a social event for many of Zurich's wealthiest women. The contents of his lectures were often directly applicable to personal psychological issues and peppered with insightful observations about a broad range of cultural matters. Eager for intellectual stimulation and enlightenment, some of the women formed study groups to discuss his lectures and the sources he cited. These *Zürichberg Pelzmantel*—"fur-coated ladies" from the most affluent part of town—became Jung's devoted acolytes. They "marched with poise and self-assurance into his every lecture, commandeering the best seats and thereby earning the enmity of the students, who had to stand at the rear of the auditorium."[15] Deirdre Bair, in her remarkably detailed biography of Jung, summarizes and even essays an analysis of Jung's charismatic and inflated personality at this juncture in his life.

> Jung seems always to have taken his good looks and good health for granted, but now, with so many women eager to fall at his feet, he became conscious of the power over others, particularly women, his

> handsome physical appearance gave him. As the women fluttered before him, his numerous flirtations grew increasingly dangerous and, by extension, increasingly exciting. And, as he could not hope to achieve satisfaction from being the principal provider in his current situation because Emma's fortune was simply too vast, it was easier as well as more interesting and more personally satisfying to find *power* through approval and affection elsewhere. His problem was that the strong-willed Emma was ready to put the damper to his flame with her flat-out assertion that she would divorce him rather than suffer further, deeper humiliation. He knew she meant it.[16]

The "further, deeper humiliation," probably refers to those flirtations, a number of which may have gone beyond mere flirtation, as well as Jung's tangled relationship with Sabina Spielrein, who publicly intimated she was having an affair with him. The salacious gossip provoked by the situation included a rumor that he would divorce Emma and marry Spielrein.

The power relationship between Freud and Jung

When, in 1907, Jung began his association with Freud, he was taking a calculated risk with his career; for he was fully cognizant that the pioneer of psychoanalysis was a *persona non grata* in academic circles. On the other hand, having married the second wealthiest heiress in Switzerland, Jung did not have to be concerned about employment. Jung's initial pleasure in Freud's approval and his deference to the older man was expressed in his stated desire to "'enjoy' the friendship 'not as one between equals but as that of father and son.'"[17] Both men must have known that such a relationship inevitably entailed conflict. Freud was the first to voice his suspicion of a secret death wish on the part of the son toward the father, and Jung, needing to assert his independence, eventually rebelled against Freud's paternal authority.

In the beginning, however, Jung basked in Freud's fatherly feelings toward him. He confessed to Freud, in the context of their intimacy, that there was a "hysterical" component to his personality that needed "to make an impression on people and to influence them."[18] Freud assured him that these were precisely the traits that made him a good teacher and leader. Jung also admitted that a "feeling of inferiority towards you frequently overcomes me," and concomitantly, that he was pleased by Freud's attention: "I am, after all, very receptive to any recognition the father bestows."[19]

In later years as their association became strained, Emma Jung, protective of both men, tried to reframe the nature of their relationship. Why, she wrote to Freud, was he looking at Jung "with a father's feeling: 'He will grow, but I must dwindle'?" Why did Freud think that in his mid-50s, he had to pass on the reins of succession instead of basking in "well-earned fame and success?" She concluded, "Don't be angry with me. . . . with warm love and veneration."[20] But her kindly advice either fell on deaf ears or came too late.

After their joint visit to Clark University in 1909, both men found an interest in exploring the psychology of religion. Since this was primarily Jung's concern, an unconscious rivalry may have sparked Freud's pursuit of the topic. They had been discussing the need for applying the principles of psychoanalysis to the cultural sciences, and Freud lamented the dearth of scholars of mythology and religion who could do such work, "otherwise we will have to do it all ourselves."[21] Jung interpreted the complaint as an expression on Freud's part that he considered him "unfit for *this* work."[22] Evidently, Jung felt that the application of psychoanalysis to religion and mythology was his special bailiwick and his pride was piqued. When Freud asked for advice about material that would eventually appear in *Totem and Taboo*, Jung was pleased but added, "It is, though, very oppressive to me, if you too become involved in this area, the psychology of religion. You are a dangerous competitor, if one wants to speak of competition."[23] In response to Jung's feeling that by calling for scholars in myth and religion he was questioning his capacity in these areas, Freud wrote: "Just rest easy, dear son Alexander, I will leave you more to conquer than I myself have managed, all psychiatry and the approval of the civilized world, which regards me as a savage!"[24]

Freud was slow to respond to Jung's 1912 publication, *Transformations and Symbols of the Libido*. He critiqued the first part of the work, but Jung was anxious about the second part, where he abandoned Freud's sexually based concept of libido. By this time, also, their personal relationship had cooled. Emma Jung, always the mediator, saw Freud's reticence in a favorable light, writing to Freud that by withholding his views "he permitted Jung a semblance of independence that did not 'reinforce this father–son relationship.'"[25]

Freud had other "sons" besides Jung, among them Karl Abraham, who had worked for three years at Burghölzli under Bleuler and Jung, Sandor Ferenczi and Ernest Jones. All were jealous of each other and watchful for any sign of favoritism on the part of the patriarch. When Freud praised a paper by Ferenczi, Jung wrote confessing to "an ignoble feeling of envy."[26] When Ferenczi tried to drive a wedge between Freud and Jung, playing on Freud's reservations about "Zurich occultism," Freud wrote to Ferenczi that he understood how much Ferenczi wanted to "triumph," but, Freud warned, he would, "see to it that you will not succeed."[27] When Abraham expressed negative feelings about Jung and the Zurich group, Freud responded that he hoped Abraham's "competitiveness" was not clouding his judgment, adding, "Why cannot I harness Jung and you together, . . . your precision and his élan?"[28] As for the highly extraverted and overtly ambitious Ernest Jones, Jung encountered his own shadow in the man, comparing him to a "little bulldozer, eager to bury him and take his place with Freud."[29] It is true that Jones, perhaps more than any other of Freud's disciples, was resentful of Jung's privileged position and spared no effort to exacerbate the differences and tensions between the two men, resorting to gossip, slander and outright lies.[30]

Jung knew his favored status aroused envy and jealousy among Freud's followers. With the founding of the first psychoanalytic journal and Jung's appointment as editor, "political machinations were frenzied, as all of Freud's followers jockeyed for position."[31] When Jung was elected president of the International Psychoanalytic Association, Freud's Viennese colleagues were dismayed that he handed over so much power to Zurich and succeeded in modifying the terms of the office: Jung's presidency was limited to two years instead of being permanent. But Freud was adamant in wanting Jung as his heir. In a letter to Ludwig Binswanger drafted in the midst of his struggles with Adler, he wrote, "when the realm I have founded is orphaned . . . no one but Jung should inherit it all."[32]

Ernest Jones, in his biography of Freud, writes that Jung's failure to perform his duties as president and head of the international psychoanalytic movement and not the theoretical disagreement over the concept of libido was responsible for Freud's increasing disillusionment with Jung. Freud had counted on Jung to liaise among the various societies, supervise the administrative work of congresses and edit the *Jahrbuch*. Freud hated administrative work and wanted to be free to pursue his research and writing. At the same time, he wanted to maintain control of the psychoanalytic movement and hoped that Jung, his presumed heir, would serve as his surrogate. He expected the energetic younger man, who loved to lecture and travel and was fluent in German, English and French, to shoulder these responsibilities. Freud was dismayed that Jung seemed uninterested in the prestige and power the position entailed, and seemed to have other priorities. Freud may have also been falsely confident because of Jung's Swiss heritage, with its reputation for probity and attention to detail; it soon turned out that Jung, like Freud, had no interest in administrative work. Jung came to resent the time these responsibilities took away from his own research and writing, and expressed his frustration in a curt and abrupt manner toward his colleagues. No doubt his impatience was compounded by his personality, as Alphonse Maeder observed, "Jung was, in his own way, as authoritarian as Freud; he had no understanding or nor taste for exchanging points of view with collaborators. He was very short with them . . . and made all the decisions."[33] Also, Jones noted, Jung "worked best alone and had none of the special talent needed for cooperative or supervisory work with other colleagues. Nor had he much taste for business details, including regular correspondence. In short he was unsuited to the position Freud had planned for him as President of the Association and leader of the movement."[34] I think it noteworthy that as much as both Freud and Jung loved authority, power was their secondary motivation; when faced with a choice between the exercise of power and the pursuit of creative endeavors, each opted for the latter.

As one reads the correspondence between the two men during the period of their estrangement (1912–13) and follows Jung's reactions, it is fairly clear that Freud did not want to be rid of Jung; on the contrary, he did everything he could to hold on to him. Rather, it was Jung's desire for independence, an aspect of his power drive, that did not let him rest. He also must have felt guilty because of his disavowal of the central tenet of psychoanalysis and consequent disloyalty to Freud. He knew that the libido theory was the touchstone that divided Freud's followers from his enemies and consequently expected Freud to ostracize him, as he had ostracized Adler. Jung, therefore, looked for any sign of disapproval from Freud, and simultaneously, for a pretext to separate and establish his independence. At first he found the disapproval in Freud's reticence about *Symbols of Transformation*. But Freud temporized and refused to use their differences about the concept of libido as a reason for a break. Jung then made a great fuss about Freud's visit to Ludwig Binswanger in Kreuzlingen, a Swiss town not far from Zurich, without informing Jung or inviting him to visit.

When the two men met at a gathering of European presidents of the various Psychoanalytic Associations in Munich in September 1913, they had a tête-à-tête to sort out their differences. They began by trying to straighten out "the Kreuzlingen gesture" as Jung had dubbed it. According to Freud's account of their meeting, Jung admitted that Freud had indeed informed him about the visit and it was his own oversight that made him think otherwise. Jung also acknowledged that he had feared for a long time that his intimacy with Freud, or with anyone else for that matter, would infringe on his independence. Jung confessed that he construed Freud according to his father complex, and was afraid of Freud's censure of his modifications of the libido theory and even of Jung's convoluted style of writing. He admitted that he was wrong to be mistrustful and that it hurt him to be judged as a fool caught up in a complex. Freud continued his account:

> I spared him nothing at all, told him calmly that a friendship with him could not be maintained, that he himself gave rise to the intimacy which he then so cruelly broke off; that things were not at all in order in his relations with men, not just with me but with others as well. He repels them all after a while. All those who are now with me have turned from him because he threw them out.[35]

Freud admitted to one mistake on his part: in a condescending manner, he said that he had misjudged Jung, believing him to be "a born leader." He now realized that Jung was "immature" and "in need of supervision." At the end of the meeting, and in spite of their personal estrangement, Jung promised, "You will find me completely with the cause."[36] But Freud did not believe him and rightly so, for evidently, in the presence of the older man, Jung still could not assert his independence and capitulated to his father complex. That complex, I believe, was at the root of the "kernel of dishonesty" Freud sensed in Jung, when he later reflected on their conversation.[37]

After their talk, they joined others at a luncheon and there was a brief discussion about Karl Abraham's recent essay on the monotheist pharaoh Akhenaten. Someone mentioned Akhenaten's destruction of his father's cartouches on stele and other monuments. There was a difference of opinion about the reasons for the pharaoh's behavior, with Jung insisting that Akhenaten's act was "not as an act of resistance against his father but because he was a creative man."[38] In the course of the discussion Freud fainted. This was the second time Freud had fainted in Jung's presence; the first time was in Bremen in 1909, as they were leaving for their lecture tour in the United States. In both instances the circumstances were similar: Freud's perception of an Oedipal death wish towards him on Jung's part. But it seems also possible that Freud projected his own murderous paternal impulses onto Jung. In his account of the incident, Jung writes that when Freud regained consciousness he appeared utterly helpless and terribly old, and looked at him "as if I were his father, or his mother."[39] Ernest Jones reports that when Freud regained consciousness he uttered, "How sweet it must be to die."[40] Clearly Freud had death on his mind. But, as Louis Breger interprets the statement, it "expressed both his wish to be the passive recipient of love and care and the deathlike fear associated with the disappointment of this longing."[41] Freud told Jones his fainting spell was unfortunate because it made him lose "a portion of [his] authority." Initially, Freud attributed the incident to fatigue, lack of sleep and too much smoking.[42] Upon reflection, however, he recalled he had fainted in the same room of the Park Hotel in Munich 16 years before, during a quarrel with his erstwhile friend Fliess. In a letter to Binswanger, Freud confessed, "repressed feelings, this time directed against Jung, as previously against a predecessor of his, naturally play the main part."[43]

It took several more months and an exchange of letters before the break was final. In the meantime, Jung tried Freud's patience to the extreme, saying that he would stand by him in public, but writing in his letters "what I really think of you." No doubt, he continued, "you will be outraged by this peculiar token of friendship, but it may do you good all the same."[44] Freud finally put an end to their misery: "Take your full freedom . . . and spare me your supposed 'tokens of friendship.'"[45]

The breach was long overdue, for the fact is that Jung had not been standing by Freud in public. In a series of lectures in the United States in the fall of 1913, immediately after his meeting with Freud in Munich, Jung described Freud's concept of the Oedipus complex and his theory of libido as narrowly sexual and stated that it should be regarded "in the more general sense of passionate desire."[46] He presented his deviations from Freud "not as contrary assertions but as illustrations of the organic development" of psychoanalytic theory.[47] This formulation was disingenuous, for already in the summer of that year, Jung wrote to Ernest Jones that his extension of Freud's libido theory in *Symbols of Transformation* was bound to destroy his friendship with Freud:

> I knew that Freud never will agree with any change in his doctrine. And this is really the case. He is convinced that I am thinking under the domination of a father complex against him and this is all complete nonsense. It would break me, if I were not prepared to see it through, the struggle of the past year where I liberated myself from the regard for the father. If I will go on in science, I have to go on through my own path.[48]

The statement with respect to his father complex is contradictory: why the need for liberation if there was no domination? Not only that, the fact is that Jung did not establish his independence on his own by ending the relationship with Freud. Instead, he forced Freud's hand, thereby still giving him the ultimate authority. It appears Jung needed a setting of boundaries—a father's "No!" He provoked Freud to stand by his authority and exercise it. In this respect, Freud served as Jung's *Gegenspieler* and Jung owes him a great debt, both personally and intellectually. Although Freud and Jung went their separate ways, they are, in fact, intimately bound together. And if over time it happens that Jungian psychology does indeed inherit the field Freud founded, the two men will always be viewed as father and son, the one coming first, the other his heir.

The last letter in *The Freud/Jung Letters*, after a gap of ten years, is from 1923. Addressed by Jung to "Dear Professor Freud," the letter refers a patient for treatment. There is no record of a response by Freud, but Freud did accept the patient. I would like to think that the interaction was an attempt on their part at renewing relations; but nothing came of it. Still, the referral by Jung and Freud's acceptance of the patient do point to the possibility that they might have like to be reconciled. The letter is signed, "With respectful regards, Very truly yours, Dr. Jung."[49] Unfortunately, as the section below on Jung and the Nazis will demonstrate, the possibility of any future reconciliation was torpedoed by Jung's machinations during the 1930s when, under the cover of the Nazi attack on psychoanalysis, he sought to supplant the dominance of Freudian psychology with his own.

The power drive: Jung and his colleagues

The official venue for Jung's followers in Zurich was the Psychological Club. The club was endowed by Edith Rockefeller McCormick, daughter of John D. Rockefeller Sr. and the wife of Harold McCormick, heir to the International Harvester fortune. Both Edith and Harold McCormick were in analysis with Jung during the early 1900s and Edith McCormick eventually became a Jungian analyst.

Similar to Freud's association with the Vienna Psychoanalytic Society, Jung held no official position in the club, but with Emma serving as chair, there was little doubt about who held the reins of power. Jung would walk into the club with Toni Wolff on one arm and Emma on the other "with an air of invincibility about him."[50] They entered, as one member recalled, as "a phalanx of power, as if everyone should bow to

Their Majesties."[51] There were three arm chairs reserved for them in the front row; Jung's in the middle, Emma's and Toni's to either side of him. If they did not attend the chairs remained empty. Many members were offended by Jung's blatant bigamous behavior; they sympathized with Emma and were openly hostile to Toni. When Alphonse Maeder, who liked Toni, broached the subject with Jung, Jung exploded: tell them I'll "take her on my knee and hold her there throughout every meeting until they stop hounding her."[52]

During the early years of the club, 1916–18, Jung's presentations consisted of reports on his progress with *Psychological Types*. But even in a circle of sympathetic colleagues, his demeanor was authoritarian. He "became biting and sarcastic if anyone dared to differ" with his point of view "and frequently held the unfortunate person up to ridicule."[53] Eventually, the club members were so cowed that they only asked questions of clarification. Tina Keller, one of Jung's earliest colleagues, was "frequently 'repelled' by him because when others offered their views, 'he could be so sarcastic. He made fun of people in an unfeeling way.'"[54] Keller put her finger on the shadow side of the power drive—absence of Eros.

The issue of Jung's difficulties with Eros surfaced in his discussions with Hans Schmid-Guisan, a Basel physician and psychotherapist, who was also working on the issue of typology. Schmid and Jung knew each other before Jung's break with Freud and were close friends and colleagues. They even intended to publish their correspondence in which they hammered out the initial concepts of Jung's later typology.[55] Both agreed that there were two major types—introverts and extraverts. They also agreed that the introvert was characterized by thinking and the extravert by feeling. Appropriately enough, each of them represented one of the types: Jung, introversion and thinking; Schmid, extraversion and feeling. At this point, Jung had not yet defined feeling as a rational evaluative function and they often spoke of feeling as Eros.

It is disheartening, reading Deirdre Bair's summary of their dispute, to watch how between two reflective individuals, who also happened to be good friends, the misunderstandings typical of opposing types progressively took over the discussion and irrevocably altered the nature of their friendship. Schmid believed "feeling is life;" Jung thought "thinking is life." Jung argued that the "highest value of analysis" lies in knowledge.[56] Schmid contended that "life can take the place of analysis," but in a spirit of compromise was willing to grant that life "can also be a realization of thinking."[57] Jung accused Schmid of being a nineteenth-century romantic and "simply going ahead with relationships."[58] Schmid countered that Jung, with his introverted thinking, was deficient in his understanding of feelings. He pointed out that they espoused "a completely different set of premises," which Schmid defined as two different "ideals," each limited in its validity.[59] Jung, in good typological fashion, insisted that his set of premises was superior and instead of two different *ideals* he thought they were actually speaking about two different *truths*.[60] As the dispute continued in this vein, Schmid observed that if they went on "counter-asserting like this without listening to the other's argument, we shall very soon come to an unedifying dispute about competence."[61] He also sought to keep their theoretical disagreements separate from their personal relationship. But Jung let his side of the correspondence dwindle.

Once Schmid realized they had reached an impasse, he adopted a role similar to that which Jung had taken with Freud toward the end of their friendship and became unsparing in his criticism of Jung. He accused Jung of failing to understand "the most valuable attribute" of the extravert—his ability to love.[62] What is more, he reproached Jung with a failure to accord love a proper place in three areas of his life: in his work, notable by the absence of the theme of love or by its denigration; in his relationships with those close to him; and in his unfeeling reactions to Schmid himself.[63] By those close to him, Schmid clearly meant Emma Jung and Toni Wolff and had in mind the humiliation both suffered because of Jung's lack of empathic feeling. He added: "I will, by God, never bring out this evidence, for it is up to these people themselves, once they have become independent individuals who also acknowledge their own emotional lives, to react to your reactions."[64] Jung was furious with the first two accusations and denied them; as for the third, he acknowledged that there was a "strangely affective, often almost ironically spiteful tone" in his attitude toward Schmid's extraverted concept of love.[65] Jung's admission notwithstanding, their correspondence and creative collaboration came to an end.

Jung then proceeded to develop his typology in keeping with his own predilections, but thanks to Schmid's Eros and, one must add, Jung's surprising tolerance, the two men did remain on friendly terms. Periodically, Schmid still offered an unstinting critique of Jung's "truth." For instance, Schmid did not think much of Jung's Bollingen retreat, describing it as a "'bitterly true' Zurich Lake Idyll":

> In a tower at the Obersee you . . . have adopted the heritage of Nietzsche, a father to no one, a friend to no one, completely self-sufficient, fulfilled by yourself. Across the way, here and there, live a few other male and female introverts, each in his own tower, loving

> humanity in those "farthest away," thus protecting themselves from the devilish love of their "neighbors."[66]

To rub it in, he added a coda: "And now and then they . . . meet each other on the lake, each in his/her motor boat, and prove to each other the existence of human dignity."[67] He also told Jung that with his introversion and lack of Eros he had constructed "a way of life that required the world to respond to him just as he wanted."[68] That construction, of course, is an expression of power. Schmid's critique again confirms the fundamental misunderstanding between extraverts and introverts. It also discloses his regret at not having been able to convert Jung to the perspective of Eros.

As Jung worked to complete his typological model, it is not clear when he separated introversion from thinking and extraversion from feeling and began to regard extraversion and introversion as independent categories that can be combined with any of the four functions. Jung did not take Schmid's perspective into account and allowed no room for Eros in his typology; he defined feeling as a purely rational evaluative function. In their correspondence neither man had mentioned intuition and sensation, which together with feeling and thinking became the four functions of Jung's typology. Schmid's daughter Marie-Jeanne Boller-Schmid, who, interestingly enough, served as Jung's secretary from 1932 to 1952, claimed that Toni Wolff suggested the inclusion of these two functions.[69] The editors of the *Collected Works*, on the other hand, credit Maria Molzer with the discovery of the intuitive type.[70]

By the time of the publication of *Psychological Types* in 1921, Jung had overcome the severe psychological disorientation that plagued him for years after his break with Freud. It is noteworthy that in contrast to his intense preoccupation with the unconscious material welling up in him during these years, his intellectual work was devoted to a description of conscious functioning. His "confrontation with the unconscious," as his psychological breakdown has come to be called, however, was the more important endeavor, and accounts in large measure for his arrogant behavior. For anyone who has engaged the unconscious at its turbulent life-threatening depths, and comes through unscathed, attains a good deal of self-confidence. The encounter is a hero's journey, a confrontation with the possibility of psychological disintegration, an ego death, which may at times lead to physical death. A successful engagement with the depths of the unconscious, however, leads to an assimilation of archetypal energy by the conscious ego personality.

The resulting combination of self-confidence and psychic energy is felt by admirers as charisma and by opponents as arrogance—and that indeed is how almost everyone who met Jung at this time experienced him. In Jung's own terms, this is the psychic inflation characteristic of a mana-personality.[71] The problem afflicts individuals who undergo a shamanic or spiritual training that brings with it an experience of an ego-identification with the archetype of the self.

Jung's inflation was evident during meetings at the club, when he permitted himself liberties that would have been intolerable in anyone else. If he didn't like a speaker or the contents of the talk, "he would sit throughout the lecture . . . harrumphing and guffawing" or talking loudly to Toni Wolff, ostensibly oblivious to the uncomfortable reaction of both speaker and audience.[72] No one, apparently, dared say anything to him. After four years Emma stepped down as chair and, after an interim year, Toni Wolff's brother-in-law Hans Trüb took her place. He wanted to address the situation and proposed a "measure to censure." Maeder seconded the motion, but no one else joined in the attempt to bring Jung's behavior in line.[73]

Prior to Trüb's election Maeder, one of Jung's most loyal supporters during and after his break with Freud, was asked to chair the club and was also nominated by Jung to serve as the first president of the Swiss Association for Psychoanalysis. He declined both positions, openly telling Jung, "You nominate me, but in the background all the strings are in your hand. Only what you want will be done, only what you say will be accepted."[74] A more power-oriented person would gladly have accepted the positions simply for the sake of the title and the prestige. But Maeder evidently was motivated by Eros rather than power. His friends and acquaintances reported that he radiated "a warmth nearly unheard of for a psychiatrist," thawing even Jung.[75]

Hans Trüb was younger than Maeder, and had no personal knowledge of Jung's power struggles with Bleuler and Freud. From all accounts, Trüb, like Maeder, was an Eros type; hence their friendship and similar attitude. From his Eros standpoint, Trüb criticized Jung's approach to psychotherapy as too intellectual and rejected Jung's research into the mythological and cultural aspects of the unconscious as irrelevant to the treatment of patients. He considered the therapeutic relationship as a shared "companionship" in which the doctor suffers with the patient, and wrote a book entitled *Healing Through Meeting*.[76] He came to believe that individuation was not complete without a feeling of social responsibility and the cultivation of relationships with others.[77] (One can hear echoes of Adler's *Gemeinschaftsgefühl*.) As an Eros type, he emphasized the importance of personal relationships and was shocked to hear Jung's rejoinder: "Personal relationships don't count very much for me."[78] Deirdre Bair reports that Trüb "found this remark so shocking that, as his archive shows, he spent the next twenty years, indeed the rest of his life, brooding about what Jung might have meant and trying to puzzle it out in various kinds of writing."[79]

As the new chair of the Psychology Club, he sought to make the club serve as a forum for diverse ideas, arguing that, an exchange among interested colleagues, after all, was its original purpose.[80] In December 1923, he invited the religious philosopher Martin Buber to address the club. Buber had recently published his book, *I and Thou*, which champions the principle of Eros in people's relationships with others and the world. Trüb had met Buber the previous year and the philosopher became "one of the most important influences on his life and thought" and thus "an indirect participant in Trüb's eventual clash with Jung."[81] Jung was not pleased by the introduction of ideas different from his own and successfully lobbied to keep members away so that the audience was embarrassingly small.[82]

Even before this incident, Jung's response to Trüb's temerity to censure him for his callous, anti-social behavior was livid: "Heads will roll over this!"[83] Jung, Emma and Toni quit the club and did not return until Trüb resigned, which happened shortly after the Buber fiasco. Jung's withdrawal was a transparent power manoeuvre, and in the end he prevailed. Once Trüb was gone, Jung returned to the club, Toni became chair, and ruled in Jung's stead for the next 20 years with an iron hand. Needless to say, there were no further attempts to present any views other than those of Jung. Jung's animus against Trüb, whom he originally befriended and who was Emma's analyst, was implacable. He refused to have anything to do with him, and in later years, when Trüb and his wife came to hear Emma speak at the club, Jung simply ignored them. Emma, on the other hand, maintained a social relationship with the Trübs, but made it clear that publicly, she had to side with her husband.

When the C. G. Jung Institute was founded in 1948, Jung again demonstrated his power drive. He insisted on a governing board or curatorium of his own choosing with himself as president. When, in spite of his advocacy, the club members twice voted to reject one of his choices, Jolande Jacobi, he "pulled some very private strings," to persuade several members to change their vote and have her approved.[84] Prestige and power considerations primarily determined his choice of board members. They included: Carl A. Meier, Jung's loyal disciple and professor at the Swiss Federal Institute of

Technology (ETH); Kurt Binswanger, whose name carried international recognition; Liliane Frey-Rohn, daughter of the president of the ETH; and the extraverted, power oriented Jolande Jacobi. The members served for life or as long as they wished, and all power in the institute resided in their hands.

Jung's authoritarian attitude was one of his chief characteristics, and the formation, composition and nature of the curatorium reflected that stance. Even after he had a secure, world-renowned reputation, his tolerance of dissenting views was minimal. In a classic Freudian way, having "murdered the patriarch," he, then, apparently identified with Freud's personality to assuage his guilt. No doubt Jung had his own propensity for authoritarian behavior, but that propensity was strengthened; for he now replaced the patriarch, and, if not in content, then certainly in demeanor, completely identified with Freud. Like Freud, therefore, he welcomed new ideas only if he could show that he had already thought of these ideas, but may not as yet have elaborated them. Similarly, any changes and correction of his theories was his sole prerogative and he entertained dialogue and criticism as long as he was the final arbiter.[85] Jung was not pleased when original thinkers, such as Sabina Spielrein, Philip Wylie and Victor White, who accepted and admired his theoretical constructs, elaborated his ideas in their own way. Each was eventually cut off.

As Freud pointed out to him, Jung seemed to have a particularly difficult time relating to men and keeping them as his colleagues. Freud explained the problem as fear of homosexual intimacy. Indeed, Jung had experienced an adolescent encounter with a man he admired who then shocked him with sexual advances. But Jung's own explanation for his problems with men was that men in psychology "always need to best other men."[86] In this respect he was, perhaps unconsciously, speaking of himself. He noted that he had no problems with men who had established reputations in other fields; but that, of course, begs the question, for they were not competing with him. He also offered another strange explanation for his difficulties with men. The problem, he thought, lay in the fact that men "have a harder time accepting their anima than women [do in accepting their animus]."[87] It is not clear what he meant to say by this. But since the anima is concerned with emotions and relationships, is Jung perhaps inadvertently pointing to a problem from which he himself suffered, namely his inadequate Eros? For that inadequacy certainly accounts for his difficulties with men and once again demonstrates that Power was his chief motivation and Eros, his undeveloped shadow.

In summarizing Jung's relationships with his male followers and colleagues, Deirdre Bair writes that in the last decade of his life, the situation remained the same as it had been from the beginning of his professional career, once he broke with Freud and established his own psychology. She observes:

> There were those who came originally as acolytes interested inspreading his gospel; if they did not drift away, he severed communication with those who had the temerity to question his authority or to offer creative addenda or new insights into his method. The other group consisted of men who came to call on him at Bollingen and stayed, in effect, to sit at his feet, listen to his words, and collect and disseminate everything he said exactly as he said it. This group includes a number of his historiographers who produced books that rank today among the most frequently cited documents in the history of psychoanalysis and the biography of Jung. When they presented his views exactly as he wanted them, Jung tolerated some and befriended others; when they wanted to build upon his work or explain it for their own purposes, he either tolerated them with a certain degree of prickliness or else dismissed them outright.[88]

Bair's account is an objective appraisal of the situation. But in defense of Jung—and Freud for that matter—no one evaluates creative people in the arts in this manner. No one, for instance, criticizes a composer, a painter or playwright for being intolerant of criticism and not allowing others to contribute to or expand their creative work. Yet, in the arena of ideas, there is a feeling that democratic principles apply, that authors of psychological or philosophical theories should be amenable to criticism and engage with those who want to change or elaborate upon their creative initiatives. Both Freud and Jung, like the primeval patriarch Jehovah who was jealous on account of his project, the children of Israel, were possessive of the work they fathered. Each used his power drive to defend his work against all who sought to "bastardize" it. Adler, with all his *Gemeinschaftsgefühl* and Social Democrat convictions, was no different in this respect. Perhaps this is putting the case strongly, but I think the founders of depth psychology would agree with my defense, and with the artistic and religious analogies I employ.

The above argument, of course, stems from my view that depth psychology is a field of knowledge and not a science. Freud, Adler and Jung spoke to their work as *Wissenschaft*, which, in English, is usually translated as "science," while in German, the term means "knowledge," or area of study. They did not think of their work as a science in the strict sense of the term, that is, as a discipline based on detached observation and experimentation. The scientific method is not an appropriate instrument for validating and evaluating data in a field in which the essential components encompass a mixture of symbolism, emotional reactions, feeling judgments, intuitive understanding, and contradictory or paradoxical assumptions and behavior. At best, depth psychology—and I use the term to include all theories based on the study of the unconscious—adheres to the principles of empiricism, that is, knowledge founded on experience. In its practical application depth psychology is a craft, which, in the hands of a master, becomes a form of art. Similarly, when its theoretical principles are addressed by such creative individuals as Freud, Adler and Jung, the conceptual vision opened by these pioneers is breathtaking and inspirational. Thus, in addition to their ground-breaking contributions to psychiatry and psychology, their work has influenced developments in education, literature, art, philosophy, mythology and, in the case of Jung, religious studies and theology.

The power drive: Jung and the Nazis

Discussions of Jung's involvement with the field of psychology in Germany during the Nazi era are clouded by issues of his purported collaboration and alleged anti-Semitism.[89] Jung's power considerations in this context are hardly mentioned. Looking at his activities during this time from the perspective of his personal ambition and power drive may explain more about his motivations than his alleged anti-Semitic or pro-Nazi sympathies.

Given his power drive and his ambition, Jung was not above settling scores and making use of an opportunity to press his advantage. Anger at the dismissive and negative criticism of his work by Freud and his adherents must have influenced his attitude and behavior. Jung's organizational activities on behalf of psychotherapy in Germany and worldwide are, therefore, obfuscated by his conflict with Freud. The Nazi attack on Freudian psychology provided Jung with a chance to even the score with his former mentor and to promote his psychology, or at least to bring it to equal prominence with Freud's in the international psychotherapeutic community. No doubt his inferior Eros also played a role and accounted for the shockingly insensitive attitudes evident in a number of his political statements during this dark period in history.

In my book, *Jung and Politics*, I argued that Jung's initial stance toward Nazi Germany was based on a therapeutic attitude. Diagnosing the Nazi phenomenon as a collective psychosis, he approached the problem in the manner with which he would treat a patient undergoing a psychotic episode. Jung knew from his personal experience that an intense encounter with the unconscious, in spite of the inherent disorientation and potential danger of being swept away by irrational forces, also carried the possibility of a creative renewal. Consequently, he did not want to summarily dismiss and condemn the events taking place in Germany, and hoped that with time the crisis would pass and the nation return to its senses.[90] He was far from alone in that expectation. Freud, too, is said to have remarked that "a nation that produced Goethe could not possibly go to the bad."[91] In 1935, two years after Hitler seized power and the persecution of Jews became official government policy, even the usually hard-nosed Churchill was not ready to condemn Hitler:

> We cannot tell whether Hitler will be the man who will once again loose upon the world another war in which civilization will irretrievably succumb, or whether he will go down in history as the man who restored honour and peace of mind to the great German nation and brought it back serene, helpful and strong, to the forefront of the European family circle.[92]

With his therapeutic standpoint, Jung clearly hoped to contribute to the latter positive developments. Of course, to anyone of Jewish heritage, a tolerant attitude toward Hitler and the Nazis could only be regarded as callous disregard of the plight of German Jews and supportive of anti-Semitism. For Jung's broadminded attitudes were held in the face of Hitler's openly anti-Semitic diatribes in *Mein Kampf* and the official 1933 decrees on boycotting Jewish businesses, stripping "non-Aryans" of all essential rights and condoning anti-Semitic and racist behavior on the part of the German population. Jung's callousness certainly cannot be explained by his therapeutic stance but can be understood as stemming from power consideration; he saw the situation as an opportunity to further his personal and professional ambitions and to satisfy his need for domination and power.

Jung's involvement with the Nazis began with his assumption of the presidency of the International General Medical Society for Psychotherapy in April 1933. The society was an umbrella association that sought to further dialogue among the three major schools of depth psychology, their off-shoots, and other theoretical approaches. Jung and Adler were among the 399 "charter" members when the society was incorporated in 1928. They were joined by many notable independent thinkers, among them Karen Horney, Wilhelm Reich and Frieda Fromm-Reichman.[93] Another member who was to play a pivotal role in the society was Matthias Heinrich Göring, a cousin of Hermann Göring, the future *Reichsmarschall* and second most powerful man in Nazi Germany after Hitler. Freud and other conservative depth psychologists did not join and regarded the association as a conglomeration of "wild psychoanalysts" with unorthodox psychotherapeutic theories and orientations.[94] Ernst Kretschmer, one of the most reputable psychiatrists in Germany, was elected as president, with Jung as vice-president. According to the society's statutes, the vice-president would automatically succeed the president upon the expiration of his term.

Jung was thrilled with these developments. The International Society for Psychotherapy provided legitimacy as well as a forum for his school of depth psychology and served to counterbalance the domination of Freudian theory in the field, particularly in Germany. Jung's analytical psychology had garnered professional recognition in the United States and England, but in terms of scientific and academic prestige in the early part of the twentieth century, Germany was the country that really mattered. Jung's activities and prominence in the German headquartered International Society for Psychotherapy attracted a good number of followers and a C. G. Jung Association was established in Berlin in 1931.

When Hitler came to power in 1933, Ernst Kretchmer's reaction was widely quoted: "There's something strange about psychopaths. In normal times we write expert evaluations of them; in times of political unrest they rule us."[95] In their drive for total control of Germany, the Nazis forced all institutions and organizations to subordinate their activities to their political ideology. Kretschmer refused to serve as president of a "conformed" International General Medical Society for Psychotherapy. The critical comments he dispensed about Hitler, he knew, would eventually force him to resign. He, therefore, began to make plans for Jung to take over as president. Kretschmer hoped that as a Swiss citizen Jung could better withstand the pressure of the Nazis than native Germans, preserving "a modicum of independence for the society."[96] Indeed, Jung did try to convince those with misgivings about the functioning of the society within the political context in Germany that as a Swiss he could maintain a neutral position and, in that manner, serve the overall interests of the organization.

Jung seemed eager to take over the presidency. Endeavoring to appease the Nazi hierarchy by stating that "there are political frontiers even in science," he called for an understanding of the "special circumstances of the time" which forced German doctors "to make a political declaration of faith."[97] He reasoned that his role was to wait out what he and others saw as a temporary aberration in Germany while maintaining the legitimate activities of the International Society outside that country. Of course, these arguments can also be seen as rationalizations for his ambition and his power drive.

To place Jung's attitude and activities in a historical context, it is important to note that Freud also took a pragmatic stand and urged compromise, if not outright appeasement, for the sake of preserving the existence of psychoanalysis in Germany. When Max Eitington, one of Freud's earliest and most loyal followers, was forced to resign because of his Jewish heritage, first as chair of the German Society for Psychoanalysis and then as director of the Berlin Psychoanalytic Institute, Freud, to assuage Eitington's feelings, wrote to him that the overall interest of psychoanalysis required the institute to remain open "so that it may survive these unfavorable times."[98] Ernest Jones, with Anna Freud's support, insisted that all Jewish members of the institute resign. A good number of them protested; Eva Rosenfeld, in particular, complained that if they followed his advice they were agreeing "to become their own executioners."[99] But Jones, anticipating Nazi demands and hoping to forestall the dissolution of the organization, forced all Jews to resign. In the end, the policy failed to produce the desired results. Eventually, "cleansed" of Jewish membership and Freudian terminology, the institute was incorporated into the "conformed" German Psychoanalytic Society.

Freud, Jung and many others felt that if psychotherapy was to have a future it had to maintain a firm foundation in Germany, hence their willingness to compromise and work with the Nazis. Jung had another agenda as well, namely countering the dominance of the Freudians in Germany and Austria. However, in the face of the anti-Semitic onslaught against Freud and his followers, Jung was careful to point out "that he was 'not an opponent of the Jews,' merely 'an opponent of Freud's.'"[100] He explained that he opposed Freud because of "his materialistic and intellectualistic and—last but not least—irreligious attitude and not because he is a Jew."[101] However, Jung continued:

> In so far as his theory is based in certain respects on Jewish premises, it is not valid for non-Jews. Nor do I deny my Protestant prejudice.

> Had Freud been more tolerant of the ideas of others I would still be standing at his side today. I consider his intolerance—and it is this that repels me—a personal idiosyncrasy.[102]

Jung's statement that were it not for Freud's lack of tolerance he would still be "standing by his side" was courageous, but nullified by his inopportune argument that Freud's theory rests upon Jewish premises, and in that regard, is invalid for non-Jews. In order to outflank Freud, he succumbed to an opportunistic stance that played directly into the hands of the Nazis. Desiring to defeat Freud, he provided a cover for the Nazis who condemned psychoanalysis as a "Jewish science." I believe that in large measure it was Jung's objective to defeat Freud and the prominence of Freudian psychology that explains his speaking of "the differences between the Germanic and the Jewish psychology," espoused in complete disregard of the anti-Semitic fever raging in Nazi Germany.[103] Jung's explanation that he was referring only to differences in "national psychology" and not acknowledging the validity of "racial psychology," hardly addressed the political implications of his statement.[104] By pointing out such differences, Jung continued, he meant no "devaluation of Semitic psychology" any more than it would be a devaluation of Chinese psychology to make a distinction between Western and Eastern psychology.[105] Perhaps, in a politically neutral context it is possible to entertain such distinctions, but in the racially charged atmosphere of his day, it is difficult to find any excuse for Jung's statements other than the blindness caused by his personal agenda of defeating Freud and Freudian psychology. Additionally, Jung's attitude reveals the emotional lacuna with respect to Eros already evident in his exchanges with colleagues and friends.

Every shadow has its light and no doubt there were also valid humanistic reasons for Jung accepting the role of president of the International Society in those perilous and uncertain years. In a response to Gustav Bally, a German psychoanalyst who fled Nazi Germany and published an attack on Jung in the *Neue Züricher Zeitung* (27 February 1934), Jung explained his reasons for acceding to the presidency. He could have, he writes, as a prudent neutral, withdrawn into the security of Switzerland, washed his hands of the whole thing and not risked his skin and exposed himself "to the inevitable misunderstandings which no one escapes who, from higher necessity, has to make a pact with the existing political powers in Germany."[106] Interestingly enough, Jung appeals to Eros as an explanation for his decision: "Should I sacrifice the interests of science, loyalty to colleagues, the friendship which attaches me to some German physicians, and the living link with the humanities afforded by a common language—sacrifice all this to egoistic comfort and my different political sentiments?"[107] As things stood, he argued, "a single stroke of the pen in high places would have sufficed to sweep all psychotherapy under the table" and that, Jung felt, had to be avoided at all costs "for the sake of suffering humanity, doctors, and—last but not least—science and civilization."[108] In many ways, Jung was true to his words and did what he could to help his Jewish colleagues. Deirdre Bair comments that in Jung's unpublished correspondence from 1934 onward there are many notarized statements signed by Jung accepting financial responsibility for foreigners admitted to Switzerland. He also wrote numerous letters to acquaintances in the United States and England asking them to accept and help Jewish emigrants. Jung treated many Jewish patients at this time without payment and helped raise funds for German Jewish immigrants.

There is also ample evidence that Jung did everything in his power to outmaneuver Nazi attempts to rid the International Society of its Jewish members. As editor of the society's journal, the *Zentralblatt für Psychotherapie*, he tried to keep the journal neutral and inclusive of all theoretical perspectives and retained Rudolf Allers, who was Jewish, as editor of the book review section of the journal in spite of Nazi protests. When Jung learned that at the 1934 conference in Bad Nauheim the statutes of the society were to be conformed to Nazi policy, meaning that all Jewish members would be expelled, Jung actually managed to subvert Nazi intentions. He asked Vladimir Rosenbaum, a Zurich attorney, to rewrite proposed new statutes with sufficient obfuscations and loopholes to prevent the exclusion of Jewish members from the society. In his post-war recollections, Rosenbaum reports he was skeptical of Jung's attempt to outwit the Nazis. "Pardon me, Herr Jung, but you really are *very young*," making a pun with his name, which in German does mean "young."[109] Jung turned on him in hurtful rage, "How so? . . . Why do you say this?"[110] Rosenbaum tried to explain that he seemed to be "caught in an illusion," for in fact Jung was powerless "to do anything that would help the Jews."[111] Jung would not be put off: "I know this, but I want to! I must indeed try!"[112]

With Rosenbaum's help, Jung did manage to preserve the professional status of the society's Jewish members. They were expelled from the German chapter but maintained individual membership in the International Society, both within Germany and in other countries, if they emigrated. After his work on the statutes Rosenbaum wrote to Jung that he wanted to straighten something out between them. He confessed that because of Jung's involvement with Nazi Germany he had harbored the suspicion that Jung might be anti-Semitic. But after their meeting he was convinced otherwise: "For if you were an anti-Semite, you would precisely not have gotten yourself into a tight spot! . . . I am glad . . . that I can tell you this of all things at this very moment. Allow me kindly to shake your hand."[113]

There is a coda to the story between Rosenbaum and Jung. In 1937 Rosenbaum was arrested for channeling money and armaments to anti-fascist forces in Spain. After being freed from jail, disbarred, penniless and newly divorced, he asked Jung if he could attend the meetings of the Psychological Club. Jung was impressed by the significant dreams Rosenbaum had had while in jail, and gave his permission. The club members however panicked. They told Jung that with Rosenbaum's anti-fascist reputation, it was politically too dangerous to have him join the club or even to attend its meetings.

At this point the story takes a bizarre and unverifiable turn. Jung is said to have sent a letter to Rosenbaum, asking him to come and see him at his retreat in Bollingen. When he arrived Jung did not invite him in, but met him at the gate and said, "Even a mortally injured animal knows when to go off alone and die."[114] I can certainly see Jung making such a statement, for it is in keeping with his character. As sensitive and empathic as he could be during his therapeutic sessions, outside the consulting room he was often brutal and heartlessly cruel. I can also imagine Jung blurting out such a statement if Rosenbaum came to Bollingen uninvited, intruding on Jung's privacy. But it is difficult to envision Jung taking the trouble to invite him to Bollingen, which is not a simple trip, and then meet him at the gate with that pronouncement.

In any case, the story is not finished. Rosenbaum moved to Ascona, Switzerland and within several years established himself as a respected antiques dealer. Olga Fröbe, who hosted the annual scholarly Eranos conferences in Ascona, always invited Rosenbaum to the meetings and made certain to seat him either next to Jung or in his direct line of vision. Fröbe's daughter, brain-injured from birth, had lived in a German institution from which she was taken and murdered by the Nazis. Olga Fröbe clearly felt Jung owed Rosenbaum an apology and hoped the proximity would force reconciliation. But her stratagem apparently had no effect on Jung and the two men never re-established their previously cordial relationship. Again, Jung's lack of Eros is evident in his inability to acknowledge a feeling mistake and rectify it.

By 1936, Jung became openly critical of Hitler and took a dismal view of the future of Germany. He described the situation as one in which "one man, who is obviously 'possessed,' has infected a whole nation to such an extent that everything is set in motion and has started rolling on its course towards perdition."[115] Still, he continued to function as president of the society and editor of the *Zentralblatt* in spite of increasingly embarrassing and compromising machinations on the part of Matthias Göring and the Nazi contingent of the society. Jung waged an ongoing battle with the Nazi leadership of the "conformed" German section of the International Society. For instance, he countered Göring's plans to hold the 1938 meeting of the society in Germany and managed instead, to have the conference in Oxford, England, where upon British insistence, "non-Aryan" lecturers were invited to participate.

Jung also persuaded Hugh Crichton-Miller, a distinguished British psychiatrist and founder of the Tavistock Clinic, to accept the vice-presidency of the society in the face of Göring's "objections to a non-German holding the position."[116] In reaching out to Crichton-Miller, Jung was deliberately seeking to bolster British influence in the society, at the same time preparing for his own eventual departure, as the vice-president automatically became the next president. Jung was reelected president of the International Society at the Oxford conference, and Göring, in a letter to Jung, pleaded with him to stay on: "At this time no one but you can represent our association. I am convinced that other psychotherapeutic movements would try to dominate our association if you do not remain its chairman. Also, for political reasons I think it best if the chairman comes from a small neutral state."[117] Göring's mention of "other psychotherapeutic movements" that would try to dominate the association was a clear reference to the Freudians and appealed to Jung's own political interests.

After the Oxford conference, Jung again thwarted Göring by having the Dutch extend an invitation to host the next scheduled meeting. Jung continued to work with Göring and his cohorts until 1939 when he resigned in response to a second request by the Dutch chapter. Dutch members of the society made their first request for Jung's resignation in 1936; even at that time they felt him too closely identified with Göring's anti-Freudian stance and his goal of "conforming" the activities of the International Society to Nazi ideology. Jung, in response, blamed the Freudians in the Netherlands and not just the German chapter for the Dutch stand. He viewed the criticism as a personal attack. Nevertheless, exactly because of the Dutch anti-Nazi sentiments, Jung sought to have the next meeting of the society in the Netherlands.

By 1939, however, Jung was ready to resign. The ever-increasing power of Germany and the Nazi success in establishing a totalitarian regime, overtook his attempts to maintain a semblance of independence and neutrality for the society. Göring, aware of the political cover that Jung's name provided, delayed accepting his resignation. Jung, therefore, wrote another letter of resignation in July 1940, which Göring finally accepted. Göring then placed Jung's name on the list of banned authors in Germany.

Such, in brief, is Jung's involvement with the Nazis. One should not think that his work on behalf of the International Society for Psychotherapy dominated his life during these years. On the contrary it was something he did almost peripherally, assigning much of the bureaucratic work to others. During these years he maintained a full analytic practice and continued his research and writing. He also traveled to Palestine, Egypt, India, the United States and various countries in Europe, giving lectures during most of these trips. He tried to come to terms with events in Germany by giving a weekly seminar, from 1934 to 1939, on Nietzsche's *Thus Spake Zarathustra*. Like many people, he felt that Nietzsche's philosophy—with its image of the *Übermensch* (superman) and advocacy of instinctive life—was a precursor of Nazi ideology.

By accepting the presidency of the International Society for Psychotherapy in 1933, Jung gambled that he could outflank Freud, and enhance his own prestige and that of his school of psychology. His efforts failed: as an intellectual and a psychologist, Jung was out of his depth in politics. Because of his association with the Nazis and his insensitive and politically damaging statements about the differences between Jewish and non-Jewish psychology, Jung's reputation was tarnished. As a consequence, to this day, his work is summarily dismissed by many people and his contributions to depth psychology are held suspect. Some scholars, Jungians included, purport to find an explanation for Jung's political stance in his theory of the collective unconscious, with its family, clan, tribal, national and transnational layers.[118] I do not share that view, for as I have sought to demonstrate, Jung's politics and statements during the Nazi era were primarily motivated by power considerations and not by an inherent bias embedded in his theoretical formulations.

As early as 1934, Jung knew that by dealing with the Nazis he had "fallen afoul of contemporary history."[119] Yet he persisted in the pursuit of his goals. His attempt to pursue his political agenda under the cover of Nazi ideology failed miserably and accomplished the opposite of what he had sought. After the war he admitted that he had "slipped up" in his expectation that something positive might emerge out of the initial upsurge of spirit and enthusiasm that marked the revival of Germany during the early 1930s.[120]

Reflecting upon Jung's activities under the Nazis, it is possible to conclude that Freud was correct in his premonition that Jung sought his demise; but in keeping with his Oedipal notions, Freud took the matter much too literally and personally. What Freud may have sensed, and what perhaps accounted for his fainting spells in Jung's presence, was the power drive and the competitive nature of Jung that would indeed, in time, seek to supplant Freud and his work.

In 1938, after the Austrian *Anschluss*, Jung and Franz Riklin Sr., who had known Freud in earlier days, dispatched Riklin's son to Vienna with 10,000 dollars to help finance Freud's escape to England. Franz Riklin Jr. reported that Freud was adamant in declining the money, insisting repeatedly, "I refuse to be beholden to my enemies."[121]

Jung's admission that he had "slipped up" comes from a letter written by Gershom Scholem, a renowned scholar of Jewish mysticism, to Aniela Jaffe.[122] In 1947, Scholem received an invitation to the Eranos meeting in Ascona and talked about it with Leo Baeck. Prior to the war Leo Baeck was a rabbi and professor of religion in Berlin who courageously stayed with his Jewish community until deported to Theresienstadt in 1943. He had known Jung quite well before the war but when he visited Switzerland in 1946 did not bother to get in touch with him. Jung learned that Baeck was in Zurich and extended an invitation. Baeck declined. Jung then came to his hotel and they had a long talk during which Baeck confronted him with the accusations of his alleged anti-Semitic and pro-Nazi sympathies. Jung defended himself, citing the conditions he felt he had to work with given the circumstances. But in the end he confessed, "Well, I slipped up." Baeck repeated the phrase to Scholem several times and it remained vividly in his memory. Scholem also said that during their talk Baeck and Jung cleared up everything between them and parted reconciled and on good terms. Baeck urged Scholem to accept the invitation to Eranos, and indeed Scholem did go and participated in the meetings with Jung.

In hindsight, I think that Jung's statement to Rabbi Baeck that he "slipped up" was a "Freudian slip" that inadvertently referred to an accident in 1944 when Jung slipped on ice and broke the fibula in his leg. Only in part did it refer to "the slippery ground of politics," as Marie-Louise von Franz interprets the statement.[123] I believe Jung's subsequent heart attack and illness must also be seen in the light of a guilty conscience and, perhaps, as an atonement for his power-ridden activities and insensitive attitude. The archetypal dreams and visions he experienced during that near-death illness have to be placed in their historical and personal context.

Thus, it was hardly pure coincidence that he imagined the nurse, who nightly brought him food that she had warmed, as an old Jewish woman who "was preparing ritual kosher dishes for me," or that he saw himself in one dream "in the Padres Rimmonim, the garden of pomegranates," where the Kabbalistic mystic marriage of Malkuth and Tifereth, the female and male principles of the Godhead, was taking place.[124] Nor can it be simply chance that he felt he was Rabbi Simon ben Jochai "whose wedding in the after life was being celebrated."[125] The garden of pomegranates then changed to the city of Jerusalem, where the Marriage of the Lamb was consummated. The final image was that of a classical amphitheater, in a magnificent green landscape, and on stage, on a flower-bedecked couch, "All-father Zeus and Hera consummated the mystic marriage, as it is described in the *Iliad*."[126] In every case, he felt, somehow, that he himself was the marriage and was not merely a witness or an observer, indicating the integration of the opposite principles within the archetype of the self in his own psyche.

If dreams and visions are compensatory to conscious attitudes, then these dramatic images served to bring Jung closer to his Judeo-Christian heritage and reunite him with the Jewish people from whom he had become emotionally estranged because of his worldly ambition and his unempathic, rational attitude. These are scenes of the triumph and celebration of Eros, the overcoming of Power in the embrace of Eros. Such was the message and compensation that Jung had to experience in the imagery that would make the deepest and most lasting impression on him—that of the mystical *hieros gamos*, the sacred marriage. When he said to Rabbi Baeck, "I slipped up," those words emerged from the above experience: from his fall, his heart attack, his brush with death—and from the grace that healed his soul and balanced his Power drive with Eros.

Pneuma

As much as Jung was enamored with power in his personal behavior and professional activities, his primary motivation was Pneuma—the world of ideas, concepts, theory, insight, vision and inspiration. Looking at Jung's life-long preoccupation with the various manifestations of the psyche and the subjects he pursued in his research and writings, there can be little doubt that Pneuma was his first and last love; and within the realm of Pneuma, he was particularly fascinated by religious and spiritual issues.

One need only peruse his autobiography, *Memories, Dreams, Reflections*, and the titles of his other writings to note his profound concern with religious questions and with the spiritual aspect of psychology. His doctoral thesis was devoted to a study of spiritualistic phenomena and he retained a life-long interest in ESP, closely following the parapsychological experiments of J. B. Rhine at Duke University. Numerous Jung essays explore the nature of spirit in its various manifestations; those with the term "spirit" in their title include: "the Psychological Foundations of Belief in Spirits"; "Spirit and Life"; "The Phenomenology of the Spirit in Fairytales"; "The Spiritual Problem of Modern Man"; "Paracelsus as a Spiritual Phenomenon"; and "The Spirit Mercurius." But even these are far outnumbered by books and essays concerned with religious and spiritual issues that do not include spirit in their titles. In fact, almost all of Jung's mature writings expound on religious and spiritual topics: *Psychology and Religion*; *Aion*; *Psychology and Alchemy*; *Mysterium Coniunctionis*. Significant essays on these matters include: "The Psychology of the Transference"; "A Psychological Approach to Dogma of the Trinity"; "Transformation Symbolism in the Mass"; his commentaries on "The Secret of the Golden Flower"; "The Tibetan Book of the Dead"; "The Tibetan Book of Great Liberation"; a seminar on "The Psychology of Kundalini Yoga"; and the as yet to be published seminar on the "Spiritual Exercises of Ignatius Loyola"; in addition, there are the essays on "The Psychology of Eastern Meditation," "The Visions of Zosimos," "The Philosophical Tree," and his studies of the mandala in "Concerning Mandala Symbolism" and "A Study in the Process of Individuation." If one compares the subject matter of Jung's work with that of Freud or Adler, Jung's concern with the realm of Pneuma is readily confirmed. In contrast, Freud's and Adler's major contributions to depth psychology and significant publications concentrate on practical and clinical psychological issues.

Dreams and visions

Aside from his professional work, Jung also had a personal relationship with the world of Spirit, and that connection was dramatically revealed in his dreams and visions. A number of Jung's friends and colleagues felt that his accident in the winter of 1944, when he broke his leg and ten days later suffered a heart attack, was a synchronistic event similar to his breakdown during World War I. Near death and in an altered state of mind, for weeks Jung was engulfed by dreams, visions and hallucinations. Uncannily, the dreams and visions returned to themes Jung experienced in dreams during his 1938 trip to India. On that trip, too, his stay in a hospital, necessitated by a severe bout of amoebic dysentery, was marked with vivid dreams, which at the time he found difficult to understand.

Fowler McCormick, his traveling companion on the trip to India, reported that immediately before his illness, Jung was troubled with dreams of red. McCormick conjectured that these dreams had to do with the goddess Kali and the evidence of animal sacrifice they constantly encountered in their travels. I think these were the day-time stimuli that triggered the dreams. For, given his visions of blood prior to World War I, I believe these day-time associations and his dreams of red again pointed to the forthcoming events that would overwhelm Europe and a great deal of the world in another sea of blood. The image of red might also refer to the post-war spread of communism in Europe, China and other parts of the globe.

Jung's other dreams in 1938 centered on the Grail legend. In one dream, he was with a group of people on a quest to recover the Grail. Their goal was to return it to the castle of the Grail from which it had been taken and where it was needed that evening for a "celebration of the Grail." The castle of the Grail stood on an unknown island, divided in half by a sea channel, off the coast of southern England. His companions had fallen asleep and Jung realized he would have to swim across the channel alone and retrieve the Grail from an uninhabited house on that part of the island: "I knew one thing for sure: I have to reach that Grail."[127]

Jung considered the dream one of the most important dreams of his life. On the journey home from India, he reviewed his Grail dreams and concluded that they sought to take his attention away from the fascinating religious sights and impressive surroundings of India, and forcibly turn it back to "the too-long-neglected concerns of the Occident, which had formerly been expressed in the quest for the Holy Grail as well as in the search for the philosophers' stone."[128] It was as though the dream was saying, "What are you doing in India? Rather seek for yourself and your fellows the healing vessel, the *sevator mundi*, which you urgently need. For your state is perilous; you are all in imminent danger of destroying all the centuries have built up."[129] On his way home, when his ship docked in Bombay (now Mumbai), he never ventured ashore, but instead, buried himself in the study of an alchemical text.

Immediately before and during World War II, Jung's creative efforts were devoted to the study of alchemy. He had recently completed the first section of *Mysterium Coniunctionis*, when he broke his leg in February 1944. The dreams and visions that assailed him at this time began with a similar experience he had during his Indian illness. Then, as now, he saw himself floating high above the earth over the island of Ceylon (Sri Lanka) and saw the ocean and the outlines of the Indian sub-continent.[130] But this time his vision expanded to include the "reddish-gold" desert of Arabia, the Red Sea, a bit of the Mediterranean and a glimpse of the snow-covered Himalayas.[131] These images, interestingly enough, also echo alchemical symbols he was working with in *Mysterium*. Jung knew he was on the verge of departing from the earth. His memories of India also returned in a dream of a tremendous block of stone that reminded him of stones on the coast off the Gulf of Bengal, some of which had been hollowed out into temples. The stone in his dream was such a temple. As he entered this rock temple, he felt his earthly existence, its desires, goals and experiences, being sloughed off, so that at the end of this "extremely painful process" he felt emptied out, yet at the same time, strangely full: "There was no longer anything I wanted or desired. I existed in an objective form."[132] Once inside the temple, he saw a black Hindu sitting in a lotus posture in silent meditation. The rock temple and the meditating Buddha-like figure are symbols of the self.

Later, while recuperating, Jung had another dream of the Hindu. In this dream he was on a biking trip and came across a small wayside chapel. He went inside and to his surprise, instead of the cross or a statue of the Virgin on the altar, there was only a beautiful flower arrangement. In front of the altar and facing him sat a yogi in a lotus posture in deep meditation. When Jung looked him more closely, he realized the yogi had his face. "I started in profound fright, and awoke with the thought: 'Aha, so he is the one who is meditating me. He has a dream, and I am it.' I knew that when he awakened, I would no longer be."[133] Again, the mediating yogi is a self-image, this time clearly indicating the parallel identity and relationship between the temporal ego and the eternal self.

The other dreams during his illness consisted of the *hieros gamos* variations discussed above. In each case, Jung felt as if he were also somehow the marriage that was taking place. Unlike his Indian dreams of red and of the Holy Grail, these dreams were clear in their meaning. They were death dreams, indicating that he was on the verge of dying: marriage is one of the symbols associated with death, since at death the person is thought to unite in an eternal bond with the soul. Jung later told Marie-Louise von Franz, his collaborator on the *Mysterium* book, the marriage dreams during his illness confirmed that what he had written so far on the subject was valid.

Finally, the dreams also related to Jung's own process of individuation, which, in religious terms, is the experience of the mystical union of one's soul with God. The dreams of the Grail spelled the beginning of the quest for wholeness; the later dreams of marriage pointed to a culmination of that quest. He had recovered the Grail. To the extent that his personal task coincided with the collective events around him, Jung's dreams of wholeness intimated the end of World War II. On the other hand, since dreams and symbols are multifaceted and not time specific, his dreams of the coniunctio, in which the opposites can confront one another either in enmity or love,[135] also extend to the Cold War period and the persistent threat of a violent confrontation between the two newly emergent superpowers.

It is important to keep in mind, Jung contends, that what is realized in dreams is not yet realized in life. Dreams merely point to the potential that is now active and inherent in the psyche. That potential needs to be embodied in one's daily life and made an integral part of one's personality. Intellectual insight is not sufficient to realize the psyche's purpose for the dream. In the last days of his life, in June 1961, Jung had a dream in which he saw a large round block of stone in a high bare place with the inscription, "This shall be a sign unto you of wholeness and oneness."[136] The large round block of stone, reminiscent of the rock temple in his earlier dream, is a symbol of the philosophers' stone. The dream seems to indicate that Jung's 1944 coniunctio visions finally achieved their concrete realization within his personality. But, that wholeness is accorded reality in the beyond and not in this world.

As Jung was beginning to recover from his 1944 illness, Barbara Hannah, a close associate, and Emma Jung went to visit him in the hospital. He told them that during his recovery he felt as if his body had been dismembered, cut up into pieces and then slowly collected and put together again; Jung also felt that he had to do most or all of the reassembling himself.[137] Such an experience of dismemberment and recollection resembles a shamanic initiation and parallels the Egyptian myth of the dismemberment of Osiris. Jung was released from the hospital after D-Day, toward the end of June 1944, and entered upon a long convalescence. Not until April 1945, as the war was winding down in Europe, did he feel well enough to visit his Bollingen retreat.

Since I have outlined the synchronicity of Jung's major illnesses and concurrent historical conditions, I think it is worthwhile to recount his deathbed visions. Marie-Louise von Franz reports that one of Jung's daughters gave her notes of Jung's last dreams and visions. On the page was a line going up and down with the words, "The last fifty years of humanity" and several remarks about the "final catastrophe being ahead."[138] Von Franz also reports that the last time she saw Jung, he had a vision in her presence: "I see enormous stretches of earth devastated, but thank God it's not the whole planet."[139]

Conclusion

These are sobering visions, and one can only hope that either Jung was mistaken, or that, as von Franz says in her interview, a miracle happens and we are able just to slip around the corner and avoid the catastrophe. Given our history as a species and the absence of a parallel ethical development that matches our technological capabilities, I can only hope against hope, but cannot allow myself to be too naïve and optimistic. As the late comedian George Carlin quipped, "That's what I like to see, weapons of mass destruction in the hands of people with ancient ethnic and religious hatreds." Hatred may not even be required; sheer stupidity will do! On the other hand, I take consolation in the fact that Christ was mistaken about the timing of the end of the world when he prophesized that it would take place within a generation after his death. Perhaps, in spite of his visions foretelling the two world wars, Jung was mistaken as well. I also think an individual whose psyche is closely integrated with the collective unconscious, may experience his personal death in transpersonal terms. After all, end of the world visions and dreams are fairly common in people who are psychotic: the death of the ego personality appears to the psyche as the end of the world. But these are speculations, and most likely rationalizations and defensive attempts to ward off facing up to what is a real possibility for our times—in the same manner that we avoid the thought of our own personal death. Unlike the psychotic's vision, or the apocalyptic visions of the end of the world in the past, our situation is different: we actually possess the means of destruction to make the vision a reality. I can only pray these archetypal visions do not possess us, as they have a tendency to do, so that we concretize them in the world. In this regard, the current popular expectation of Armageddon is not a salutary phenomenon. For expectations have a way of being realized. They can set forth a dynamic that becomes inevitable, in the manner of a self-fulfilling prophecy.

I suppose it is only fair that our ability to create life and to conquer nature goes hand in hand with our ability to destroy life and put an end to what has taken nature billions of years to bring to fruition. We may yet regret having eaten of the fruit of the Tree of Knowledge that has made us, as the serpent promised, like unto God. In this context, the Revelation of St. John is not to be taken literally, but must be seen in its personal and historical context. In the psyche of the beloved disciple, who was consciously identified with the archetype of love, the Revelation depicts an "enantiodromia", the swing of the pendulum from one extreme to the other, and discloses the unconscious aggression, anger, violence and hatred that such a one-sided identification called forth. Historically, the book may be read as a prophetic vision of archetypal dynamics underlying the Christian era and of the culminating change of consciousness we are witnessing as that era draws to a close. In that sense, the Revelation is a metaphor for the revolutionary transformation of the collective Christian psyche as it is confronted with a new incarnation of the God image. The emergence of this new archetype of the self into the collective consciousness of our time, the "Christification of many," to which I alluded at the end of the previous chapter, is the prophesized second coming of Christ. The Second Coming, therefore, is a metaphor to be understood psychologically and spiritually.[140] Serious distortions ensue when societies attempt to concretize an archetypal symbol. One need only think of the communist ideology, that other recent collective dream of paradise, and the moral, emotional and intellectual distortions that translated into horrendous physical suffering, torture and death for millions of people.

The Revelation of St. John shows in bold relief the shadow side of the God of Love. In his book, *Answer to Job*, Jung struggled to understand and come to terms with the dark side of God as it was disclosed in the Book of Job and the Revelation, also known as the Apocalypse of John. He writes:

> Since the Apocalypse we now know again that God is not only to be loved, but also to be feared. He fills us with evil as well as with good, otherwise he would not need to be feared; and because he wants to become man, the uniting of his antimony must take place in man. This involves man in a new responsibility. He can no longer wriggle out of it on the plea of his littleness and nothingness, for the dark God has slipped the atom bomb and chemical weapons into his hands and given him the power to empty out the apocalyptic vials of wrath on his fellow creatures. Since he has been granted an almost godlike power, he can no longer remain blind and unconscious. He must know something of God's nature and of metaphysical processes if he is to understand himself and thereby achieve gnosis of the Divine.[141]

"Everything," Jung concludes, "now depends on man: immense power of destruction is given into his hand, and the question is whether he can resist the will to use it, and can temper his will with the spirit of love and wisdom."[142] The call for self-knowledge, in the context of Jung's own mistake when he allowed his unconscious power drive to motivate his activities during the Nazi era, gives a poignant tone of contrition and urgency to his statement. We can only hope that his mistake and the lessons he learned from having been caught by his own shadow will be heeded by others, before it is too late and we follow the example of Germany on the road to collective suicide.

10
Conclusion

Power, Eros, Pneuma, Physis

When used in a responsible manner, typology seeks to understand the unique attributes of every person and, in the process, to foster tolerance and communication among disparate individuals and cultures. My introduction of archetypal-motivational typology (AMT) stems from a desire to further these values and aims. As the term "archetypal" implies, AMT is based on Jung's conception of the unconscious as composed of a personal and transpersonal level. In Jung's view, archetypes are psychological configurations analogous to the physiological instincts, or "natural incentives," to use a contemporary euphemism, and, therefore, common to all human beings.[1] Consequently, by identifying a number of basic attributes of the archetypal psyche, it is possible to develop a typology that applies across a broad spectrum of human attitudes and behavior. I focus on the archetypes of Power, Eros, Pneuma and Physis, because these are fundamental ways that all human beings interact with the world.

Power has its evolutionary origins in the aggressive and territorial instincts, in the need to dominate and control the environment for the sake of survival. Eros, the desire for connection, also serves survival needs through propagation of offspring and attachment to family, herd and species. Physis originates in the necessity of all living beings to apprehend and manipulate external reality. And Pneuma is expressed in the proclivity for a symbolic relationship to reality, a tendency already present in the ritual behavior of animals and particularly evident in the artistic, mythological and conceptual expressions of human beings.

Soul and Spirit

These four archetypes seem to encompass the basic motivations of human beings. They are concerned with survival and provide ways of responding to the physical, relational and symbolic aspects of reality. Soul and Spirit, the two other archetypes that comprise the six categories of AMT, add their characteristic tone to the entire personality and to the behavioral expression of the four archetypes.

I am aware of the fact that Pneuma, as a motivational area of interest, and spiritedness, as a temperamental predisposition, make use of the same archetype. But, archetypes are mutable and have more than one form of expression. Any confusion between the two can be clarified by consulting the separate descriptions of Pneuma and spiritedness in Chapters 2 and 4. The touchstone for the use of the same archetype in these two different ways is experiential reality, which generally substantiates the typological distinction I propose.

Another possible confusion may arise from the fact that soulfulness is related to Eros, since it shares some of its attributes, such as the preference for reflection over action and the capacity for personal love. People with a soulful temperament, therefore, are often mistaken for Eros types. Spirited types, on the other hand, because of their decisive and active nature may be mistaken for Power types. And both, Eros types (with their need for connections) and spirited types (with their penchant for action) can be seen as extraverts. Hence, the usefulness of the Archetypal-Motivational Typology Scale (see Addendum), which allows for a more objective assessment of a person's typology than one based solely on intuitive insight or external observation.

Yet another area of confusion with respect to my use of the terms soul and spirit is Jung's use of *anima* (the Latin term for soul), for the archetypal personification of the unconscious in men and *animus* (the Latin term for spirit), for the archetypal personification of the unconscious in women. Jung's theory assumes that because men's consciousness is identified with spirit and women's consciousness with soul, the unconscious is then saddled with carrying the physiological and psychological contra-sexual elements present in all human beings. If, for cultural or psychological reasons, the conscious identity of a man becomes feminine and that of a woman masculine, the unconscious compensation is necessarily reversed.

Jung's notion of animus and anima is gender based and has caused a great deal of controversy both within and outside Jungian circles. Archetypal-motivational typology uses the archetypes of soul and spirit as expressed in temperament without regard to gender, so that it is possible to speak of both men and women as either soulful or spirited. Spirit, therefore, is not restricted to the conscious attitude of men and the unconscious of women; nor is soul limited to the consciousness of women and the unconscious of men. Expanding the use of soul and spirit in this manner does not constitute a rejection of Jung's definition of anima and animus, but simply indicates that the archetypes of soul and spirit need not be tied to gender.

All six categories of archetypal-motivational typology are archetypes, and therefore readily lend themselves to mythological descriptions, for mythology is a store-house of archetypal motifs depicted in personified images and narratives. These personifications and stories express the universal structures and contents of the human psyche as arrayed in the distinctive attributes of a specific culture: for example, the "great mother" archetype is universal, but each culture has its own representation of it. A mythological description of the archetypes gives them a specificity that helps to curtail theoretical speculations with little regard for empirical reality. Conceptually, for instance, it appears that the archetypal motivation of Pneuma and the temperamental quality of spiritedness make use of the same archetype. Empirically, however, that archetype has different manifestations that can be readily demarcated.

In addition, mythology specific to particular civilizations provides insight into the motivational characteristics of various cultures. For instance, it is startling to discover that the Judeo-Christian creation myth is an expression of the power archetype. The Western founding myth begins with a command: "Let there be Light." As for Eros, the opposite of Power, there appear to be only isolated instances in the Western world of groups and nations motivated primarily by this archetype. Evidently, a thousand years of Christianity, with its message of love and forgiveness, has had little effect on our society. As witnessed by the horrors of the twentieth century, and the unremitting, undeclared wars of this new century, too often the drive for domination and control reigns supreme.[2]

The archetypes of Pneuma and Physis, on the other hand, seem to have found a fairly balanced presence in the cultural history of the West. The concretizing tendencies of ancient Egypt, the pragmatism of Rome, and the materialism of the modern era are expressions of Physis. Medieval Christianity, the Renaissance, the Enlightenment and the Romantic period are manifestations of Pneuma. The mythological amplification of these four archetypes, therefore, points out the cultural characteristics of an era. It goes without saying that individuals whose personal typology happens to coincide with the cultural dominants of their day fare better in those cultures than individuals whose typology is at odds with the spirit of the time.

Freud, Adler and Jung

After establishing a typology based on unconscious archetypal motivations and providing a general description of extraverted and introverted Power, Eros, Physis and Pneuma personality types, it seemed appropriate to demonstrate the value of archetypal-motivational typology by applying its categories to the life and work of the three founders of the psychology of the unconscious, Freud, Adler and Jung. In undertaking that analysis, I was cognizant of the fact that Jung became interested in typology because he felt that the disagreements among his colleagues were based on a divergence in temperament. However, the typology he created in an attempt to address this issue did not succeed in illuminating the conflicts between Freud and Adler and between himself and his two colleagues.

Although I did not set out to formulate a typology to address the problem, fortuitously, the categories of Power, Physis, Eros and Pneuma were directly applicable to the personalities and theories of the three men and identified significant temperamental differences among them. Freud was a Physis type, Adler an Eros type and Jung a Pneuma type. In addition, my typology revealed that Freud and Adler shared Physis as one of their consciously deployed motivations, while Freud and Jung shared Power as their secondary motivation. These shared motivations, however, did not ensure theoretical consensus or personal accord. For instance, because of their shared Physis, both Freud and Adler based their theories on the physiological development of the child. However, Adler did not agree with Freud's initial emphasis on the primacy of the sexual drives and his rejection of a separate aggressive instinct. Freud and Jung exhibited Power as their secondary consciously deployed motivation, but after an attempt to merge their worldly ambitions, their respective Power drives forced them to go their separate ways. Still, issues of Power were not directly responsible for their disagreements and parting. The personal and theoretical reasons for their separation were complex and I have sought to address them in the above chapters. But once Freud and Jung parted, their Power drives were clearly in evidence, as each sought to disparage and undermine the theories and influence of the other.

Of the three, only Adler was an extravert and as long as he was alive, his practical and sociologically oriented form of depth psychology presented an alternative to the introverted and individually biased theories of Freud and Jung. If Adler had not died in 1937, but lived on into his 80s, as did Freud and Jung, the character and influence of depth psychology, at least in the United States, probably would not have been dominated by Freudian psychology and its emphasis on internal psychic drives and personal pathology. The extraverted, pragmatic culture of North America was a natural match for Adler's approach to psychology. He enthusiastically immigrated to the United States in the early 1930s and was an effective advocate of the humanistic and sociological perspective that came to fruition only during the 1960s and 70s with the work of Rollo May, Carl Rogers and Abraham Maslow, the latter a former student of Adler's.

In addition to shedding new light on the similarities and differences among Freud, Adler and Jung, my typological analysis of the three men also led to a surprising discovery: each of the pioneers of depth psychology created a theory based on his inferior unconscious motivations. Freud was a Power Physis type, with Eros and Pneuma as his shadow motivations. When he analyzed his unconscious, he therefore encountered the archetypes of Eros and Pneuma. Since unconscious contents tend to coalesce and contaminate one another, his Eros was imbued with spiritual qualities, turning his sexual theory into a quasi-religious dogma. The fact that so many secular people found his theory compelling, in all likelihood, stems from the fact that their spirituality had no overt channel of expression and, as with Freud, become attached to the sexual aspects of the archetype of Eros. Indeed, there is probably a direct correlation between the loss of religious belief in the modern era and the rise of the fascination with sexuality.

Adler was a Physis Eros type, with Pneuma and Power as his inferior motivations. When he analyzed his unconscious, he discovered his Power drive and made it the leitmotif of his theory. His inferior Pneuma motivation, on the other hand, was expressed in the missionary fervor with which he espoused the value of *Gemeinschaftsgefühl*, or community feeling. In this connection it is worth noting that his wife Raissa and many of his close friends and acquaintances were socialists who sought to recruit Adler to their cause. But, like Raisa, they tended to be Power types whose unconscious Eros motivations found an outlet in their socialistic or nationalistic feelings. In contrast, Adler was an Eros type, and his inferior Power drive was subsumed by his extraverted Eros, leading him to emphasize community feeling rather than government and laws.

Jung was a Power Pneuma type, with Eros and Physis as his inferior motivations. The archetype of Physis, which is concerned with matter, accounts for Jung's fascination with alchemy. His inferior Eros is evident in his alleged womanizing as a younger man and in his later preoccupation with the problem of *coniunctio*, the alchemical union of opposites, and its frequent erotic symbolism: for example, the Rosarium pictures Jung used to elucidate the psychology of the transference. In my experience, Jung's psychology attracts Pneuma types whose Eros tends to be comprised by their spirituality or by some form of artistic expression. As we have seen, Jung felt Freud's attempt to reduce these cultural manifestations to the sexual drive was a direct assault on Pneuma. For Jung, Pneuma had its own archetypal autonomy and was not an epiphenomenon of sexual libido, no matter how broadly defined or interpreted.

Looking at the theoretical contributions of the three founders of depth psychology from the perspective of archetypal-motivational typology, reveals not only the motivations responsible for their personal and conceptual interests, but also provides a comprehensive view of the human psyche. Each theory alone is not complete, but requires the counterbalancing contribution of the others. That does not mean, however, that an eclectic approach to the psyche is best. On the contrary, such a perspective has only an abstract and theoretical validity. In practical terms, as archetypal-motivational typology demonstrates, people separate into different types and are therefore innately drawn to Freudian, Adlerian or Jungian psychology. As there are Eros, Power, Physis and Pneuma types, there are also Freudian, Adlerian and Jungian types. No one type is superior to the other. Each temperamental attitude brings its own unique perspective on reality, but needs the others to provide the necessary counterpoint.

Archetypal cores of the four functions

In the introductory chapter to this book I alluded to the possibility that the four motivational archetypes central to archetypal-motivational typology may also serve as archetypal cores of the four functions delineated in Jung's seminal book, *Psychological Types*. Power/Logos is the archetypal nucleus of the thinking function; Eros is the archetype underlying the feeling function; Pneuma is the core archetype of intuition; and Physis, of sensation. This does not mean, though, that an Eros motivated person, for example, is invariably a feeling type or that a Physis oriented individual is necessarily a sensation type. As I have noted previously, archetypes and functions are malleable and responsive to historical, sociological and cultural circumstances and pressures.

Nevertheless, when the motivational typology of Freud, Adler and Jung is compared with their functional preferences there is a direct correlation between the two. In my opinion, Freud was a Power-Physis type; originally he may have been a feeling-sensation type, but in later life he seems to have moved to sensation-thinking. Adler was a Physis-Eros type with dominant feeling and sensation as his secondary function. Jung's principal motivation was Pneuma with Power as his secondary drive; initially, he was a thinking-intuitive type but in later life he may have privileged intuition over thinking. Thus, in Freud's case, Physis was the archetypal core of his sensation and Power/Logos the basis of his thinking function. With Adler, Eros was the archetypal core of his dominant feeling and Physis, the core of his sensation function. Jung's intuition was directly related to his archetypal Pneuma orientation and his thinking, to his Power/Logos drive.

Three individuals hardly provide conclusive evidence about the correlation between the four archetypes and the four functions, particularly since the estimation of their characters is, to a large extent, a matter of speculation. Further considerations along these lines, therefore, need to await a statistical analysis comparing the personality types identified by the Archetypal Motivational Typology Scale and the typological preferences recognized by the Myers-Briggs Type Indicator or similar functional typology tests.[3]

Power and Eros

My interest in formulating a typology began with Jung's insight concerning the opposing relationship between Power and Eros. As a political theorist, I was interested in understanding the motivations behind the drive for power. Of the three founders of depth psychology, Adler alone addressed this issue directly.

It seems to me that given the contemporary preoccupation with politics, it is imperative to understand the power motive and its role in the personal and public domain. As Adler wrote almost 100 years ago, "The struggle for power has a psychological aspect, the description of which appears to us today as an urgent duty."[4] Adler's contribution was his observation that the drive for power is motivated by feelings of inadequacy. In popular terms, his thesis is illustrated by the Napoleon complex: a diminutive man compensating for his size by amassing power. But the thesis applies to groups as well. Any circumstance that diminishes or demeans an individual or a group of people, from socio-economic inequality to racial prejudice, activates the power motive in those burdened by these real or perceived inferiorities. Too often political and human relations remain mired in a vicious cycle of violence between the privileged and the disenfranchised, between the oppressors and the oppressed. "For human nature," Adler states, "generally answers external coercion with counter coercion."[5]

Without disputing Adler's thesis concerning the compensatory character of power, my typology assumes that the will to power is also a normal expression of human nature. Indeed, I regard the power drive as a basic structural component of the psyche. It follows that I view the need for domination and control by some individuals as a temperamental bias and not a compensatory response to feelings of inadequacy. From Adler's perspective, the psychological dynamics involved consist of a tension between weakness and power. From my perspective, the dynamic tension is between Eros and Power, between the desire for connection and the drive for domination. Actually, in his post World War I idea of *Gemeinschaftsgefühl*, Adler came to a similar conclusion and in his later work emphasized that the mature response to feelings of weakness or inadequacy was the cultivation of community feeling and not the striving for superiority. He even went so far as to consider *Gemeinschaftsgefühl* an "innate potentiality" present in all human beings, which, incidentally, is Jung's definition of an archetype.[6]

The problem is that, in Adler's words, "the present stage of our culture and insight still permits the power principle to prevail."[7] And where Power is not tempered by Eros, it readily degenerates into intolerance, violence and tyranny. If there is a way to halt the dominance of the power principle and the resulting lack of civility in domestic politics and recourse to violence in foreign affairs, it can only be, Adler concludes, through the "miracle of *Gemeinschaftsgefühl* which we must perform and which will never succeed through the use of power."[8] Adler acknowledges that this miracle has been the aim of "all great reformers of mankind [who] have always intuitively placed mutual aid above the struggle for power."[9]

But how exactly are we to perform the miracle of Eros? I think the nature of the problem has to be posed in somewhat different terms. One can not simply give up Power and cultivate Eros. These two archetypal forces, really gods, as they should be rightly called, inherently belong together. Their joined nature is depicted in such iconic images as the Hindu Shiva-Shakti, the Taoist yin-yang and the alchemical king and queen. The essential nature of each is best realized in conjunction with the other, as they balance and complement one another. Distortions and difficulties arise when one archetype dominates or when they are split apart. Power tempered by Eros, Eros joined with Power is the formula that may bring about the miracle Adler has in mind. Yet, in the propagation of this miracle, Eros must take the lead. For Eros is the great uniter, the archetype capable of reconciling all opposites into a paradoxical, but tempered whole: "a warring peace, a sweet wound, a mild evil."[10]

Pneuma and Physis

The need for a balanced relationship between Power and Eros that is apparent from the above description applies to the other archetypal pair as well, Pneuma and Physis. They belong together and when one overshadows or becomes separated from the other, inevitable perversions arise. In Western Europe, the emergence of Christianity during the later stages of the Roman Empire ensured the preeminence of Pneuma for almost a millennium. Everyone is familiar with the temporal consequences of the overly spiritual and patriarchal attitude, especially when combined with Power: subjugation of women, exploitation of the lower classes, annihilation of indigenous peoples, colonization of non-Western countries and an arrogant attitude toward nature. In the twentieth century, this shadow side of Pneuma culminated, as Jung observed, in "a false spirit of arrogance, hysteria, woolly-mindedness, criminal amorality, and doctrinaire fanaticism . . . [and became] a purveyor of shoddy spiritual goods, spurious art, philosophical stutterings, and Utopian humbug, fit only to be fed wholesale to the mass man of today. That is what the post-Christian spirit looks like."[11]

Beginning with the Renaissance, however, Physis has made a steady advance on Pneuma. The focus on the material universe has brought with it an increase in scientific knowledge and technological prowess. The contemporary breakthroughs and advances in medicine, space exploration, computer science, astronomy, and theoretical and applied physics are probably beyond anything people even in the nineteenth century could imagine.

Culturally, the emergence of Physis as the ruling archetype of our day is evident in many areas. We see this in the attention paid to the body: the return to natural childbirth and breastfeeding; working out, aerobics and yoga; massage; tattoos; body piercing; and open sexuality. Then, there is the new-found respect for nature: environmentalism; ecology; eco-psychology, the Green movement; advocacy of a sustainable life style; setting aside nature preserves and protection of wildlife. Include here also the fascination with food: preference for local and seasonal organic produce; natural ingredients; cooking shows; chef competitions; and a proliferation of gourmet products. Nor can one ignore the current preoccupation with Wall Street and the economy, with money making, wealth, real estate, houses, gardens and the ceaseless acquisition of material goods. Shopping malls are the new temple grounds where families go to spend their Saturdays and Sundays, the former Sabbath days of spiritual dedication. The shadow side of this new materialism is evident in reality shows, in the fascination with the scandals of people in power and in the popularity of confessional memoirs.

From an historical perspective, Western culture has moved from one extreme to the other: from an exclusive preoccupation with spirit and the deprecation of matter, to a fascination with all things natural and material. This new trend is often accompanied by a marked disdain for matters of culture and spirit. Even religion, when taken seriously, as it is in the United States and in the Muslim world, is espoused by a fairly large portion of the population in a literal way, with no regard for tolerance and reasonable discourse.

A balance needs to be found and we do not know what miracle will bring that about. Some contemporary religious thinkers, for example, promote the ideal of finding the sacred in everyday life. Others, contrary to the Biblical injunction for human beings to "have dominion . . . over all the earth" (Genesis 1:26), advocate stewardship rather than rule over God's creation: Eros rather than Power. Certainly, an understanding of the nature of Physis, the ruling paradigm of our day, may help us temper its more extreme expression so that it does not take a series of social and environmental crises to bring the problem of imbalance to public awareness.

Individuation and wholeness

In the preceding discussion, I have addressed some of the problems that arise when one side of the archetypal pairs of Eros–Power, Pneuma–Physis dominates the other. What is true in the cultural and social sphere is also true on the personal level. Individuals need to acknowledge their archetypal-motivational character and then make a concerted effort to compensate for their temperamentally biased motivations. This entails Eros types recognizing that the desire for union and relationship can turn into a compulsion that respects no boundaries. Power types have to pay attention to Eros, both in their personal and social interactions, and not simply use their unconscious Eros, with its charismatic energy, to further their aspiration for domination and control. Physis types would do well to accord the realm of ideas and spiritual strivings serious consideration so that they do not succumb to the fleeting moments of ecstasy associated with alcohol, drugs and sexual addictions. And if Pneuma types develop a healthy regard for material reality and resist their inclination to theorize and fantasize, they will be less likely to suffer from unpleasant real-life surprises, such as financial disasters.

Fortunately, in the course of confronting one's inherent temperament and compensating for any one-sidedness, a person is actually helped in this endeavor by the archetype of the self. For the aim of this archetype is to bring about a union of the conscious and unconscious aspects of the personality. Within this organizing center of the psyche these motivational opposites are amalgamated into a paradoxical, yet harmonious whole, so that they interact with, rather than repel each other.

On a transpersonal level, the inherent complementary interaction of all opposites is expressed, for example, by the law of dharma in Hinduism and the "way" in Taoism. These concepts helped to confirm Jung's discovery of the paradoxical nature of the archetype of the self. He then sought to give these ancient truths a personal psychological representation with his ideas of *the process of individuation* and *striving for wholeness*.

Initially, however, individuation means to become the unique person that one's innate potentialities portend, and that call may, at first demand, a certain imbalance. A gifted politician, for example, will naturally focus on Power at the expense of Eros. An emphatically related individual will embrace Eros and ignore Power. A philosopher will prefer Pneuma over Physis. An engineer will value Physis over Pneuma. A penchant for one's inherent temperamental disposition marks the first stage of individuation.

The second phase calls for the cultivation of wholeness. At this point, an attempt is made to moderate one's temperamental biases in favor of a more complete expression of personality. The satisfactions and accomplishments obtained from the expression of the dominant archetypal drives now give way to a cultivation of the neglected motivations. With that, as the leading motivations are moderated by the infusion of their complementary opposites, their expression becomes less clear and direct. The result is a sense of disorientation: Power types feel diminished; Eros types frustrated; Pneuma types limited; and Physis types unmoored.

The development of one's inferior motivations is a disconcerting and difficult enterprise, but only the person who has taken her or his natural inclinations to task and balanced the opposing tendencies can be said to be a whole, or *cultivated* individual. Individuation is a life-long effort and rarely ever completed. Yet, without an attempt to rein in one's given temperament, a distorted personality results; one, moreover, prone to all sorts of unintended consequences often of tragic proportions. This is why in the course of outlining his typology based on the oral, anal, phallic and genital stages of psychological development Freud was moved to concur with the ancient Greek observation that *character is fate*.

Archetypal-motivational typology, on the other hand, is based on the idea that character is not determined by early childhood vicissitudes but is a manifestation of innate motivational tendencies. Moreover, in the course of a person's life, the one-sided conscious deployment of these motivations is eventually tempered by the drive of the archetype of the self. As a result, the opposing pairs of Power–Eros, Pneuma–Physis are brought into alignment so that the inferior motivations no longer operate autonomously and the one-sidedness of the conscious personality is resolved. The attainment of an integrated psyche is a hard-won form of self-realization, seldom fully achieved. But the striving to attain such wholeness is often rewarded by the understanding that only the *unexamined* character is fate.

Appendix I: Jungian Archetypal Typologies

Between 1913 and 1920, when Jung was constructing the typological model presented in *Psychological Types*, he had not yet elaborated the concept of the archetype, nor had he fully realized the dominant role archetypes play in personal psychological development. However, once his conception of the archetypal organization of the collective unconscious was in place, his followers began to introduce typologies based on archetypes. (I provide a cursory summary of these typologies in this Appendix. A full treatment of Jungian archetypal typologies together with an account of typologies based on Jung's conscious functions, such as the Myers-Briggs Type Indicator, will be presented in a companion volume to this book.)

The first to propose a typology based on Jung's conception of the archetypal nature of the psyche was his associate Toni Wolff. Wolff thought that Jung's typology held an implicit masculine bias. She proceeded to remedy the situation with her essay, "Structural Forms of the Feminine Psyche," in which she outlined a typology based on the archetypal configuration of the feminine unconscious.[1] We must assume Jung was aware of her work and may have even contributed to it in some manner. She imagined the psyche of women to be composed of four archetypes: mother, hetaira (the ancient Greek term for a courtesan), medium and amazon. In an identical manner to the four functions in Jung's typology, she arranged the archetypes in opposing pairs, mother–hetaira, medium–amazon. Although the mother and hetaira are opposites, both are characterized by their need for a personal connection to men. The medium and amazon, on the other hand, function independently of a personal relationship to men. Wolff assumes that every woman has this fourfold archetypal psychic structure; however, a woman may not be aware of the archetypal roles she plays or of the dominant archetype with which she is identified. At one point in her life, for example, she may function out of the hetaira or amazon energy and at another time, inhabit the mother or medium role. The four-fold underlying structure is always present, and a certain fluidity is possible, indeed, desirable, if a woman is not to become one-sided and identified with only a single aspect of her femininity.

Other followers of Jung took a different tack in exploring the notion of archetypes and typology. Emma Jung, M. Esther Harding and Marie-Louise von Franz focused on the archetypes of the animus and the anima and their influence on the character of women and men. They did not outline an overt typology, but their descriptions of the animus and anima lend themselves to a classification of individuals based on a relationship to those archetypes. For instance, Emma Jung, in *Animus and Anima*, describes four stages of a woman's relationship with the animus. The first stage entails a fascination with a man of physical prowess, the second with a man of action, the third with a man of the word, and finally, with a man of wisdom.[2]

M. Esther Harding was one of Jung's early adherents. Her book, *The Way of All Women*, portrays six different types of women characterized by certain typical attitudes based on their relationship to men: the instinctive anima woman; the innocent child-like woman; the dark, full-blooded passionate woman; the passive, cold, distant woman; the *femme inspiratrice* or muse; and the conscious, ego-centered woman. Harding also explores the nature of different types of women based on their relationship to the animus. Thus, there are women entranced by an inner figure of an ideal lover. Others fall victim to a "ghostly lover," sometimes as a consequence of a lost, dead or absent lover. The third type of woman pursues the animus through projection, and here Harding makes use of Emma Jung's distinctions among the various types of animus figures representing potential "hooks" for such projections.

Marie-Louise von Franz, in her essay, "The Process of Individuation," delineates four stages in anima development in men and animus development in women.[3] The unfolding of a man's anima proceeds from the erotically attractive woman, to the romantic beauty, to the mature woman and then to the woman of wisdom. The corresponding animus progression is the physically attractive man, the romantic man, the man of action and the man of wisdom.

With the growing interest in mythology during the 1970s in the United States, the Jungian analyst Jean Shinoda Bolen designed a feminine and masculine typology based on the classic Greek pantheon of goddesses and gods. Her books include *Goddesses in Everywoman, Gods in Everyman* and *Goddesses in Older Women*. In *Goddesses in Everywoman*, Bolen describes a typology based on seven Greek goddesses which she divides into three groups: the autonomous virgin goddesses, Artemis, Athena, Hestia; the relationship-oriented vulnerable goddesses, Hera, Demeter and Persephone; and the "alchemical goddess," Aphrodite, who combines both the autonomy and relationship characteristics of the other two groups.[4] All seven goddesses are present in the psyche of every woman and represent the totality of her personality, but the role that each goddess plays in a woman's life will vary with time and circumstances. Bolen emphasizes the importance of the ego in overseeing the multiple and often conflicting demands of the various archetypal energies.

In her companion volume, *Gods in Everyman*, Bolen finds that three father archetypes, Zeus, Poseidon and Hades, and five son archetypes, Apollo, Hermes, Ares, Hephaestus and Dionysus, characterize masculine psychology. In *Goddesses in Older Women*, Bolen adds the goddesses of wisdom, rage, mirth and compassion to the ones she treated in her earlier book.

Perhaps inspired by the work of Bolen, Jungian psychotherapists Jennifer and Roger Woolger in their book, *The Goddess Within*, introduce a feminine typology based on six Greek goddesses: Athena, Artemis, Aphrodite, Hera, Persephone and Demeter. These goddesses "in various combinations, underlie every woman's behavior and psychological style."[5] They arrange the six goddesses in a goddess wheel with the great mother as the central archetype that gives rise to the other six manifestations of the feminine deities. The Woolgers further illustrate that the six goddesses can be placed in complementary or opposing dyads with each dyad associated with a dominant psychological trait: Athena and Artemis are the dyad of independence; Hera and Persephone, the dyad of power; and Aphrodite and Demeter, the dyad of love. Additionally, one of the goddesses of each dyad is essentially introverted—Artemis, Persephone, Demeter, while the other is extraverted—Athena, Hera, Aphrodite.

Like Bolen, who was inspired by feminist concerns to explore the archetypal structure of the feminine psyche, Jungian oriented psychotherapists Robert Moore and Douglas Gillette, motivated by their unease about the plight of men in contemporary American society, created a similar archetypal exposition of the masculine psyche. They acknowledge the adolescent nature of many contemporary American men and offer a developmental model of the mature masculine psyche. Four archetypes of "Boy psychology," the divine child, the precocious child; the Oedipal child and the adolescent hero are described.[6] These four then provide the basis for the mature archetypal constellations of king, magician, lover and warrior. Moore and Gillette do not mention that these mature masculine figures correlate with Toni Wolff's four archetypes that characterize the feminine psyche: mother, medium, hetaira and amazon. Perhaps Wolff's essay served as their model. The one disparity between the two schemas is that of the king and the mother. Many women will immediately point out the power bias: men see themselves as kings, but view women as Eros-biased mothers, not queens. Moore and Gillette note that the function of the hero archetype is to separate the boy from the unconscious, which in men is experienced as feminine, in order to establish an independent, individual masculine standpoint. The hero, however, is a transitional figure who needs to make way for the mature archetype of the king, or in less grandiose terms, for the father or the mature adult man.

The role of the hero archetype, this time in the psychological development of both women and men, is the theme elaborated by a scholar of leadership theory and practice, Carol S. Pearson. She explores these ideas in her books, *The Hero Within* and *Awakening the Heroes Within*. The books are inspired by the motif of the hero archetype described by Joseph Campbell in *The Hero with a Thousand Faces*.

Initially, Pearson alludes to "six inner guides, or archetypes, that help us . . . traverse the unpredictable dilemmas of the maturation process":[7] orphan, innocent, wanderer, warrior, altruist and magician. In her second book, Pearson deletes the archetypes of wanderer and altruist and adds eight others for a total of 12: caregiver, seeker, lover, destroyer, creator, ruler, sage and fool. In her terms, the innocent, orphan, caregiver and warrior belong to the preparatory stage of the hero's journey and are concerned with survival and ego formation. The seeker, destroyer, creator and lover archetypes inform the heart of the journey and relate to self-discovery and self-expression; through these archetypes a connection with the transpersonal psyche, with soul, is found. The ruler, magician, fool and sage belong to the stage of the hero's return after overcoming the obstacles along the way and are expressions of the archetype of the self. Each fosters personal authenticity from which genuine contributions flow to the community.

There is an implicit typology present in Pearson's schema. An individual may identify with one or two of the archetypes at each stage of the maturation process, with the orphan and the warrior, for example, in the first stage. Sometimes the identification is life-long and used to traverse all phases of the journey. She does not, therefore, expect every person to identify with each of the 12 archetypes as they move through life. Pearson does not emphasize the typological aspects of the archetypes. She is primarily interested in their influence at various stages of life and describes a fluid picture in which various archetypes emerge during the course of one's life. However, as the titles of her books indicate, the hero archetype is at the center of her model and each of the 12 archetypes is related to the hero's journey.

The Jungian analyst, John Beebe, also uses typology to examine the process of maturation but links this process to Jung's notion of individuation. He accepts Jung's typology and then adds an archetypal image to each of the four functions. Thus, in Beebe's view, the superior function has the attributes of a hero—strong, self-sufficient and effective. He associates the auxiliary function with parental figures, either helpful or critical. The tertiary function is represented by a child, either divine or wounded, and connected to the Jungian notion of *puella* and *puer aeternus*, the eternal adolescent girl or boy. He links the inferior function with the anima and animus, for they are usually seen as a bridge to the unconscious.

Not satisfied with the essentially positive images of the four functions, Beebe eventually demarcated their shadows. Thus the dominant conscious function and its hero archetype are undermined by the opposing personality, which is avoidant, passive-aggressive and paranoid. The mother and father archetypes of the auxiliary function have the controlling witch and inflexible senex as their shadows. The trickster is the shadow of the puer and puella. The demonic personality is the shadow of the anima and animus and works to undermine an individual's self-esteem and relationships with others.

Beebe's creative elaboration of Jung's typology opens a fertile area of further research and exploration. But, there is a serious problem with his formulation as a generally applicable model because, as he himself readily acknowledges, it describes his personal psychology. The images of hero, parents, puer and anima as representations of the four functions emerged from his dreams and self-reflection and not from clinical observation.[8] It remains to be seen to what extent his archetypal images of the four functions can be generalized to others.

The above summary of Jungian archetypal typologies provides the historical and theoretical context in which I introduce archetypal-motivational typology. These earlier typologies rely upon the personification of various psychological traits which are linked to different developmental stages. Additionally, the archetypes of the hero, of the Greek deities and of the personifications of animus and anima are associated with specific roles and modes of behavior. By contrast, the archetypal motivations of Power, Eros, Physis and Pneuma determine the attitudes and behavior of every individual, regardless of the above mythic roles with which an individual may identify during the course of her or his personal development. Some combination of the four motivational principles will invariably influence the behavior and goals of each of the goddesses and gods and the personifications of animus and anima. For example, the hero-identified person can pursue his or her aims motivated by either Eros or Power as styles of behavior and focus on either Pneuma or Physis concerns.

The primary import of the Power, Eros, Physis and Pneuma archetypes is readily apparent in their mythological amplification. While the gods and goddesses and the personifications of anima and animus are anthropomorphic representations of qualities associated with the later evolution of the human psyche, the four archetypal motivations are metaphorically linked to the non-human elements and forces present in creation myths: Physis refers to earth, Pneuma to air, Soul to water, Spirit to breath and air. Eros, in the Orphic tradition, is the first being to emerge out of the primordial unity of the cosmic egg, a symbol of the universe before its creation. Power is closely related to Logos and the Word, which is central to the Judeo-Christian creation myth and God's command: "Let there be Light."

Appendix II: Primacy of Spirit in the *I Ching*

The earliest Chinese world view is encapsulated in Taoism in which the source of all existence is the unknown, undifferentiated, dynamic void called the Tao, or the Way. The Tao is usually described as the mother and compared to water, which "wins its way by softness. Like a deep ravine, it is shadowy rather than brilliant."[1] In contrast to Taoism, which emphasizes the primacy and the creative power of yin, of containing emptiness, the *I Ching*, at least as it has been handed down from the time of Confucius (551–479 BCE), emphasizes the dominance of yang, of active energy. The Confucian overlay is also evident in the extraverted emphasis in the commentary, which focuses on hierarchical filial and social obligations.[2]

In his commentary therefore, Confucius underscores the primacy of *ch'ien*: "Great indeed is the generating power of the Creative; all beings owe their beginning to it."[3] The "creative" has even usurped the form-giving aspects of the receptive: "The clouds pass and the rain does its work, and all individual beings flow into their forms."[4] The commentary proceeds to state that "creative activity is revealed in the gift of water, which causes the germination and sprouting of all living things."[5] Even water is now the gift of the spirit. The earlier Taoist notion, however, can still be found in the statement that the creative begot all things, but they were brought to birth, sustained and nourished by the receptive.[6] The receptive "takes the seed of the heavens into itself and gives to beings their bodily form."[7] Giving bodily form, limitation in time and space, is the chief characteristic of the receptive. In contrast, as we saw previously, the creative is "unrestricted in any fixed conditions in space and is therefore conceived of as motion."[8] But the next sentence is telling: "Time is regarded as the *basis* of this motion";[9] and time is an attribute of the receptive. Clearly, time is an inherent element of motion; the two are dependent upon each other and one cannot rightly speak of the primacy of one or the other.

In the commentaries we read that "the Receptive is dependent upon the Creative."[10] Moreover, we are told that "the Creative is the generating principle, to which all beings owe their beginnings, *because the soul comes from it.*"[11] In the explanation of the hexagram *k'un* we read:

> The Receptive must be activated and led by the Creative; then it is productive of good. Only when it abandons this position and tries to stand as an equal side by side with the Creative, does it become evil. The result then is opposition to and struggle against the Creative, which is productive of evil to both.[12]

Obviously, no such warning applies to *ch'ien* usurping or trying to stand as an equal side by side with the receptive, for *ch'ien* is now conceived as primary and superior to *k'un*! Where have the lack of opposition and the complementarity of the two principles gone? Need I point out that with the primacy of the "male-paternal," the "female-maternal" becomes the source of evil. The receptive must now be kept in its place and instead of being an equal active, generative, and balancing power with the creative, it is transformed into a passive, subservient principle. All its previous activity, including the generation of soul and the giving of material form, are assigned to *ch'ien*. In the West, the same change of archetypal dominants is found in the gradual emergence of the heavenly creator father gods over the previously, if not dominant, at least coequal earthly creator mother goddesses. This is not a political statement, but simply a description of the change of the archetypal dominants that rule various periods of history. Today, the matriarchal archetype seems to be gaining in influence and it remains to be seen whether a balance will be struck between *ch'ien* and *k'un* once again, or whether the pendulum will simply swing from one extreme to the other.

Addendum: Archetypal-Motivational Typology Scale

Please circle either a *or* b *for each statement. Even if both apply, please make a choice. Try not to think too much about the questions and answer as quickly as you can.*

1. Do you find meeting many people
   a. exhausting, or
   b. energizing?

2. Do you prefer
   a. cloudy and overcast days, or
   b. bright and sunny days?

3. Would you say you are more
   a. practical, or
   b. theoretical?

4. Are you emotionally more
   a. spontaneous, or
   b. controlled?

5. Do you prefer
   a. being alone, or
   b. being with others?

6. Do you like to
   a. mull things over, or
   b. move things forward?

7. Do you feel art
   a. needs to have social relevance, or
   b. is for art's sake?

8. In your daily routine, do you
   a. go with the flow, or
   b. have a definite schedule?

9. Is it more relaxing for you to
   a. stay at home, or
   b. socialize?

10. Would you say you prefer
    a. a leisurely pace, or
    b. a lively pace?

11. Do you find facts
    a. interesting, or
    b. not interesting?

12. Would you say you are more
    a. cooperative, or
    b. competitive?

13. Do you tend to cultivate
    a. a few close friends, or
    b. many friends and acquaintances?

14. Are you basically
    a. moody, or
    b. cheerful?

15. Are you drawn to
    a. practical knowledge, or
    b. theoretical knowledge?

16. When you first meet someone are you
    a. open and accepting, or
    b. cautious and circumspect?

17. Do you feel comfortable voicing your opinion
    a. sometimes, or
    b. most of the time?

18. When you get angry do you
    a. sulk and smolder, or
    b. lose your temper?

19. Do you find philosophy
    a. unimportant, or
    b. important?

20. Do you prefer
    a. synthesis, or
    b. analysis?

21. Are you more
    a. private, or
    b. sociable?

22. Which affect you more
    a. images, or
    b. words?

23. Would you say you are more
    a. realistic, or
    b. idealistic?

24. Do you enjoy doing things for others
    a. most of the time, or
    b. some of the time?

25. Do you enjoy rallies and crowds
    a. hardly ever, or
    b. sometimes?

26. Are you mostly
    a. sensitive and personal, or
    b. objective and rational?

27. Would you say you are more interested in
    a. concrete everyday issues, or
    b. cultural and spiritual matters?

28. Do you like having a leadership position
    a. sometimes, or
    b. most of the time?

29. Do you prefer to work mostly
    a. alone, or
    b. with others?

30. Do you respond more to
    a. feelings and emotions, or
    b. ideas and concepts?

31. Do you live more
    a. in the here and now, or
    b. with an eye on the future?

32. Which is more important
    a. sociability, or
    b. leadership?

33. Do you interact easily
    a. mostly with close friends, or
    b. with almost everyone?

34. Is your approach to exercise
    a. reluctant and erratic, or
    b. disciplined and enthusiastic?

35. Are you more interested in
    a. science, or
    b. art?

36. Do you take a stand
    a. with some hesitation, or
    b. with little difficulty.

37. In company, do you generally prefer to
    a. listen, or
    b. talk?

38. Are you drawn more to
    a. valleys, or
    b. mountains?

39. Is it more important
    a. to be realistic, or
    b. to be principled?

40. Are you more interested in
    a. connections and similarities, or
    b. differences and uniqueness?

41. When the phone rings at home do you
    a. let someone else answer, or
    b. answer it yourself?

42. Do you like to
    a. day dream and fantasize, or
    b. think and figure things out?

43. Do you get more excited by
    a. concrete facts, or
    b. abstract ideas?

44. Is it important for you to feel in control
    a. sometimes, or
    b. almost always?

45. Do you pay more attention to
    a. your inner world, or
    b. the world around you?

46. Would you say you prefer
    a. to grasp the complexity of things, or
    b. get to the heart of the matter?

47. When investigating a problem do you
    a. stick to the facts, or
    b. imagine various possibilities?

48. Do you believe that "where there's a will there's a way,"
    a. sometimes, or
    b. most of the time?

49. When everyone is excited by something do you
    a. hold back a bit, or
    b. jump on the bandwagon?

50. Do you prefer music that is
    a. moody and relaxing, or
    b. lively and spirited?

51. Do you think religion should be concerned primarily with
    a. humanitarian and social values, or
    b. spiritual and eternal values?

52. Do you find that winning is important
    a. sometimes, or
    b. most of the time?

53. If you have a free evening do you prefer to
    a. stay at home, or
    b. go out on the town?

54. Would you say you are
    a. slow and deliberate, or
    b. quick and impatient?

55. Do you prefer
    a. biographies and historical novels, or
    b. fiction and fantasy?

56. Are friendships
    a. primary and essential, or
    b. important and helpful?

AMT Scale Scoring

Place either a or b after each number corresponding to your answers on the test.

I Orientation Introversion–Extraversion	II Temperament Soul–Spirit	III Area of interest Physis–Pneuma	IV Style of behavior Eros–Power
1. A	2. B	3. B	4. B
5. A	6. A	7. B	8. A
9. A	10. A	11. A	12. B
13. A	14. A	15. B	16. B
17. A	18. b	19. B	20. B
21. A	22. B	23. B	24. A
25. A	26. B	27. B	28. B
29. A	30. A	31. B	32. B
33. A	34. A	35. B	36. A
37. A	38. A	39. A	40. A
41. A	42. A	43. B	44. B
45. A	46. A	47. B	48. B
49. B	50. A	51. B	52. B
53. A	54. A	55. B	56. A

Add the a's and b's in each column.

a. 13 b. 1	a. 11 b. 3	a. 2 b. 12	a. 5 b. 9

Notes: A score of 10–14 indicates a strong tendency, 5–9 a fair tendency and 0–4 a weak tendency in the characteristics designated by each column.

A score of seven a's and seven b's in any one column suggests a balance between the two orientations, temperaments, areas of interest or styles of behavior.

An identical score in two or more columns is possible (for example, nine a's and five b's in column II and nine a's and five b's in column III) and simply implies that the strength of the tendency designated by each column is the same.

However, if the final score is the same in columns III and IV, both the "area of interest" and "style of behavior" are dominant motivations and, depending on circumstances, either can serve as the secondary motivation.

Whether the scores in the third and fourth columns are identical or not, every reader should refer to both descriptions of the areas of interest and style of behavior for a full account of the motivations that influence personality. For example, an extraverted (fourteen b's, zero a's) spirited (five b's, nine a's) Pneuma (four a's, ten b's) Power (three a's, eleven b's) type needs to read the sections on both the extraverted Pneuma type and the extraverted Power type in Chapter 3.

Notes

References to the English translation of the *Collected Works of C. G. Jung*, Bollingen Series XX, volumes 1–20 (Princeton: Princeton University Press, 1954–1979) are indicated as *CW* followed by volume and paragraph number. References to *The Standard Edition of the Complete Psychological Works of Sigmund Freud*, vols. 1–24, ed. and trans. by James Strachey, in collaboration with Anna Freud, assisted by Alix Strachey and Alan Tyson (London: Hogarth Press, 1953–74) are indicated as *SE* followed by volume and page number.

Foreword and Preface

1. A colorful and well known Venezuelan Jungian analyst and writer, author of, among other works, *Cultural Anxiety*.
2. See Johnson, *Jung's Compass of Psychological Types*, also http://www.giftscompass.com.
3. Jung, *Memories, Dreams, Reflections*, p. 207.
4. Ibid.
5. Personal communication.
6. Ibid.
7. Ibid., p. 209.
8. Von Franz, "The Inferior Function," in *Lectures on Jung's Typology*.
9. Jung, *CW* 7, para. 78.
10. Jung, *CW* 16, para. 79.
11. Ibid.
12. As the white spot in the dark area of yin and the black spot in the white area of yang indicate, each archetype has an element of the other within it. Thus Eros has some Power motivation and Power some Eros; similarly, Pneuma has within it a kernel of Physis and Physis a germ of Pneuma.
13. William James, *Pragmatism: A New Name for Some Old Ways of Thinking* (New York London Toronto: Longman's Green & Co., 1947), pp. 8–9.
14. Jung, *CW* 6, para. 91.
15. Deirdre Bair, *Jung: A Biography* (Boston New York London: Little, Brown and Company, 2003), p. 722, note 50.

1 Introduction: Typology

1. Jung acknowledged the role astrology played in the history of typology but did not make use of its categories, at least in his writings. In his essay, "Synchronicity: An Acausal Connecting Principle," he undertook an astrological experiment to see if there was a synchronicity, or a meaningful coincidence, between married couples and certain astrological conjunctions

in their horoscopes. One of Jung's daughters, Gret Baumann-Jung became a respected astrologer. The British psychologist, Jungian analyst and astrologer Liz Greene, has correlated the categories of modern astrology with Jungian psychology in such books as *Development of Personality*, *Dynamics of the Unconscious* and *Mythic Astrology*.

2. In the West, the idea of the four elements has its origins in pre-Socratic times. Aristotle added ether as a fifth incorruptible element of which the heavenly bodies are composed. The Hindu schema also has ether as a fifth element. The Chinese version has five elements: wood, metal, earth, water and fire. The absence of air and the addition of wood and metal make the Chinese system markedly different from the Western and Indian ones.
3. In the seventeenth-century anthology, *Theatrum Chemicum Britannicum*, the alchemist David Lagneus associated the four humors and their colors with the four stages of the alchemical opus: the melancholic-black with *nigredo*; the phlegmatic-white with *albedo*; the choleric-yellow with *citrinitas*; and the sanguine-red with *rubedo*. See C. G. Jung, *CW* 14, para. 390, note 113.
4. It is worth noting that aside from their reliance upon astrology, the ancient Egyptians had a mythologically based typology related to the contending gods Seth and Horus. Seth was the god of chaos, of storms and thunder; Horus, the god of order, of civilization and kingship. The Seth type of person was hot-tempered, emotional and instinctive; the Horus type was self-possessed and moderate in behavior. Interestingly enough, the two personality types were taken into account in the interpretation of dreams. See Geraldine Pinch, *Egyptian Myth: A Very Short Introduction* (Oxford: Oxford University Press, 2004), p. 87.
5. In the twentieth century, a somatically based typology was proposed by the German psychiatrist Ernst Kretschmer and the American psychologist William H. Sheldon. Sheldon relied heavily on Kretschmer's classification of asthenic, athletic and pyknic types, essentially changing the nomenclature to ectomorph, mesomorph and endomorph. The thin asthenic-ectomorph is sensitive, artistic, apprehensive and introverted. The muscular athletic-mesomorph is energetic, active and aggressive. The plump pyknic-endomorph is relaxed, even-tempered and sociable. Jungian psychologists Tara and James Arraj seek to integrate Jung's psychological types with Sheldon's somatotypes in *Tracking the Elusive Human: A Practical Guide to C. G. Jung's Psychological Types and W. H. Sheldon's Body and Temperament Types and Their Integration*, vols. 1 and 2 (Chiloquin, OR: Inner Growth Books, 1994).
6. Jung, *CW* 6, para. 254.
7. David Hume, *Of the Standard of Taste and Other Essays*, ed. John W. Lenz (Indianapolis: The Library of Liberal Arts, 1975).
8. Schiller, Friedrich, *On the Aesthetic Education of Man*, trans. and Introduction by Reginald Snell (Mineola, NY: Dover Publications, Inc., 2004), p. 80. Cited in Jung, *CW* 6, para. 171.
9. Jung is reported to have said that "*Psychological Types* was written entirely on the basis of the material contained in thirty pages of his *Red Book*." (See Stephan A. Hoeller, *The Gnostic Jung and the Seven Sermons to the Dead* (Madras, India/London, England: The Theosophical Publishing House, 1989), p. 6. With the recent publication of *The Red Book* we now know that these pages

refer to the *Liber Primus*, the first part of *The Red Book*. When Jung recorded his visions and fantasies in this part of the book, he had not yet formulated the concept of archetype. He, therefore, interpreted the figures of Elijah and Salome as representative of his thinking and feeling functions. Since the feeling function was personified by Salome, he also identified feeling with pleasure; a far cry from his eventual definition of feeling in *Psychological Types*, as a rational evaluative function. Only after some years did he refer to Elijah and Salome as the archetypal principles of Logos and Eros. (See *The Red Book: Liber Novus*. ed. Sonu Shamdasani. Preface by Ulrich Hoerni. trans. Mark Kyburz, John Peck and Sonu Shamdasani. New York, London: W. W. Norton & Co., 2009. pp. 247–48 and C. G. Jung, *Analytical Psychology: Notes of the Seminar Given in 1925*, ed. William McGuire, Bolingen Series XCIX (Princeton, NJ: Princeton University Press, 1989), pp. 88–90.

10. Jung, *CW* 6, para. 830.
11. Jung, *CW* 7, para. 78.
12. Geoffrey Chaucer, *The Canterbury Tales* (London: Penguin Books, 1977), p. 410.
13. Jung, *CW* 9i, para. 197.
14. Jung, *CW* 8, para. 251.
15. See Arthur O. Lovejoy, *The Great Chain of Being: A Study of the History of an Idea* (New York: Harper & Row, 2005).
16. John Beebe, "Understanding Consciousness through the Theory of Psychological Types, *Analytical Psychology: Contemporary Perspectives on Jungian Analysis*," eds. Joseph Cambray and Linda Carter. (Hove and New York: Brunner-Routledge, 2004), pp. 105–112. Please see Appendix I for additional material on Beebe's model.
17. Silas L. Warner, "Freud's Antipathy to America," *Journal of the American Academy of Psychoanalysis, 19* (1), (1991) p.149.
18. Essays on these various typologies can be found in *Who Am I? Personality Types for Self-Discovery*, Robert Frager, ed., (New York: G. P. Putnam's Sons, 1994).

2 The Archetypes of Power, Eros, Pneuma and Physis

1. Edward F. Edinger, *Anatomy of the Psyche: Alchemical Symbolism in Psychotherapy*, (La Salle, Ill.: Open Court, 1985), p. 191.
2. In *Psychopathology and Politics*, a 1930 work that pioneered the application of Freudian psychology to politics, the political scientist Harold D. Lasswell describes individuals who pursue their power orientation in the realm of politics. He conjectures that the "most aggressive, power-lusting individuals in modern society find their way into business, and stay out of the legislature, the courts, the civil service, and the diplomatic service" (p.45). But even in the corporate world, "the man who cherishes power must achieve some measure of socialization or he is outlawed" (p. 50). Among those power oriented individuals who pursue power in politics, Lasswell finds three functional types: the administrator, the agitator and the theorist. Composite types are also possible, for example, Lenin who combined all three (p.54). Lasswell also proposes a definition of the *homo politicus*: an individual who is

able to displace his or her private motives onto the public realm and rationalize the displacement in terms of the public good (pp. 261–2).

3. Jung, *CW* 14, para. 1.
4. Jung, *CW* 16, p. 167.
5. In her book, *Eros and Chaos: The Sacred Mysteries and Dark Shadows of Love*, Veronica Goodchild challenges the usual mythological paradigm that chaos gives rise to order. Instead, she explores the premise that "chaos is a harbinger of eros" (p. 1).
6. Robert Graves, *The Greek Myths* (Baltimore, Maryland: Penguin Books, 1968), vol. 1, p. 58, 15. 1, p. 145, 39, j.
7. Peter Gay, *Freud: A Life for Our Time* (New York and London: W. W. Norton & Co., 1988), p. 40.
8. Jung, *CW* 9i, para. 167.
9. Analytical philosophers and deconstructionists adhere to the principle of Logos, of discrimination and differentiation, and in this context, therefore, one can speak of another opposition, that between Eros and Logos. Freud's psychoanalysis, for example, is ruled by the principle of Logos, as are the disciplines of clinical psychology and psychiatry. Jung's analytical psychology, on the other hand, seeks a balance between analysis and synthesis.
10. Jan Christiaan Smuts (1870–1950) was a prominent South African military leader, statesman and philosopher. In his 1926 book, *Holism and Evolution*, he advanced the thesis that nature evolves though the creation of unified wholes that are then greater than the sum of their independent parts. Shortly after the publication of the book, Albert Einstein concluded that his theory of relativity and Smuts' concept of holism would inform human thought in the coming millennium. He also stated that Smuts was one of the few people in the world who understood his theory of relativity.

    Smuts applied the idea of holism to his international political activities. He supported the establishment of the British Commonwealth. The League of Nations was implemented according to his designs and he wrote the preamble to the United Nations Charter. Domestically, however, he was a vocal supporter of segregation and white supremacy; in time, he modified his stand slightly in response to pressure from the international community.
11. *A Dictionary of Symbols*, eds. Jean Chevalier and Alain Gheerbrant, (London: Penguin Books, 1996), p. 87.
12. Ibid., p. 57.
13. Ibid., p. 121.
14. Jung, *CW* 14, para. 1.
15. Jung, *CW* 9ii, para. 368.

3 Power, Eros, Physis and Pneuma Personality Types

1. The eight personality types described in this chapter are not identical with the results on the Archetypal-Motivational Test Scale, which include the secondary motivation. However, the characteristics of the secondary motivation may be obtained by reading the section in this chapter that describes that archetype as a primary motivation. In other words, an extraverted Eros type with Matter as the secondary motivation, should read both the section

on the extraverted Eros type and the section on the extraverted Matter type. These are the two consciously deployed motivations and the descriptions in this chapter, therefore, outline both the dominant and secondary motivations. (The inferior motivation noted in the section describing the secondary motivation is then a description of the tertiary motivation.)

2. Jung, *CW* 6, para. 559.
3. On the surface, the Physis type, whether introverted or extraverted, seems to correlate with the sensation type in Jungian typology. Jung's typology describes conscious mental functioning and defines the sensation type as someone who apprehends inner or outer reality—depending on whether the type is introverted or extraverted—in a quick, precise and objective manner. In my terms, that functioning in itself does not necessarily mean that such an individual is oriented toward the material universe. A person can be a sensation type and chiefly motivated by the archetype Pneuma or Spirit, in which case, the sensation function is used to classify ideas or concepts rather than concrete data. The entire orientation of the psyche towards physical or material reality, and not just the primacy of the sensation function, is what defines the Physis type.
4. Harold D. Lasswell, *Politics: Who Gets What, When, How*. (New York: Meridian Books, 1972.)

4 Soulful and Spirited Temperaments

1. I question the Myers-Briggs attempt to assign the preferred attitude between extraversion and introversion to the dominant function and the less preferred attitude to the auxiliary function. This is a theoretical notion with little empirical evidence to support it. The idea assumes that both the superior and secondary functions remain exclusively bound to either extraversion or introversion. I am not certain that is the case. An introverted thinking sensation type, for instance, can call upon a degree of extraversion in the use of the thinking function and remain with the introverted attitude in the use of the secondary function. The arrangement also runs counter to the tendency of many Jungian analysts to consider both the dominant and the auxiliary functions under the sway of the dominant attitude of either introversion or extraversion.
2. *Man and His Symbols*, C. G. Jung et al. (Garden City, NY: Doubleday & Co., 1964), p. 77.
3. Jung, *CW* 9i, para. 183.
4. *The Way and Its Power*, trans. Arthur Waley (London, 1934) quoted in C. G. Jung, *CW*8, para. 918.
5. Ibid., para. 919.
6. Jung, *CW* 14, para. 155.
7. Ibid.
8. Jung, *CW* 9i, para. 66.1
9. Every archetype contains its opposite. The anima therefore is the archetype of both life and death. For a description of these two sides of the anima, see Marie-Louise von Franz, "The Process of Individuation," in *Man and His Symbols*. In his early work, *Re-Visioning Psychology*, James Hillman emphasizes the death aspect of the soul, or anima; in his later writings, the anima becomes the living sensuous experience of the world. See his essay, "Anima Mundi: The Return of the Soul to the World" in *The Thought of the Heart and The Soul of the World.*

10. In *The Wounded Scholar: Research with Soul in Mind*, the Jungian oriented phenomenologist, Robert D. Romanyshyn articulates a soulful approach to scholarly research in contrast to Logos oriented scholarship. He proposes a hermeneutic methodology, which, unlike traditional hermeneutics, takes the unconscious into account. *The Soulful Scholar: Research with Soul in Mind* is probably a more felicitous and accurate title for this ground-breaking book.
11. *The I Ching or Book of Changes*, The Richard Wilhelm Translation rendered into English by Cary F. Baynes, Foreword by C. G. Jung, Bollingen Series XIX (Princeton: Princeton University Press, 1971), p. lvi.
12. Ibid., p. 3.
13. Ibid., p. 10. See Appendix II for a discussion of the primacy of spirit in the *I Ching* in comparison to the equivalence of value placed on soul (yin) and spirit (yang) in Taoism.
14. Ibid., p. 3.
15. Ibid., p. 453.
16. James Hillman, *Re-Visioning Psychology* (New York: Harper& Row, 1975), p. 69.

5 Temperament and Theory: Freud, Adler and Jung

1. In the 1932 exchange of letters between Einstein and Freud about the possibility of avoiding future wars, Freud described, as he put it, "our mythological theory of instincts:" the struggle between Thanatos and Eros. Then he added, "It may perhaps seem to you as though our theories are a kind of mythology and, in the present case, not even an agreeable one. But does not every science come in the end to a kind of mythology like this? Cannot the same be said to-day of your own Physics?" (Freud, "Why War?" *SE* XXII, 199) An illustration of Freud's statement is provided by the contemporary theoretical physicist, Stephen Hawking, in *A Brief History of Time*. Hawking describes the nature of the universe prior to the big bang as *infinitely small, infinitely dense*, and *infinitely hot* (my emphasis). The condition transcends all scientific laws and theories, while the terminology and concepts involved are clearly mythological, to say the least.
2. Alfred Adler's pioneering work was *A Study of Organ Inferiority*, in which he argued that the cause of most neuroses is to be found in congenital physiological weaknesses. The organism and psyche inevitably seek to compensate for these inferiorities with a striving for superiority, but that striving may also lead to overcompensation: the classic example is Napoleon whose diminutive stature lead to a titanic drive for power.
3. Jung, *MDR*, p. 356.
4. Ibid., p. 358.
5. Edward F. Edinger, *Ego and Archetype: Individuation and the Religious Function of the Psyche* (Middlesex: Penguin Books, 1986), p. xiii.
6. Laurens van der Post, *Jung and the Story of Our Time* (New York: Pantheon Books, 1975), p. 17.
7. Jung, *CW* 6, para. 539.
8. William James, *Pragmatism: A New Name for Some Old Ways of Thinking* (New York London Toronto: Longman's Green & Co., 1947), pp. 6–7.

9. Ibid., pp. 7–8.
10. Jung, *CW* 7, para. 59.
11. Ibid., para. 60.
12. Jung, *CW* 6, para. 91.
13. Bair, p. 285.
14. Ibid. Jung's diagnosis of Freud as neurotic leads me to think of the three men in terms of their pathological predispositions: Freud was a neurotic type with an undertone of hysteria, Adler, a manic-depressive type and Jung, a schizophrenic type.
15. Ibid., p. 722, fn. 50. In his biography of Freud, Louis Breger, *Freud: Darkness in the Midst of Vision* (New York: John Wiley & Sons, inc., 2000), argues that Freud's early childhood was indeed traumatic: a brother was born when Freud was 11 months old and his mother stopped breastfeeding him; the boy, named after the mother's brother who died just before the child was born, himself died eight months later and the mother withdrew into a prolonged period of mourning. After that, a new sibling arrived almost every year until Freud's tenth year. The Czech nanny who loved and admired the young Freud was arrested for petty thievery and disappeared from his life when he was two and a half. His father's business failed shortly thereafter and the family moved from Freud's childhood home first to Leipzig and then to Vienna. Breger observes that Freud tended to gloss over this early period, presenting it in his autobiographical statements as an essentially happy childhood; and his earlier biographers took him at his word. Breger thinks Freud's insistence on the Oedipus complex as the central theme of his theory was a defensive move compensating for an absent mother and a passive father. Turning the tables on him, Breger argues that the presence of the Oedipus complex within Freud's own unconscious represented a wish-fulfillment on Freud's part for a loving mother and a strong father.
16. Ibid.
17. Jung, *CW* 6, para. 55.
18. C. G. Jung, *Letters*, Vol. 2 (London: Routledge & Kegan Paul, 1976), p. 347.
19. Ibid., p. 348.
20. Gay, p. 475.
21. Jung, *Letters*, vol. 2, p. 350.
22. Von Franz and Hillman, p. 61.
23. Ibid.
24. Ibid.
25. Ibid.
26. Ibid.
27. Bair, p. 722, note 50.
28. Ibid.
29. *The Freud/Jung Letters: Correspondence between Sigmund Freud and C. G. Jung*, ed. William McGuire, Bollingen Series XCIV (Princeton: Princeton University Press, 1974), p. 472.
30. Ibid. Horace Gray, who with Jane and Joseph Wheelwright designed the Jungian Type Survey, disputes Freud's assessment of himself as an intuitive type and argues that he was in fact a sensation type with feeling as his secondary function. Gray also accepts Jung's initial argument that Freud was an extravert. I think Gray's erroneous conclusion that Freud was a sensation

type stems from Freud's Physis motivation. Gray's assessment can be found in "Freud and Jung: Their Contrasting Psychological Types," *Psychoanalytic Review*, 36(1), January 1949, pp. 22–44.

31. Jung, *CW* 6, para. 577.
32. Ibid.
33. Henri F. Ellenberger, *The Discovery of the Unconscious: The History and Evolution of Dynamic Psychiatry* (New York: Basic Books, 1970), p. 508.
34. Ibid.
35. Jung, *CW* 6, para. 630.
36. *The Individual Psychology of Alfred Adler: A Systematic Presentation in Selections from his Writings*, edited and annotated by Heinz L. Ansbacher and Rowena R. Ansbacher (New York: Harper & Row, 1967), p. 5.
37. Bair, p. 286.
38. Gay, p. 475.
39. Freud, *SE* XVIII, 38.
40. Ibid., p. 402 note.
41. Ibid., p. 402.
42. Jung, *CW* 7, para. 79.
43. Ibid., para. 78.
44. Ibid.
45. Ibid.
46. Freud, *SE* XXII, 95
47. Ibid., p.211.
48. The ongoing contemporary fascination with UFOs demonstrate, the tendency to explain and experience all phenomena in terms of one's world view. In the past, these objects seen in the heavens would have been associated with angels or gods and not with space ships and aliens. The title of Jung's study of UFO sightings indicates the contemporary bias: *Flying Saucers: A Modern Myth of Things Seen in the Skies*. Since the publication of Jung's book in 1958, the once distant sightings have turned more concrete and personal. The mythologist Glen Slater observes that during the intervening decades "speculations about visitors from outer space have become more detailed and intense," so much so that they now include accounts of experiences of abductions by aliens. (Glen Slater, "Aliens and Insects," *Varieties of Mythic Experience: Essays on Religion, Psyche and Culture*, eds. Dennis P. Slattery and Glen Slater (Einsiedeln, Switzerland: Daimon Verlag, 2008), p. 193. See Whitley Strieber's *Communion: A True Story*, a best seller account of an alien abduction experience and Susan A. Clancy's scholarly study, *Abducted: How People Come to Believe They Were Kidnapped by Aliens* (Cambridge, MA: Harvard University Press, 2005.) Interestingly, the alien visitors are envisioned as hybrid mechanical and insect-like creatures. Slater refers to this combination of advanced technology and regressive instinctuality as a *technomyth* and argues that the image represents the split in the contemporary psyche between "an oppressive, autonomous mechanization of existence on one side, and a neglected, regressed, instinctive nature on the other" (Slater, *op. cit.*, p. 205).
49. Jung. *MDR*, p. 150.
50. Ibid.
51. Phyllis Bottome, *Alfred Adler: Apostle of Freedom* (London: Faber and Faber LTD, 1957), p. 120.

52. Ibid.
53. Ibid., p. 121.
54. Ibid., p. 123.
55. Ibid., p. 122.
56. Jung, *MDR*, p. 168.
57. Jung, *CW* 6, para. 93.
58. Ibid.
59. Bottome, p. 15.
60. Jung, *CW* 8, para. 827, note 12. Perhaps one can also find evocative meaning in the names of Rank (slim, slender) and Reich (rich, abundant).
61. Jung, *MDR*, p. 227. The Bollingen Stone is a square block about 20 inches thick on which Jung chiseled words and images that came to him from the depths of his being. He considered this stone together with the Bollingen Tower symbolic representations of his personality.
62. Jung, *CW* 6, para. 93.
63. Jung, *MDR*, pp. 149–50.
64. Jung, *CW* 6, para. 91.
65. *The Individual Psychology of Alfred Adler: A Systematic Presentation in Selections from His Writings, op. cit.*, p. 167.
66. See Chapters 1 and 2 in *Two Essays on Analytical Psychology*, CW7.
67. "From the beginning I felt the Tower as in some way a place of maturation—a maternal womb or a maternal figure in which I could become what I was, what I am and will be. It gave me a feeling as if I were being reborn in stone. It is thus a concretization of the individuation process, a memorial *aere perennius*. During the building work, of course, I never considered these matters. I built the house in sections, always following the concrete needs of the moment. It might also be said that I built it in a kind of dream. Only afterward did I see how all the parts fitted together and that a meaningful form had resulted: a symbol of psychic wholeness." Jung, *MDR*, p. 225.
68. Jung, *CW* 4, para. 774.

6 Sigmund Freud: Introverted Spirited Power Physis Type

1. Ernest Jones, *The Life and Work of Sigmund Freud* (New York: Basic Books, 1955), vol. 1, p. 60.
2. Jones, vol. 2, pp. 404–5.
3. Gay, p. 99.
4. Ibid., p. 124.
5. Bair, p. 210.
6. Gay, p. 157.
7. Ibid., p. 316. The repressed rage the essay contains explains why he published it anonymously. He finally let out his anger in *The History of the Psycho-Analytic Movement*. *SE* XIV.
8. Gay, p. 217.
9. Isidor Sadger. *Recollecting Freud*. ed. Alan Dundes (Madison, Wisconsin: University of Wisconsin Press, 2005), pp. 40–1.
10. Ibid., p. 55.

11. Jones, vol. I, p. 162.
12. Freud, "Why War?" vol. XXII, 213. (Emphasis added.)
13. Ibid., 212.
14. *Sigmund Freud: Psychoanalysis and Faith, Dialogues with the Reverend Oskar Pfister* (New York: Basic Books, 1963), eds. Heinrich Meng and Ernst L. Freud, trans. Eric Mosbacher, p. 118.
15. Freud, *Group Psychology and the Analysis of the Ego, SE* XVIII, 127.
16. Gay, p. 230
17. Ibid.
18. Jones, vol. I, pp. 22–3.
19. Siegfried Bernfeld, "Freud's Scientific Beginnings," *The American Imago,* VI (Sept. 1949), p. 163.
20. Jones, vol. I, p. 31.
21. Gay, p. 25. Peter Gay's translation of this passage differs markedly from that of the *Standard Edition* which replaces the phrase "greed for knowledge" with "curiosity."
22. Gay, p. 24.
23. Ibid., p. 157.
24. Ibid.
25. Ibid.
26. Bair, p. 163.
27. Ibid., p. 164.
28. Ibid.
29. Freud, "Character and Anal Eroticism," *SE* IX, 175.
30. Gay, p. 23. In a footnote added in 1914 to the *Interpretation of Dreams* Freud writes: "We have also learned from psycho-analysis of neurotic subjects the intimate connection between bed-wetting and the character trait of ambition" (*SE* IV, 216). I tend to regard bed-wetting as a regressive tendency, a desire to return to the womb. Deliberate, adolescent pissing-contests certainly can be associated with competition and ambition. The adult Freud's neurotic urge to urinate in public places requires a more sophisticated explanation than either regression or ambition.
31. Freud, *Interpretation of Dreams SE* IV, 216.
32. Ibid.
33. Bair, p. 164.
34. Ibid., p. 161.
35. Ibid.
36. Ibid., p. 164.
37. Freud, *Interpretation of Dreams, SE* V, 546.
38. Gay, p. 171.
39. Ibid., p. 33.
40. Ibid., p. 156.
41. Freud, *Totem and Taboo, SE* XIII, 33–4.
42. Freud, *Jokes and their Relation to the Unconscious, SE* VIII, 109.
43. Gay, p. 165.
44. Freud to Jones in English, 8 February 1914. Freud Collection. D2. Library of Congress. Quoted in Gay, pp. 167–8.
45. Gay, p. 46, footnote.
46. Freud, *Interpretation of* Dreams, *SE* IV, 41–2.

47. Freud, *Three Essays on the Theory of Sexuality, SE* VII, 219 and 217. As evidence for such sexualization of the entire body, Freud can point to early representation of female goddesses covered with breasts or eyes (analogues of the vulva) and of male gods associated with trees, bulls and Hermes pillars. Actually, these figures are imaginal attempts on the part of the psyche to convey the generative aspects of nature and not of the human body. As a Physis type, and having rejected Jung's formulation of the collective unconscious and the archetypes, Freud concretized the symbolism in the human body and regarded mythological images as sublimated expressions of physiological processes. In this respect, the mythologist Joseph Campbell, who is considered a Jungian because of his reliance upon the concept of universal archetypes, is actually closer to Freud than to Jung. Campbell argues that all mythical images are manifestations of biological energies (see Chapter 2 section on Projection).
48. Gay, p. 119.
49. See *Psycho-Analytic Notes on An Autobiographical Account of a Case of Paranoia, SE* XII, 4–5.
50. Gay, p. 55.
51. Ibid., p. 274.
52. Ibid.
53. Ibid., p. 275.
54. Paul Ferris, *Dr Freud: A Life* (Washington, D.C.: Counterpoint, 1997), p. 138.
55. Gay, p. 632.
56. Ibid., p. 337.
57. Bair, p. 447.
58. Jung, *CW* 7, para. 78.
59. Freud, *Moses and Monotheism, SE* XXIII, 123.
60. Ibid.
61. Gay, p. 606.
62. Ibid., p. 608.
63. Freud, *Future of an Illusion, SE* XXI, 30 and 24.

7 Alfred Adler: Extraverted Soulful Physis Eros Type

1. Edward Hoffman, *The Drive For Self: Alfred Adler and the Founding of Individual Psychology* (Reading, MA: Addison-Wesley Publishing Co., 1994), p.50.
2. Sigmund Freud, *Collected Papers*, vols. I–V (London: The Hogarth Press, 1949), vol. III, p. 281.
3. *The Individual Psychology of Alfred Adler: A Systematic Presentation in Selections from his Writings*, op. cit., pp. 47–8.
4. *The Freud-Jung Letters: The Correspondence between Sigmund Freud and C. G. Jung*, William McGuire, ed., Bollingen Series XCIV (Princeton, N.J.: Princeton University Press, 1974), 3 Dec, 1910, p. 376.
5. Hoffman, p. 69.
6. *Minutes of the Vienna Psychoanalytic Society*, vols. 1–4, Herman Nunberg and Ernst Federn, eds. (New York: International Universities Press, 1962–75), vol. 3, p. 147.

7. James E. Lieberman, *Acts of Will: The Life and Work of Otto Rank* (New York: Free Press, 1985), p. 126.
8. Sigmund Freud to Ernest Jones, (in English), August 9, 1911. Freud Collection, D2, LC).
9. *The Individual Psychology of Alfred Adler*, p. 179.
10. Hoffman, p. 281.
11. Ibid.
12. Alfred Adler, *Superiority and Social Interest: A Collection of Later Writings*, Heinz L. Ansbacher and Rowena R. Ansbacher, eds. (Evanston, IL: Northwestern University Press, 1964), pp. 307–8.
13. *The Individual Psychology of Alfred Adler*, p.34.
14. Ibid., p. 30.
15. *Minutes of the Vienna Psychoanalytic Society*, vol. 3, p. 147.
16. Phyllis Bottome, *Alfred Adler: Apostle of Freedom* (London: Faber and Faber, 1957), p. 61.
17. Hoffman, p. 36.
18. Ibid., p. 37.
19. *The Individual Psychology of Alfred Adler*, p. 40.
20. Ibid., p. 41.
21. *The Individual Psychology of Alfred Adler*, p. 42.
22. Bottome, p. 75.
23. Ibid, p. 19.
24. Ibid, p. 61.
25. Henri F. Ellenberger, *The Discovery of the Unconscious: The History and Evolution of Dynamic Psychiatry* (New York: Basic Books, 1970), p. 608.
26. Silas L. Warner, "Freud's Antipathy to America," *Journal of the American Academy of Psychoanalysis*, 1991, 19 (1), p. 149.
27. Bottome, p. 122.
28. Ibid, pp. 114–16.
29. Ibid, p. 121.
30. Ibid., p. 123.
31. Hoffman, p. 50.
32. *Science*, vol. 311, Issue 5765, 3 March 2006, pp. 1248–49.
33. Hoffman, p. 5.
34. Ibid., p. 7.
35. Ibid., p. 8.
36. Bottome, p. 125.
37. Freud, *SE* XX, 110.
38. Bottome, p. 256.
39. *The Individual Psychology of Alfred Adler*, p. 370.
40. Ibid., p. 375.
41. Ibid., p. 376.
42. Bottome, p. 26.
43. Ellenberger, p. 584.
44. Bottome, p. 55.
45. Hoffman, p. 234.
46. Jung, *CW* 16, *The Psychology of the Transference* (epigraph to the Introduction).
47. Bottome, p. 48.

48. Hoffman, p. 20.
49. Ibid.
50. Ibid. p. 308.
51. Ibid. p. 321.
52. Gay, p. 615.
53. Jones, vol. II, p. 130.
54. Bottome, p. 113.
55. Ibid., p. 114.
56. Ibid., p. 36.
57. Hoffman, p. 304.
58. Ibid., p. 305.
59. Ibid., p. 315.
60. Abraham Maslow, "Tributes to Alfred Adler on his 100th Birthday," *Journal of Individual Psychology*, 26 (1), 1970, p. 13.
61. Ellenberger, p. 594.
62. Ibid., p. 588.
63. Hoffman, p. 321.
64. Bottome, p. 72.
65. Ellenberger, p. 594.
66. Hoffman, p. 326.
67. Ibid.
68. Ellenberger, p. 645.
69. Ibid.
70. *Minutes of the Vienna Psychoanalytic Society*, vol. 3, p. 147.
71. Ibid.
72. Ellenberger, p. 638. My paraphrase of Ellenberger's summary.
73. Ibid., p. 641.
74. Viktor Frankl, "Tributes to Alfred Adler on his 100th Birthday," *Journal of Individual Psychology*, 26 (1), 1970, p. 12.
75. *The Collected Clinical Works of Alfred Adler*, 12 vols. ed. Henry T. Stein. Bellingham, WA: Classical Adlerian Translation Project.

8 C. G. Jung: Introverted Soulful Power Pneuma Type: Part I

1. Bottome, p. 116.
2. Jung, *MDR*, p. 383.
3. Bottome, p. 72.
4. Ibid. p. 62.
5. Jung, *CW* 10, para. 457.
6. Jung, *CW* 9, para. 516.
7. Ellenberger, p. 609.
8. Ibid.
9. Liliane Frey-Rohn, *From Freud to Jung: A Comparative Study of the Psychology of the Unconscious* (New York: G. P. Putnam's Sons, 1974), p. 77.
10. Bair, p. 500.
11. Jung, *CW* 8, para. 545.
12. Ibid.

13. *The Individual Psychology of Alfred Adler*, p. 57.
14. Ibid.
15. Ibid., p. 58. Emphasis added.
16. Bottome, p. 20 and p. 75.
17. Jung, *CW* 4, p. 87.
18. Ibid., paras. 237–8. Emphasis in original.
19. In his writings, Jung uses the "libido" and "psychic energy" interchangeably, and for him the term "libido" always carries an expanded, non-sexual meaning.
20. Jung, *CW* 8, para.10.
21. Ibid. Emphasis added.
22. Francis Crick, *The Astonishing Hypothesis: The Scientific Search for the Soul* (New York: Charles Scribner's Sons, 1994), p. 3.
23. *Newsweek*, "What Dreams Are Made Of," August 9, 2004, p. 45.
24. Jung, *CW* 8, para. 10.
25. Ibid.
26. Jung, *CW* 8, para. 79ff and *CW* 5, para. 203ff.
27. Jung, *CW* 5, para. 214.
28. *C. G. Jung Letters*, vol. 2, p. 350. Here, Jung errs in crediting Adler with coining a term for synchronistic phenomena. Adler used the German word *junctim* (a parliamentary term for two or more unconnected proposals brought together to be voted on as a unit) for two disparate emotions or thoughts for the purpose of intensifying an affect, for example, an agoraphobic linking the fear of going shopping with the fantasy of a stroke or of there being germs in the street. See *Freud/Jung Letters: The Correspondence between Sigmund Freud and C. G. Jung*, ed. William McGuire (Princeton, NJ: Princeton University Press, 1974), p. 531 and *The Individual Psychology of Alfred Adler, eds.* Heinz. L. Ansbacher and Rowena R. Ansbacher (New York: Harper & Row, 1976), p. 283.
29. *The Individual Psychology of Alfred Adler*, p. 89 and p. 95.
30. Jung, *CW* 8, para. 74.
31. Ibid., para. 798.
32. Jung, *MDR*, p. 5.
33. Ibid., p. 16.
34. Bair, p. 26.
35. Jung, *MDR*, p. 12.
36. There is a connection between the phallic image in Jung's dream and the figure of Telesphoros that Jung carved on the Bollingen Stone. See C. A. Meier, *Healing Dream and Ritual: Ancient Incubation and Modern Psychotherapy* (Einsiedeln: Daimon Verlag, 1989), Plates 6 and 7, page36.
37. Jung, *MDR*, p. 36.
38. Ibid., p. 39.
39. Ibid., p. 41.
40. Ibid., pp. 41–2.
41. Bair, p. 397.
42. Jung, *MDR*, p. 30.
43. Ibid., pp. 30–1.
44. Bair, p. 32.
45. Jung, *MDR*, p. 32.
46. Bair, p. 33.

47. Jung, *MDR*, p. 32.
48. Ibid., p. 33.
49. Ibid.
50. Although Jung's fantasy life as a child may have been more intense and dramatic than that of many other children, he was no different in the intimate connection all children have to the inner world. Children live in a mythological state of mind, in mystical connection with nature and immersed in a world of archetypal images, rituals and fantasies. With the still dominant Enlightenment bias toward rationality and the Freudian emphasis on consciousness and the reality principle, our contemporary Western approach to child-rearing and education—with notable exceptions, such as the Waldorf Schools—gives short shrift to the symbolic life of children. Parents and teachers think they have realized their responsibilities if they manage to disenchant and disconnect children from their fantasy life. What is not understood is that in so doing, we also cut off children from the source of creativity and psychological well-being. Fortunately, given the astounding sales of the Harry Potter books by J. K. Rowling, the proliferation of fantasy video games, and the perennial popularity of rock and popular music, the imaginal life of children and teenagers thrives unabated. There have been endless studies of children, encompassing their psycho-sexual, affective, cognitive, social, ethical and religious forms of development. Only Jean Piaget in *The Child's Conception of the World* and *The Child's Conception of Physical Causality* has described the mythological characteristics of childhood thinking. However, he considers these characteristics as early stages in the child's cognitive development, which is his primary area of his interest. He does not think of the child's mythological frame of reference as valuable in its own right and as a vital component in the psychological development and well-being of the child. Among Jungian writers, only Erich Neumann, in *The Origins and History of Consciousness* and *The Child,* has provided a theoretical description of the *mythological stages of childhood development*. So far, there appear to have been no empirical studies of the mythological stages of childhood similar to those of Jean Piaget. In view of the overwhelming evidence of the importance that fantasy plays in the life of children, such studies, it seems to me, are sorely needed and long overdue.
51. Jung, *CW* 6, para. 628.
52. Ibid., para. 629.
53. Ibid.
54. There have been a number of attempts to define Jung's typology disputing his own assessment that he was an introverted thinking intuitive type, with thinking as his superior function and intuition as auxiliary. Horace Gray, in "Freud and Jung: Their Contrasting Psychological Types," (*Psychoanalytic Review*, 36 (1), January 1949, pp. 22–44), thinks Jung was an introvert but that it is hard to decide whether his leading function was intuition or thinking, since both were well developed. Gray leans towards thinking as Jung's dominant function. On the other hand, Angelo Spoto, in *Jung's Typology in Perspective* (Wilmette, Illinois: Chiron Publications, 1995), argues that intuition was Jung's dominant function and thinking his auxiliary. Relying on the Myers-Briggs hypothesis that the secondary

function is opposite in attitude from the primary, he concludes that Jung extraverted his thinking function. The conclusion flies in the face of Jung's description of introverted thinking, which is essentially taken from his own experience. Spoto, however, does leave the question open by stating, "Jung just may have been a strange enough bird to have two superior functions working in both attitudes" (p.74). I believe there is some validity in Spoto's observation and in Gray's feeling that Jung's thinking and intuition were equally well developed. I would simply add that in the first half of his life, before he separated from Freud and underwent his creative crisis, Jung relied primarily upon his thinking function. His earliest writings on schizophrenia and on the word association test as well as the lectures he delivered at Fordham University in September 1912, for example, are clear, precise and logically argued. Beginning with *Symbols of Transformation*, however, as he turned inward and allowed his intuition greater play, his writing became circular and more difficult to follow.

55. Jung, *CW* 6, para. 633.
56. Ibid., para. 635.
57. Ibid.
58. Ibid., para. 634.
59. Ibid., para. 636.
60. Ibid., para. 634.
61. Ibid., para. 635.
62. Ibid., para. 634.
63. Ibid.
64. Ibid.
65. Ibid.
66. Ibid., para. 635.
67. Ibid., para. 637.
68. Bair, p. 722, note 54.
69. Jung, *MDR*, p. 193.
70. Ibid., p. 170.
71. Ibid.
72. Ibid.
73. Ibid., p. 177.
74. Ibid.
75. Ibid., p. 178.
76. Ibid., pp. 233–4.
77. Ibid., p. 175.
78. Ibid.
79. Ibid., p. 176.
80. Ibid., p. 196.
81. Ibid., pp. 196–7.
82. Jung, *CW* 6, para. 66 and C. G. Jung, *Letters*, vol. 1 (Princeton: Princeton University Press, 1973), p. 60.
83. Jung, *CW* 6, para. 93.
84. At mid-life Hillman reversed course and discovered soul in the external world, in sensuous and aesthetic experience. See his essay, "Anima Mundi: The Return of the Soul to the World," in *The Thought of the Heart and The Soul of the World*.

85. Von Franz, *Projection and Re-Collection in Jungian Psychology*, p. 189.
86. Ibid., pp. 189–90.
87. Jung, *CW* 17, para.164.
88. Jung, *CW* 8, para. 938, note 70.
89. C. A. Meier, "Science and Synchronicity: A Conversation with C. A. Meier," *Psychological Perspectives*, Fall–Winter 1988, 19 (2), pp. 320–4.
90. A good deal of work remains to be done in the area of the connection between psychology and physics. Aside from Jung's seminal essay, "Synchronicity: An Acausal Connecting Principle," the following authors discuss the issue: C. A. Meier in a number of essays and books: "Moderne Physik—Moderne Psychologie," *Die kulturelle Bedeutung der komplexen Psycholgie: Festschrift zum 60. Geburtstag von C. G. Jung,* (Berlin, 1935); *Zeitgemässe Probleme der Traumforschung* (Eidgenössische Technische Hochschulle: Kultur- und Staatswissenschaftliche Schriften, 75), Zürich, 1950; *The Unconscious in its Empirical Manifestations* (Boston: Sigo Press, 1984); and *Healing Dream and Ritual: Ancient Incubation and Modern Psychotherapy* (Einsiedeln, Switzerland: Daimon Verlag, 1989). Marie-Louise von Franz, *Number and Time: Reflections Leading toward a Unification of Depth Psychology and Physics* (La Salle & London: Open Court, 1980). Victor Mansfield, *Synchronicity, Science and Soul-Making* (Chicago, Illinois: Open Court, 1995). Michael Conforti, *Field, Form and Fate: Patterns in Mind, Nature and Psyche* (Woodstock, CT: Spring, 1999).
91. Bair, p. 124.
92. Ibid.
93. Ibid.
94. Ibid., pp. 124–5.
95. Jung, *MDR*, p. 226.
96. Ibid., p. 235–36.
97. Ibid., p. 236.
98. Ibid., p. 237.
99. Ibid., p. 190.
100. Ibid., pp. 190–1.
101. Ibid., p. 191.
102. Jung, *Letters*, vol. 2, pp. 483–4.
103. Jung, *CW* 8, para. 427.
104. Edward F. Edinger, *Ego and Archetype: Individuation and the Religious Function of the Psyche* (New York: Penguin Books, 1986), p. 101.
105. Plato, *The Symposium* (Middlesex, England: Penguin Books, 1972), p. 95.
106. Bair, p. 80.
107. Ibid., p. 211.
108. Jung, *MDR*, p. 185.
109. Ibid., p. 186.
110. Ibid.
111. Ibid.
112. Ibid., p. 187.
113. Ibid.
114. Ibid.
115. Ibid.
116. Bair, p. 192.

117. Jung, *CW*, para. 258.
118. Ibid.
119. Ibid.
120. Ibid.
121. Ibid., para. 257.
122. Ibid., para. 275.
123. *The New Jerusalem Bible* (New York: Doubleday, 1990), p. 1111.
124. Ibid., p. 976.
125. Jung, *CW* 11, para. 753. The continuing impetus for including the feminine principle in the Western notion of God is attested by the growing list of publications with such titles as *Gaia, Return of the Goddess, When God was a Woman.* The astounding popularity of *The DaVinci Code* by Dan Brown was part of this phenomenon.
126. Ibid., paras. 749 and 758.

9 C. G. Jung: Introverted Soulful Power Pneuma Type: Part II

1. Bair, p. 33.
2. Ibid., p. 29.
3. Ibid., p. 44.
4. Ibid., p. 55.
5. Ibid., p. 97.
6. Ibid.
7. Ibid., p. 57.
8. Ibid.
9. Ibid., p. 56.
10. Gay, p. 215.
11. Bair, p. 145.
12. Ibid.
13. Ibid., p. 122.
14. Ibid., p. 150.
15. Ibid., p. 98.
16. Ibid., p. 114. Emphasis added.
17. Ibid., p. 131.
18. Ibid., p. 203.
19. Gay, p. 227.
20. Bair, p. 204.
21. Gay, p. 227.
22. Ibid.
23. Ibid.
24. *The Freud/Jung Letters, op. cit.*, March 6, 1910, p. 300.
25. Bair, p. 203.
26. Gay, p. 204.
27. Bair, p. 202.
28. Bair, p. 147.
29. Ibid., p. 138 and p. 695, note 35.
30. Ibid., p. 233.

31. Ibid., p. 151.
32. Gay, p. 219, note.
33. Bair, p. 209 and p. 151.
34. Jones, vol. II, p. 142.
35. Bair, p. 235.
36. Ibid., pp. 235–6.
37. Ibid.
38. Ibid. p. 236.
39. Ibid.
40. Jones, vol. I, p. 317.
41. Louis Berger, *Freud: Darkness in the Midst of Vision* (John Wiley & Sons: New York 2000), p. 229.
42. Bair, p. 236.
43. Berger, p. 228.
44. Bair, pp. 237–8.
45. Ibid., p. 238.
46. Ibid., p. 230.
47. Ibid., p. 231.
48. Ibid., p. 233.
49. *The Freud/Jung Letters*, p. 553.
50. Bair, p. 312.
51. Ibid., p. 275.
52. Ibid.
53. Ibid., p. 285.
54. Ibid., p. 252.
55. The correspondence is now published in Hans Konrad Iselin's *Zur Entstehung von C. G. Jungs "Psychologischen Typen:" Der Briefwechsel zwischen C. G. Jung und Hans Schmid-Guisn im Lichte ihrer Freundschaft*, Veröffentlicheungern der Schweizerischen Gesselschaft für Geschichte der Medizin und der Naturwissenschaften, no 38 (Aarau: Verlag Sauerländer, 1982). Bair, p. 741, note 19. An English language edition is forthcoming: C. G. Jung and Hans Schmid-Guisan, *The Correspondence of C. G. Jung and Hans Schmid-Guisan on the Question of Psychological Types*, eds. John Beebe and Ernst Falzeder (Princeton: Princeton University Press, 2012).
56. Bair, p. 281.
57. Ibid.
58. Ibid., p. 279.
59. Ibid., p. 281 and p. 280.
60. Ibid., p. 280.
61. Ibid., p. 281.
62. Ibid.
63. Ibid., pp. 281–2.
64. Ibid., p. 282.
65. Ibid.
66. Ibid., p. 283.
67. Ibid.
68. Ibid. Bair's paraphrase of Schmid's letter to Jung.
69. Ibid., p. 742, note 24.
70. Jung, *CW* 6, para. 773, note 68.
71. Jung, *CW* 11, paras 374–406.

72. Bair, p. 312.
73. Ibid.
74. Ibid., p. 309.
75. Ibid., p. 260.
76. Ibid. The book was published posthumously with an introduction by Martin Buber.
77. Ibid., p. 313.
78. Ibid., p. 541.
79. Ibid.
80. Ibid., p. 744, note 50.
81. Ibid., p. 311.
82. Ibid., p. 313.
83. Ibid., p. 312.
84. Ibid., p. 531.
85. Ibid., p. 553.
86. Ibid., p. 366.
87. Ibid., p. 365.
88. Ibid., pp. 554–5.
89. For a detailed account of the events please see Deirdre Bair's biography of Jung, *op. cit.*, Chapter 29, "Falling Afoul of History."
90. Aniela Jaffe and Marie-Louise von Franz both speak of Jung's "therapeutic optimism" in this regard. See Aniela Jaffe, "C.G. Jung and National Socialism," in *From the Life and Work of C.G. Jung*, p. 90 and Marie-Louise von Franz, *C.G. Jung: His Myth in Our Time*, p. 64.
91. Jones, vol. III, p. 151.
92. Bair, p. 453.
93. Ibid., p. 432.
94. Ibid.
95. Ibid., p. 437.
96. Ibid., p. 439.
97. Ibid., p. 437.
98. Ibid., p. 445.
99. Ibid.
100. Ibid., p. 443.
101. Ibid.
102. Ibid.
103. Ibid., p. 447.
104. Ibid., p. 456.
105. Ibid., p. 447.
106. Jung, *CW* 10, para. 1016,
107. Ibid.
108. Ibid., para. 1017.
109. Bair, p. 449.
110. Ibid.
111. Ibid.
112. Ibid.
113. Ibid.
114. Ibid., p. 450.
115. Jung, *CW* 10, para. 388.
116. Bair, p. 456.

117. Bair, p. 458.
118. For a scathing critique of Jungian psychology and of Jung's personal attitudes with regard to racism and anti-Semitism, see Andrew Samuels, "National Socialism, National Psychology, and Analytical Psychology," *Journal of Analytical Psychology*, Part I. 37.1 January 1992): 3–28. Part II. 37.2 (April 1992): 127–48. This is a revised and expanded version of an essay first published in *Lingering Shadows: Jungians, Freudians, and Anti-Semitism.* eds Aryeh Maidenbaum and Stephen A. Martin. Boston and London: Shambhala, 1991.
119. Bair, p. 463.
120. Aniela Jaffé, *From the Life and Work of C. G. Jung* (New York: Harper & Row, 1971), p. 98.
121. See Gay, op cit., p. 779 and Robert S. McCully, "Letters: Remarks on the Last Contact between Freud & Jung," *Quadrant: Journal of the C. G. Jung Foundation for Analytical Psychology*, 20.1 (1987), pp. 73–4.
122. Ibid.
123. Marie-Louise von Franz, *C. G. Jung: His Myth in Our Time* (New York: G. P. Putnam's Sons, 1975), p. 63.
124. Jung, *MDR*, p. 294.
125. Ibid.
126. Ibid.
127. Bair, p. 429, *MDR*, pp. 280–3.
128. Jung, *MDR*, p. 282.
129. Ibid., pp. 282–3.
130. Bair, p. 497, *MDR*, pp. 289.
131. Jung, *MDR*, p. 290.
132. Ibid., p. 291.
133. Ibid., p. 323.
134. Ibid., p. 294.
135. Jung, *CW* 14, para. 1.
136. Barbara Hannah, *Jung: His Life and Work: A Biographical Memoir* (New York: G. P. Putnam's Sons, 1976), p. 347.
137. Ibid., p. 283.
138. *Remembering Jung: A Conversation about C. G. Jung and his Work with Marie-Louise von Franz*, prod. George Wagner, C. G. Jung Institute of Los Angeles, CA, 1990, 3 discs.
139. Ibid.
140. A psychological interpretation of the Revelation of St John can be found in *Archetype of the Apocalypse: A Jungian Study of the Book of Revelation* by Edward F. Edinger.
141. Jung, *CW* 11, para. 747.
142. Ibid., para 745.

10 Conclusion

1. David C. McClelland, *Human Motivation*, Cambridge, England: Cambridge University Press, 1987, p. 590. McClelland's studies of motivation are used widely in the field of organizational behavior for identifying successful managers, leaders and entrepreneurs. He describes four motive

systems: achievement motives, power motives, affiliative motives and avoidance motives. Based on the "scoring of hundreds of pages of fiction, children's text-books, and hymns throughout the history of the United States," the evidence indicates that power and affiliation-related thoughts are more common and frequent than achievement-related thoughts (*Human Motivation*, p. 602.) The conclusion supports my choice of Power and Eros as two basic archetypal motivations.

2. Conceptually, there is a similarity between the archetypes of Power and Logos. Both insist on clear distinctions, separate the opposites, and posit a hierarchical order even within the opposites: for example, heaven/earth, ruler/ruled, friend/enemy, good/evil, masculine/feminine. Eros, on the other hand, seems to be related to Chaos in which the opposites are not clearly separated, distinctions are blurred, and no hierarchical order is present. Eros seeks a union of opposites and prefers an egalitarian or federalist order based on association and cooperation. Thus, the archetypal principles of Power/Logos and Eros/Chaos have contrary aims.

   Therefore, when one comes to dominate conscious or cultural attitudes, the other must function in an unconscious manner and subterranean manner—hence the irrational acting out of Eros in Power types and the cultic and anarchic expressions of Eros/Chaos in predominantly Power/Logos societies.
3. If my thesis is correct that Power/Logos, Eros, Pnuema and Physis are the core archetypes of the thinking, feeling, intuiting and sensing functions, then I can understand how Katherine Briggs and Isabel Myers, developers of the MBTI, came to consider empathy, harmony and consensus as aspects of the feeling function. In *Psychological Types*, Jung defines feeling as a rational evaluative function and does not associate it in any manner whatsoever, with empathy and harmony in human relations. Apparently, Briggs and Myers must have intuited the connection between the feeling function and its archetypal core, Eros, and incorporated these qualities of Eros under the feeling function.
4. *The Individual Psychology of Alfred Adler: A Systematic Presentation in Selections from his Writings*, edited and annotated by Heinz L. Ansbacher and Rowena R. Ansbacher (New York: Harper & Row, 1967), p. 457.
5. Ibid.
6. Ibid. 156.
7. Ibid. 456.
8. Ibid. 457. I have substituted the original German term for its misleading translation as "social interest."
9. Ibid. 456.
10. Jung, *CW* 16. Epigraph to the Introduction of *The Psychology of the Transference*.
11. Jung, *CW* 9 ii, para. 67.

Appendix I

1. Toni Wolff, "Structural Forms of the Feminine Psyche," *Psychological Perspectives*, 31 (Spring–Summer 1995), pp. 77–90.

2. Emma Jung, *Animus and Anima* (Zurich: Spring Publications, 1978), p. 3.
3. Marie-Louise von Franz, "The Process of Individuation," *Man and His Symbols*, C. G. Jung et al. (New York: Doubleday, 1964), pp. 158–229.
4. Jean Shinoda Bolen, *Goddesses in Everywoman: A New Psychology of Women* (New York: Harper & Row, 1984), pp. 16–17.
5. Jennifer Barker Woolger and Roger J. Woolger, *The Goddess Within: A Guide to the Eternal Myths that Shape Women's Lives* (New York: Fawcett Columbine, 1989), p. 9 (italics in original).
6. Robert Moore and Douglas Gillette, *King, Warrior, Magician, Lover: Rediscovering the Archetypes of the Mature Masculine* (San Francisco: HarperCollins, 1991), Chapter 3.
7. Carol S. Pearson, *The Hero Within: Six Archetypes We Live By* (New York: HarperSanFrancisco, 1986), p. x.
8. John Beebe, "Understanding Consciousness through the Theory of Psychological Types, *Analytical Psychology: Contemporary Perspectives on Jungian Analysis*, eds. Joseph Cambray and Linda Carter (Hove and New York: Brunner-Routledge, 2004), pp. 101–2.

Appendix II

1. John Blofeld, *Taoism: The Road to Immortality* (Boston: Shambhala, 1985), p. 3.
2. An attempt to revision the *I Ching* from the original Taoist perspective can be found in a translation of the book by Stephen Karcher and Rudolf Ritsema, *I Ching: The Classic Chinese Oracle of Change* (Shaftesbury: Element Books, 1994) and in Stephen Karcher, *The Elements of the I Ching* (Shaftesbury: Element Books, 1995) and *How to Use the I Ching: A Guide to Working with the Oracle of Change* (Shaftesbury: Element Books, 1997).
3. *The I Ching or Book of Changes*, The Richard Wilhelm Translation rendered into English by Cary F. Baynes, Foreword by C. G. Jung, Bollingen Series XIX (Princeton: Princeton University Press, 1971), p. 4.
4. Ibid., p. 370.
5. Ibid., p. 371.
6. Ibid., p. 12.
7. Ibid., p. 386.
8. Ibid., p.3.
9. Ibid. (my emphasis).
10. Ibid., p. 386.
11. Ibid. (my emphasis).
12. Ibid., p. 11.

Bibliography

Adler, Alfred. *The Collected Clinical Works of Alfred Adler*. 12 vols. ed. Henry T. Stein. Bellinghma, WA: Classical Adlerian Translation Project.

—— *Superiority and Social Interest: A Collection of Later Writings*. eds. Heinz L. Ansbacher and Rowena R. Ansbacher. Evanston, IL: Northwestern University Press, 1964.

—— *Understanding Human Nature*. trans. W. Béran Wolfe. Greenwich, CT: Fawcett Publications, Inc., 1954.

Adler, Gerhard. "Methods of Treatment in Analytical Psychology." *Psychoanalytical Techniques*. ed. B. Wolman. New York: Basic Books, 1967.

Alschuler, Louis R. *The Psychopolitics of Liberation: Political Consciousness from a Jungian Perspective*. New York: Palgrave Macmillan, 2006.

Cambray, James and Linda Carter. eds. *Analytical Psychology: Contemporary Perspectives on Jungian Analysis*. New York: Brunner- Routledge, 2004.

Arraj, Tara and James Arraj. *Tracking the Elusive Human: A Practical Guide to C. G. Jung's Psychological Types and W. H. Sheldon's Body and Temperament Types and Their Integration*. Vols. 1 and 2. Chiloquin, OR: Inner Growth Books, 1994.

Bair, Deirdre. *Jung: A Biography*. Boston New York London: Little, Brown and Company, 2003.

Beebe, John. "Understanding Consciousness through the Theory of Psychological Types, *Analytical Psychology: Contemporary Perspectives on Jungian Analysis*, eds. Joseph Cambray and Linda Carter. Hove and New York: Brunner-Routledge, 2004, pp. 83–115.

—— "The Recognition of Psychological Type," in *Jungian Psychoanalysis*, ed. Murray Stein. Chicago: Open Court, 2010.

Bernfeld, Siegfried. "Freud's Scientific Beginnings," *The American Imago*, VI (Sept. 1949): 163–96.

Bettleheim, Bruno. *Freud and Man's Soul*. New York: Alfred A. Knopf, 1983.

Blofeld, John. *Taoism: The Road to Immortality*. Boston: Shambhala, 1985.

Bolen, Jean Shinoda. *Goddesses in Everywoman: A New Psychology of Women*. New York: Harper & Row, 1984.

—— *Gods in Everyman: A New Psychology of Men's Lives and Loves*. New York: HarperPerennial, 1990.

—— *Goddesses in Older Women: Archetypes in Women over Fifty*. New York: HarperCollins, 2002.

Bottome, Phyllis. *Alfred Adler: Apostle of Freedom*. London: Faber and Faber Ltd., 1957.

Breger, Louis. *Freud: Darkness in the Midst of Vision*. New York: John Wiley & Sons, Inc., 2000.

Briggs Myers, Isabel with Peter B. Myers. *Gifts Differing*. Palo Alto, CA: Consulting Psychologists Press, Inc., 1980.

Campbell, Jospeh with Bill Moyers. *Power of Myth*. ed. Betty Sue Flowers. New York: Doubleday, 1988.

Chaucer, Geoffrey. *The Canterbury Tales*. London: Penguin Books, 1977.

Clancy, Susan A. *Abducted: How People Come to Believe They Were Kidnapped by Aliens*. Cambridge, MA: Harvard University Press, 2005.

Conforti, Michael. *Field, Form and Fate: Patterns in Mind, Nature and Psyche*. Woodstock, CT: Spring, 1999.

Crick, Francis. *The Astonishing Hypothesis: The Scientific Search for the Soul*. New York: Charles Scribner's Sons, 1994.

A Dictionary of Symbols. eds. Jean Chevalier and Alain Gheerbrant. London: Penguin Books, 1996.

Edinger, Edward F. *Anatomy of the Psyche: Alchemical Symbolism in Psychotherapy*. La Salle, Illinois: Open Court, 1985.

—— *Archetype of the Apocalypse: A Jungian Study of the Book of Revelation*. ed. George R. Elder. Chicago and La Salle: Open Court, 1999.

—— *The Bible and the Psyche: Individuation Symbolism in the Old Testament*. Toronto: Inner City Books, 1986.

—— *Ego and Archetype: Individuation and the Religious Function of the Psyche*. Middlesex: Penguin Books, 1986.

—— "The Vocation of Depth Psychotherapy." *Science of the Soul: A Jungian Perspective*. eds. Daryl Sharp and J. Gary Sparks. Toronto: Inner City Books, 2002.

Ellenberger, Henri F. *The Discovery of the Unconscious: The History and Evolution of Dynamic Psychiatry*. New York: Basic Books, 1970.

Evans, Joan. *Taste and Temperament: A Brief Study of Psychological Types in their Relation to the Visual Arts*. London: Jonathan Cape, 1939.

Ferris, Paul. *Dr Freud: A Life*. Washington, D.C.: Counterpoint, 1997.

Fordham, Michael. *Jungian Psychotherapy: A Study in Analytical Psychology*. Chichester: Wiley, 1978.

Frankl, Viktor. "Tributes to Alfred Adler on his 100th Birthday." *Journal of Individual Psychology* 26.1 (1970): 12.

Frager, Robert, ed. *Who Am I? Personality Types for Self-Discovery*. New York: G. P. Putnam's Sons, 1994.

Frey-Rohn, Liliane. *From Freud to Jung: A Comparative Study of the Psychology of the Unconscious*. New York: G. P. Putnam's Sons, 1974.

Gay, Peter. *Freud: A Life for Our Time*. New York and London: W. W. Norton & Co., 1988.

Goldenberg, Naomi R. "Archetypal Theory After Jung." *Spring* (1975): 199–220.

Goodchild, Veronica. *Eros and Chaos: The Sacred Mysteries and Dark Shadows of Love*. York Beach, Maine: Nicolas-Hays, Inc., 2001.

Gray, Horace. "Freud and Jung: Their Contrasting Psychological Types." *Psychoanalytic Review* 36.1. (January 1949): 22–44.

Graves, Robert. *The Greek Myths*. 2 vols. Baltimore, Maryland: Penguin Books, 1968.

Hall, James. A. *Hypnosis: A Jungian Perspective*. New York: Guilford Press, 1989.

Hannah, Barbara. *Jung: His Life and Work: A Biographical Memoir*. New York: G. P. Putnam's Sons, 1976.

Hawking, Stephen. *A Brief History of Time*. New York: Bantam Books, 1998.

Henderson, Joseph. *Cultural Attitudes in Psychological Perspective*. Toronto: Inner City Books, 1984.

Hillman, James. *Re-Visioning Psychology*. New York: Harper & Row, 1975.

—— *The Soul's Code: In Search of Character and Calling*. New York: Random House, 1996.

—— *The Thought of the Heart and the Soul of the World.* Woodstock, CT: Spring Publications, Inc., 1997.

Hoffman, Edward. *The Drive for Self: Alfred Adler and the Founding of Individual Psychology*. Reading, MA: Addison-Wesley Publishing Co., 1994.

Hume, David. *Of the Standard of Taste and Other Essays,* ed. John W. Lenz. Indianapolis: The Library of Liberal Arts, 1975.

The I Ching or Book of Changes. The Richard Wilhelm Translation rendered into English by Cary F. Baynes. Foreword by C. G. Jung. Bollingen Series XIX. Princeton: Princeton University Press, 1971.

The Individual Psychology of Alfred Adler: A Systematic Presentation in Selections from his Writings. Edited and annotated by Heinz L. Ansbacher and Rowena R. Ansbacher. New York: Harper & Row, 1967.

Iselin, Hans Konrad. *Zur Entstehung von C. G. Jungs "Psychologischen Typen:" Der Briefwechsel zwischen C. G. Jung und Hans Schmid-Guisn im Lichte ihrer Freundschaft.* Veröffentlicheungern der Schweizerischen Gesselschaft für Geschichte der Medizin und der Naturwissenschaften, no 38. Aarau: Verlag Sauerländer, 1982.

Jacobi, Jolande. *The Psychology of C. G. Jung: An Introduction with Illustrations.* New Haven and London: Yale University Press, 1968.

Jaffe, Aniela "C.G. Jung and National Socialism." *From the Life and Work of C.G. Jung.* trans. R. F. C. Hull. New York: Harper & Row, 1971.

Jahn, Ernst and Alfred Adler. *Religion und Individualpsychologie: eine prinzipielle Auseinandersetzung über Menschenführung.* Vienna, Leipzig: Rolf Passer, 1933.

James, William. *Pragmatism: A New Name for Some Old Ways of Thinking.* New York London Toronto: Longman's Green & Co., 1947.

Johnston, James G. *Jung's Compass of Psychological Types.* Perrysburg, OH.: MSE Press, 2011.

Jones, Ernest. *The Life and Work of Sigmund Freud.* 3 vols. New York: Basic Books, 1955.

Jung, C. G. *Analytical Psychology: Notes of the Seminar Given in 1925.* ed. William McGuire. Bollingen Series XCIX. NJ: Princeton University Press, 1989.

—— *Psychological Types.* In *The Collected Works of C.G. Jung,* Vol. 6. (eds. Herbert Read, Michael Fordham, Gerhard Adler, William McGuire), Bollingen Series XX, translation by R.F.C. Hull. Princeton: Princeton University Press, 1921/1971.

—— *Memories, Dreams, Reflections.* Recorded and edited by Aniela Jaffé. Translated from the German by Richard and Clara Winston. Revised edition. New York: Vintage Books, 1961/1989.

—— *Letters,* 1906–1950. Princeton, NJ: Princeton University Press, 1973.

—— *Letters,* 1951–1961. Princeton, NJ: Princeton University Press, 1975.

—— *Man and His Symbols.* C. G. Jung *et al.* Garden City, NY: Doubleday & Co., 1972.

—— *Memories, Dreams, Reflections.* New York: Vintage Books, 1989.

—— *The Red Book: Liber Novus.* ed. Sonu Shamdasani. Preface by Ulrich Hoerni. trans. Mark Kyburz, John Peck and Sonu Shamdasani. New York, London: W. W. Norton & Co., 2009.

—— *Visions: Notes of the Seminar Given in 1930–1934.* 2 vols. ed. Claire Douglas. Princeton: Princeton University Press: 1997.

—— and Hans Schmid-Guisan. *The Correspondence of C. G. Jung and Hans Schmid-Guisan on the Question of Psychological Types*. eds. John Beebe and Ernst Falzeder. Princeton: Princeton University Press, 2012.

Jung, Emma. *Animus and Anima*. Zürich: Spring Publications, 1978

Kapleau, Philip. *Zen: Merging of East and West*. New York: Anchor Books Doubleday, 1980.

Karcher. Stephen and Rudolf Ritsema. *I Ching: The Classic Chinese Oracle of Change*. Shaftesbury: Element Books, 1994.

Karcher, Stephen. *The Elements of the I Ching*. Shaftesbury: Element Books, 1995.

—— *How to Use the I Ching: A Guide to Working with the Oracle of Change*. Shaftesbury: Element Books, 1997.

Kiersey, David and Marilyn Bates. *Please Understand Me*. Del Mar, CA.: Gnosology Books, 1984.

Lasswell, Harold D. *Psychopathology and Politics*. New York: The Viking Press, 1960.

—— *Politics: Who Gets What, When, How*. New York: Meridian Books, 1972.

Lieberman, James E. *Acts of Will: The Life and Work of Otto Rank*. New York: Free Press, 1985.

Lovejoy, Arthur O. *The Great Chain of Being: A Study of the History of an* Idea. New York: Harper & Row, 2005.

López-Pedraza, R. *Cultural Anxiety*. Einsiedeln: Daimon Verlag, 1990.

Maidenbaum, Aryeh and Stephen A. Martin. eds. *Lingering Shadows: Jungians, Freudians, and Anti-Semitism*. Boston and London: Shambhala, 1991.

Mansfield, Victor. *Synchronicity, Science and Soul-Making*. Chicago, Illinois: Open Court, 1995.

Maslow, Abraham. "Tributes to Alfred Adler on his 100th Birthday." *Journal of Individual Psychology*. 26.1 (1970): 13.

McCully, Robert S. "Letters: Remarks on the Last Contact between Freud & Jung," *Quadrant: Journal of the C. G. Jung Foundation for Analytical Psychology*, 20.1 (1987): 73–4.

McGuire, William, ed. *The Freud/Jung Letters: Correspondence between Sigmund Freud and C. G. Jung*. Bollingen Series XCIV. Princeton: Princeton University Press, 1974.

Meier, C. A. *Healing Dream and Ritual: Ancient Incubation and Modern Psychotherapy*. Einsiedeln, Switzerland: Daimon Verlag, 1989.

——"Moderne Physik—Moderne Psychologie." *Die kulturelle Bedeutung der komplexen Psycholgie: Festschrift zum 60. Geburtstag von C. G. Jung*. Berlin, 1935.

—— "Science and Synchronicity: A Conversation with C. A. Meier." *Psychological Perspectives* 19.2 (Fall–Winter 1988): 320–4.

—— *Zeitgemässe Probleme der Traumforschung* (Eidgenössische Technische Hochschulle: Kultur-und Staatswissenschaftliche Schriften. 75. Zürich, 1950.

—— *The Unconscious in its Empirical Manifestations*. Boston: Sigo Press, 1984.

Minutes of the Vienna Psychoanalytic Society, vols. 1–4. eds. Herman Nunberg and Ernst Federn. New York: International Universities Press, 1962–75.

Moore, Robert and Douglas Gillette. *King, Warrior, Magician, Lover: Rediscovering the Archetypes of the Mature Masculine*. San Francisco: HarperCollins, 1991.

Neumann, Erich. *The Origins and History of Consciousness*. trans. R. F. C. Hull. Bollingern Series XLII. Princeton: Princeton University Press, 1970.

—— *The Child*. trans. Ralph Manheim. Foreword by Louis H. Stewart. Boston: Shambhala, 1990.

The New Jerusalem Bible. New York: Doubleday, 1990.

Odajnyk, Volodymyr, W. *Gathering the Light: A Psychology of Meditation*. Boston: Shambhala, 1993. Revised edition: *Gathering the Light: A Jungian View of Meditation*. Foreword by Thomas Moore. Carmel, CA: Fisher King Press, 2011.

—— *Jung and Politics: The Political and Social Ideas of C. G. Jung*. Foreword by Marie-Louise von Franz. New York: Harper & Row, 1976. Reprint: Lincoln, NE: Authors Choice Press, 2007.

—— "The Psychologist as Artist: The Imaginal World of James Hillman." *Quadrant: Journal of the C. G. Jung Foundation for Analytical Psychology* 17.1 (Spring 1984): 39–48.

Pearson, Carol S. *The Hero Within: Six Archetypes We Live By*. New York: HarperSanFrancisco, 1986.

—— *Awakening the Heroes Within: Twelve Archetypes to Help Us Find Ourselves and Transform Our World*. New York: HarperSanFrancisco, 1991.

Piaget, Jean. *The Child's Conception of the World*. St Albans, England: Paladin, 1973.

—— *The Child's Conception of Physical Causality*. Totowa, NJ: Littlefield, Adams & Co., 1965.

Pinch, Geraldine. *Egyptian Myth: A Very Short Introduction*. Oxford: Oxford University Press, 2004.

The Republic of Plato. Translated with Introduction and Notes by Francis MacDonald Cornford. New York & London: Oxford University Press, 1945.

Romanyshyn, Robert D. *The Wounded Scholar: Research with Soul in Mind*. New Orleans, Louisiana: Spring Journal Books, 2007.

Sadger, Isidor. *Recollecting Freud*. ed. Alan Dundes. Madison, Wisconsin: University of Wisconsin Press, 2005.

Samules, Andrew. *Jung and the Post-Jungians*. London and New York: Routledge, 1985.

—— "National Socialism, National Psychology, and Analytical Psychology." *Journal of Analytical Psychology*. Part I. 37.1 (January 1992): 3–28. Part II. 37.2 (April 1992): 127–48.

Schiller, Friedrich. *On the Aesthetic Education of Man*. Translation and Introduction by Reginald Snell. Mineola, NY: Dover Publications, Inc., 2004.

The Secret of the Golden Flower: A Chinese Book of Life. trans. Richard Wilhelm. San Diego New York London: Harcourt Brace Jovanovich, 1962.

Sekida, Katsuki. *Zen Training: Methods and Philosophy*. New York and Tokyo: Weatherhill, 1985.

Sigmund Freud: Psychoanalysis and Faith, Dialogues with the Reverend Oskar Pfister. eds. Heinrich Meng and Ernst L. Freud. trans. Eric Mosbacher, New York: Basic Books, 1963.

Slater, Glen "Aliens and Insects." *Varieties of Mythic Experience*. eds. Dennis Slattery and Glen Slater. Einsiedeln, Switzerland: Daimon Verlag, 2008.

Slattery, Dennis P. and Glen Slater. eds. *Varieties of Mythic Experience: Essays on Religion, Psyche and Culture*. eds. Einsiedeln, Switzerland: Daimon Verlag, 2008.

Smuts, Jan C. *Holism and Evolution*. New York: Macmillan, 1926.

Spoto, Angelo. *Jung's Typology in Perspective*. Wilmette, Illinois: Chiron Publications, 1995.

Spranger, Eduard. *Types of Men: The Psychology and Ethics of Personality*. Halle(Salle): Max Niemeyer Verlag, 1928.

Strieber, Whitley. *Communion: A True Story*. New York: Harper, 2008.

Ulanov, Barry. *Jung and the Outside World*. Wilmette, IL: Chiron Publications, 1992.

Van der Hoop, J. H. *Conscious Orientation: A Study of Personality Type in Relation to Neurosis and Psychosis*. London: Routledge, 1999.

Van der Post, Laurens. *Jung and the Story of Our Time*. New York: Pantheon Books, 1975.

Von Franz, Marie-Louise. "The Inferior Function," in *Lectures on Jung's Typology*. New York: Spring Publications, 1971.

—— *C. G. Jung: His Myth in Our Time*. London: Hodder and Stoughton, 1975.

—— *Individuation in Fairy Tales*. Zurich: Spring Publications, 1977.

—— *On Dreams and Death*. Boston & London: Shambhala, 1986.

—— *Number and Time: Reflections Leading toward a Unification of Dept Psychology and Physics*. La Salle & London: Open Court, 1980.

—— "The Process of Individuation." *Man and His Symbols*. C. G. Jung *et al*. New York: Doubleday, 1964.

—— *Projection and Re-Collection in Jungian Psychology:Reflections of the Soul*. Chicago and La Salle, IL: Open Court, 1995.

—— *Remembering Jung: A Conversation about C. G. Jung and his Work with Marie-Louise von Franz*, prod. George Wagner, C. G. Jung Institute of Los Angeles, CA, 1990, 3 discs.

Von Franz, Marie-Louise and James Hillman. *Lectures on Jung's Typology*. Woodstock, CT: Spring Publications, 1998.

Waley, Arthur. *The Way and Its Power: A Study of the Tao Te Ching and Its Place in Chinese Thought*. London: George Allen & Unwin LTD, 1965.

Warner, Silas L. "Freud's Antipathy to America." *Journal of the American Academy of Psychoanalysis* 19.1 (1991): 141–155.

Wolff, Toni. "Structural Forms of the Feminine Psyche." *Psychological Perspectives* 31 (Spring-Summer 1995): 77–90.

Woolger, Jennifer Barker and Roger J. Woolger. *The Goddess Within: A Guide to the Eternal Myths that Shape Women's Lives*. New York: Fawcett Columbine, 1989.

Index

Page numbers followed by 'n' denotes notes.

D

E

F